PARTNERSHIP GOVERNANCE IN NORTHERN IRELAND

Partnership Governance in Northern Ireland

Improving performance

JONATHAN GREER
University of Ulster at Jordanstown, Northern Ireland

Ashgate

Aldershot • Burlington USA • Singapore • Sydney

Published by
Ashgate Publishing Limited
Gower House
Croft Road
Aldershot
Hampshire GU11 3HR
England

Ashgate Publishing Company
131 Main Street
Burlington, VT 05401-5600 USA

Ashgate website: http://www.ashgate.com

British Library Cataloguing in Publication Data
Greer, Jonathan, 1974-
    Partnership governance in Northern Ireland : improving
    performance
    1. Partnership - Northern Ireland 2. Northern Ireland -
    Politics and government - 1994-
    I. Title
    351.4'16

Library of Congress Control Number: 2001088784

ISBN 0 7546 1700 9

Printed in Great Britain by
Antony Rowe Ltd, Chippenham, Wiltshire

Contents

List of Figures

List of Tables

Preface

This book is focused on partnership governance, an area which has been gaining widespread attention from academics and public policy officials throughout many countries. Indeed, within the last two decades, partnerships have become an increasingly popular and important form of service delivery and could be described as a universal or global phenomenon. Partnership formation is now well established in advanced capitalist societies and is synonymous with policy initiatives designed to deal with complex problems such as economic development, urban regeneration and social exclusion.

The emergence of partnerships is recognition of economic, social and political changes, which have transformed the manner in which policy is made and delivered. The creation of a global economy, increasing social diversity and fragmentation in public administration has caused separation, complexity and division in the policy environment. As one means to adapt these changes, governments at every level have embraced the concept of partnerships. Partnerships have been regarded as an ideal mechanism as they can bring together organisations in the policy process to build and manage an integrative approach in an increasingly interdependent system.

Although the partnerships are being increasingly applied to a range of public policy areas and are emerging as a central feature in public administration, very little is known about how to improve the performance of partnerships. This issue has emerged as, in certain cases, partnerships have furthered the problems of administrative complexity, ineffectiveness and lack of co-ordination; the very problems which partnerships were created to resolve. In addition, concerns have been raised that partnerships are fragile mechanisms of policy implementation as they struggle to combine a wide variety of interests and are prone to conflict.

Given the uncertainties surrounding the partnership approach and the consequences for policy formulation and implementation, this book aims to provide a greater understanding of partnership governance by examining the performance of partnerships. To date, studies on improving performance have tended to be vague as partnerships have largely been regarded as one entity. By contrast, partnership is a loose term which embraces a diversity of multi-organisational relationships making it extremely difficult to define what is a successful partnership. In acknowledging the variety of partnership arrangements, this book therefore, seeks to examine the conditions which affect their performance. By providing a greater understanding of partnerships and the conditions in which they operate, this book has applied policy relevance for policy makers and partnership actors as it contributes to the debate towards creating more co-ordinated government, better service deliver and reducing pressures on public resources.

This book is set within the context of Northern Ireland, an area in which partnerships are emerging as a central feature in public administration and are being established as both multi-level and cross-cutting areas of public policy. Partnership arrangements have also been developed on a trans-jurisdictional basis, for example, on a cross-border basis with the Republic of Ireland; this interconnectedness is reshaping governance. In this case some analytical reflection on partnerships and their potential for future development is important.

This is also an important and timely book as it is located against the backdrop of ongoing political and administrative developments in Northern Ireland. After almost thirty years of civil conflict Northern Ireland is facing the prospect of peace given the paramilitary cease-fires and a negotiated settlement more commonly known as the 'Good Friday' Agreement of April 1998. Over the last two decades the transition from government to governance in Northern Ireland has been superimposed on deep historical divisions and within this book, specific focus is also given to examining how the partnership approach can address social, economic and political problems. Therefore, by critically reflecting on the partnership experience in Northern Ireland, this book will offer important insights for other countries and regions, particularly in Eastern Europe and the Developing World, which are making the transition to new models of governance.

Finally, following the 'Good Friday' Agreement new political and administrative institutions have been established in Northern Ireland with the creation of the Northern Ireland Assembly, North-South Ministerial Council and Council of the Isles. This book argues that by adopting a participative framework within Northern Ireland and on a cross-border basis, partnerships have the potential to deal with an increasingly complex and interdependent administrative and social environment by rebuilding civil society, facilitating pluralist decision making and addressing social inclusion. Moreover, it is maintained that partnerships can break down barriers and build reconciliation and trust within Northern Ireland and on the island of Ireland. Under this approach partnerships can contribute to, and work alongside, the new institutions of devolved government.

Acknowledgements

The completion of this book has depended upon the support of many others. At the outset, I would like to offer a sincere thank you to all those who provide help, advice and encouragement.

First of all, I am indebted to, Professor Colin Knox and Dr Michael Murray of the University of Ulster, whose guidance and experience were crucial in over-seeing the completion of this book. Their constant help, direction, expertise and supportive attitude have been invaluable throughout the last number of years.

Secondly, I would like to mention the contribution made to this book by Professor Colin Knox, Dr Michael Murray and Dr Joanne Hughes in conducting a qualitative evaluation of the District Partnerships for Peace and Reconciliation, funded by the Northern Ireland Partnership Board. Working with this team provided extensive research and greater analysis and insight into partnership experience in Northern Ireland.

Thirdly, I owe a large debt of gratitude to Kilian McDaid and Pat McKee of the University of Ulster who helped in the production of this book. In addition, thank you can be extended to Professor James Walsh and Dr Brendan Murtagh for their critical comments and suggestions.

I am also grateful to all those I interviewed, without their assistance this research would not have been possible. Finally, a special thanks to my parents and Patrice for their encouragement and support in setting out to write this book.

List of Abbreviations

AEBR	Association of European Border Regions
ABSAGs	Area Based Strategy Action Groups
BELB	Belfast Education and Library Board
BF	Bord Fáilte
BTA	British Tourist Authority
CBI	Confederation of British Industry
CCRU	Central Community Relations Unit
CLMC	Combined Loyalist Military Command
CPDS	Community Property Development Scheme
CRC	Community Relations Council
CRISP	Community Regeneration Improvement Scheme
DANI	Department of Agriculture for Northern Ireland
DENI	Department of Education for Northern Ireland
DHSS	Department of Health and Social Services
DoE	Department of the Environment
DUP	Democratic Unionist Party
EBRC	East Border Region Committee
EC	European Community
ECBA	Erne Charter Boat Association
EEC	European Economic Community
EEIG	European Economic Interest Group
ETI	Education and Training Inspectorate
EU	European Union
EUSSPPP&R	European Union Special Support Programme for Peace and Reconciliation
GCP	Greater Craigavon Partnership
IBEC	Irish Business and Employers Confederation
IBRA	Irish Boat Rental Association
ICBAN	Irish Central Border Area Network
IDB	Industrial Development Board
IFI	International Fund for Ireland
IRA	Irish Republican Army
IRTU	Industrial Research and Training Unit
ITB	Irish Trade Board
LACBN	Local Authority Cross-Border Networks
LEDU	Local Economic and Development Unit

MBW	Making Belfast Work
NESF	National Economic and Social Forum
NDP	National Development Plan
NIIS	Northern Ireland Information Service
NIO	Northern Ireland Office
NIPB	Northern Ireland Partnership Board
NITB	Northern Ireland Tourist Board
NSMC	North – South Ministerial Council
NWRCBG	North West Region Cross-Border Group
OTMI	Overseas Tourism Marketing Initiative
PFI	Private Finance Initiative
RDC	Rural Development Council
RTA	Regional Tourist Authority
SDLP	Social Democratic and Labour Party
SF	Sinn Féin
SRB	Single Regeneration Budget
TBI	Tourism Brand Ireland
TEDI	Tyrone Economic Development Initiative
T&EA	Training and Employment Agency
UUP	Ulster Unionist Party

1 Introduction

Introduction

One of the most striking features of contemporary language is the rise and albeit short lived, dominance of particular words and phrases, some of which emerge from specialist technical fields to become part of everyday usage. The spheres of policy making and governance are fertile breeding grounds for such fashionable terms. Expressions such as 'joined up', 'integrated', 'facilitating', not to mention 'top down' and 'bottom up' permeate the literature, and in their widespread use they seem to acquire an uncontested quality, making any rigorous analysis or critique of their underlying meaning a difficult task. The list of vogue words has been joined of late by 'partnerships', which may be described as the sine qua non of policy implementation and service delivery mechanisms. As noted by Darwin,

> Partnerships are now everywhere. Alliances, joint ventures and network forms of organisation now proliferate in the private sector. In the public sector many areas of activity, such as the health service, have been restructured into multi-organisational forms. Every part of the public sector is now exhorted to take part in partnerships, and all of the 'wicked problems' (Rittel and Weber, 1973) from economic regeneration to crime and disorder, are seen as requiring a partnership approach, usually involving both public and private sectors (Darwin, 1999, p.125).

The emergence of partnerships is recognition of economic, social and political changes, which have transformed the manner in which policy is made and delivered. Within the last two decades the creation of a global economy, increasing social diversity and fragmentation in public administration has caused separation, complexity and division in the policy environment. As a result of these changes, Bryson and Crosby comment that a fundamental paradigm shift has occurred from the world we previously lived to a shared power world in which,

> no one organisation or institution is in a position to find and implement solutions to the problems that confront us in society. In this world, organisations and institutions that share objectives must also partly share resources and authority to achieve goals (Bryson and Crosby, 1992, p.4).

National governments are finding it increasingly difficult to manage this 'no-one in charge' world. The free market and a global economy have diminished the role of national governments who lack sufficient policy levers to provide the conditions for production, while the traditional command structure of public administration is being fragmented into a series of networks (Prior, 1996). In addition, increased social diversity has created difficulties as governments do not have the necessary resources, know how and information to deal with complex social problems (Berham, 1996).

As partnerships are arrangements which envisage the convergence of different actors or sectors of influence to ensure the implementation or delivery of specific objectives, they have been seen by national governments as one means of adapting to this complex and interconnected policy environment. According to Bailey partnerships represent,

> A mobilisation of a coalition of interests drawn from one sector in order to prepare and oversee an agreed strategy for a defined area or objective (Bailey, 1994, p.293).

In facilitating co-operation between different levels of government, the private and voluntary / community sectors, partnerships are changing the nature of governance as the state takes a less pronounced role in dealing with complex problems. Thus, the notion of partnerships converges easily with the political pressures for a reduction in state activity and increased responsibility at the local level. In reshaping the nature of governance, partnerships are emerging as a central feature in public administration and their development has wide implications for the organisation and function of government and policy formulation and implementation.

Partnerships have become an increasingly popular and important form of service delivery and could be described as a universal or global phenomenon. Partnership formation is now well established in advanced capitalist societies and is synonymous with policy initiatives designed to deal with complex problems such as economic development, urban regeneration and social inclusion in the USA (De Witt *et al,* 1994; Berham, 1996), Canada (Gratias and Boyd, 1995), in Europe, for example, (Marino, 1999; Paisana and Olivera, 1999) and in Britain and Ireland (Hutchinson and Foley, 1994; Walsh, 1998).

The Partnership Approach in Northern Ireland

The partnership approach has also found favour in Northern Ireland. In Northern Ireland different types of partnerships have been increasingly applied across a wide range of different government programmes at different levels of governance, be it at the local, regional or national level or between institutions of Northern Ireland, the Republic of Ireland and elsewhere. However, over the last ten to fifteen years the rapid, diverse and *ad hoc* development of partnership arrangements in Northern Ireland has created a complex and confusing picture, at times furthering the problems of environmental complexity, ineffectiveness and lack of co-ordination; these are the very problems which partnerships were created to resolve (Cebulla, 1996). Therefore, the case of Northern Ireland suggests there are inherent limitations in the partnership approach and this has consequences for policy formulation and implementation. In this light, it would then prove valuable to examine the performance of partnerships.

Examining the Partnership Approach

Within the last decade much consideration has been focused on how to improve partnership performance, and models and steps of best practice have been identified (Combat Poverty Agency, 1995; Wilson and Charlton, 1997). This work, however, has tended to be conceptually vague as partnerships have largely been regarded as one entity. The main problem in examining partnership performance can be found when analysing the nature of partnership arrangements themselves. There are many different kinds of partnerships, they exist for different reasons, create different structures, involve different partners, operate under different conditions and set themselves different goals. In government programmes each initiative has required a different approach and it has therefore become extremely difficult to define what is a 'successful partnership'. Therefore, it must first be recognised that partnership is a loose term and that partnerships can operate under different and varying conditions.

Partnerships can represent a variety of different arrangements and can be seen to exist within a family of multi-organisational relationships. A number of commentators such as Rogers *et al* (1982), Webb (1991), Gray (1989), Mattessich and Monsey (1992) and Hall *et al* (1977) have analysed the diversity of multi-organisational relationships and have classified them into different coalition building processes. These processes have been identified and located on a multi-organisational continuum. It was suggested that *co-operation* is situated at the low end of the continuum and is a process which involves informal relationships which have no structure or planning effort. *Co-ordination* is located at the centre of the continuum and is typified by more formal relationships where there is some joint planning but authority still rests within individual organisations. *Collaboration*, on the other hand, rests at the high end of the continuum and is characterised by formal relationships, there is a new organisational structure, and mission and authority are determined by the collaboration. By recognising diversity a deeper understanding of partnerships can be sought as different approaches, processes and structures are taken into account. Given that it is not possible to outline a universal formula for a successful partnership, the purpose of this book is to examine the conditions which affect the performance of partnerships and their value in the emerging public administration system of Northern Ireland.

Book Sequence

Following the introduction, this book is divided into seven subsequent chapters. As a means to provide a deeper understanding of the partnership approach in public policy, Chapter 2 begins by tracing the theoretical roots of partnerships, examining the theories and concepts behind partnerships and identifying different types of partnership models. Following that, Chapter 2 aims to examine the different coalition building processes within partnerships and the conditions for facilitating and achieving partnership governance.

To set the context of partnership governance in Northern Ireland, Chapter 3 reviews the public sector environment in Northern Ireland and discusses the dynamics behind the partnership approach. The chapter then goes on to briefly describe the nature of partnership governance in Northern Ireland and compile a conceptual map detailing major partnership arrangements, within Northern Ireland and between Northern Ireland, the Republic of Ireland and other jurisdictions. To date, no map of the network of partnership arrangements has been completed and this will provide a valuable contribution to the study of the range and type of partnerships in Northern Ireland.

Chapters 4, 5, and 6 aim to evaluate the performance of different kinds of partnership, drawing upon case studies, in terms of their coalition building processes. From the conceptual map three partnership case studies have been selected, namely the District Partnerships for Peace and Reconciliation, the Local Authority Cross-Border Networks and the partnership relationship between the Northern Ireland Tourist Board and Bord Fáilte.

From evaluating the case studies and comparing their experience against the conditions for achieving partnership governance set out in Chapter 2, Chapter 7 develops a synthetic model highlighting both the micro and macro conditions associated with improving partnership governance. Micro conditions refer to those operating at the level of individual partnerships and include contextual, decision making, stakeholder / organisational and operation conditions. Macro conditions also influence the performance and the overall development of partnerships in public policy and these include, rebuilding civil society, and the tensions between representative and participative democracy, and political pragmatism and new idealism. By outlining a model of partnership governance this book is of central importance to policy makers and partnership actors as it will create a better understanding of partnerships and the conditions in which they operate. Through greater understanding, the book can contribute to the debate towards improving partnership performance and point in the direction towards creating more co-ordinated government, better service delivery and reducing pressures on public resources.

Chapter 7, and the book, conclude with a discussion on the value of partnerships in public administration and on the implications of the findings for future governance in Northern Ireland and the island of Ireland. It is argued that a participative partnership framework in Northern Ireland and on a cross-border basis, has the potential to deal with an increasingly complex and interdependent administrative and social environment by rebuilding civil society, facilitating pluralist decision making and addressing social inclusion. Moreover, it is maintained that partnerships can break down barriers and build reconciliation and trust within Northern Ireland and on the island of Ireland.

2 The Partnership Approach to Public Policy

Introduction

Before analysing partnership arrangements in Northern Ireland a clear understanding must first be grasped of what is meant by the term partnership. This chapter aims to provide a background to the study by analysing partnerships and gaining a deep insight into partnership arrangements, their structures, processes and procedures.

This chapter will be divided into five parts; in the first, attention will be given to the origins and roots of partnerships, explaining how they emerged and why partnerships have become such a popular approach in public policy. Following this, the second part includes a critique of partnership models in which various types of partnership arrangements are assessed and located within the context of other multi-organisational relationships. The third part discusses the advantages of the partnerships, and the fourth part, analyses the disadvantages of the approach. Finally, in part five, the conditions which facilitate partnership governance will be highlighted and examined.

The Emergence and Pervasiveness of Partnerships

In the last two decades a general rise in the popularity of the partnership approach to public policy has occurred (Tilson *et al*, 1997). Within this relatively short period of time partnerships have become a major force in public policy formulation and implementation in a number of different countries, particularly in contemporary advanced democracies. Partnerships have been applied across a wide range of government departments, for example, in economic development, education, environment and at different levels of governance be it at the local, regional, national or supranational levels. This section seeks to examine and explain common themes which have precipitated the rise of partnerships throughout contemporary advanced democracies.

There are a number of economic, social and political changes which have taken place in both the global and national spheres which help to explain the pervasiveness of the partnership approach. It is these three interlocking and changing factors which have accumulated in recent years to cause fragmentation and separation in the world order and have led to what some commentators such as, Meadowcroft (1997), Kickert *et al* (1997), Rhodes (1997) and Peters and Pierre (1998), call a paradigm shift in the process of governance.

Both national and global economic systems have experienced dramatic changes in the last twenty years. One of the most prominent changes is that the economic system is becoming more interconnected, largely due to the expansion of technology and the rise of multinational companies. This has created a global economic system in which the concepts of free trade and the market have diminished the importance of national boundaries. Alongside global interconnectedness, changes in economic organisation have led to increased diversity and division in economic production. As Healey states,

> Firms not only vary in sectors they operate in and in their size and ownership...but also in the production chains they are part of, and how they seek to add value to these chains. As a result, the firms within a region have very diverse stakes in that region, depending on the particular development strategy of each firm (Healey, 1996, p.208).

As a consequence of the interconnected global system and fragmentation of economic production, governments have found it increasingly difficult to manage their national economic systems (Prior, 1996). The problem for national governments is exacerbated in the light of increasing economic competition and pressures on public resources which has made it difficult to promote development in disadvantaged regions.

The problems resulting from the changes in the economic system are paralleled by those arising from the changes in social relations. At present, there is greater appreciation and recognition by politicians and planners of the diversity and difference in today's social world. Income, age, gender, education, ethnic background, religious group, experience of race and social orientation are now used as dimensions of difference in public policy and indeed, this can be recognised as a good thing. However, Healey (1996) has acknowledged that social diversity has also created a number of problems. Healey comments that, in the post war period, politicians and planners characterised people as aggregates, as the masses, or different classes and income groups. The recognition of being 'working class' gave people meaning to their often hard lives as people could combine in a common struggle to improve their circumstances. Recent economic and social changes have undermined the meaning of working class life and the basis both for collective organisation and neighbourhood collaboration. Healey claims that,

> Social divisions cut across each other, emphasising individuality and isolation. In many parts of British cities today, people feel cut off, isolated, marginalised and at least threatened (Healey, 1996, p.209).

Due to the recent economic and social changes many commentators now argue that a decisive shift from one globally dominant mode of democratic capitalist system has occurred to another, albeit, not yet defined post-fordist mode in which the distinguishing characteristics are according to Prior,

> supply side economic management, flexible and individualised systems of production and consumption, highly differentiated social and cultural norms and institutions and a declining role for national governments (Prior, 1996, p.93).

Not only have changes occurred in the economic and social fields but the system of public administration has also experienced a period of transition. In the last twenty years centralisation of government policy has had a profound impact on policy formulation and implementation. In Britain, for example, centralisation has been carried out by successive Conservative administrations. In various measures such as privatisation and contracting out, the role of local authorities has been diminished whereas the authority of central government and newly created government bodies and agencies has grown. The policy environment can now be characterised as more fragmented, diverse and complex as government incorporates a multiplicity of actors, each of whom has an important role to play in the policy process. For national and local government, this has led to problems of duplication, competition, inefficiency and lack of co-ordination (Rhodes, 1994). The impact of centralisation on public policy can be clearly seen in relation to urban policy. As Stewart comments,

The most visible trend to the centralisation of urban policy, however, has been the establishment of a range of initiatives which bypass the local process of planning and control and accountability and which concentrate power in Whitehall... This has created organisational proliferation and consequently fragmented local capacity (Stewart, 1994, p.135).

It can be clearly seen that the effect of the economic, social and political changes have cumulatively caused a separation, fragmentation and division in the policy environment. Bryson and Crosby (1992) comment that a fundamental paradigm shift has occurred from the world we previously lived in to a shared power world in which,

no one is in charge, no one organisation or institution is in a position to find and implement solutions to the problems that confront us in society. In this world organisations and institutions that share objectives must also partly share resources and authority in order to achieve their collective goals (Bryson and Crosby, 1992, p.4).

The current social, economic and political changes have led to calls that a new form of governance is emerging. New governance acknowledges that national governments are finding it increasingly difficult to manage in contemporary, complex, dynamic and interdependent environments. According to Meadowcroft governance is concerned with,

The challenge of governing developed industrialised democracies in more turbulent conditions, when long standing problems appear unnameable to traditional solutions and new problems are gathering pace to upset the polity, - internationalisation of economic life, increasing social complexity and differentiation, the information revolution etc. (Meadowcroft, 1997, p.439).

The debate in governance is, therefore, not concerned with whether the economic, social and policy environments have changed the role of government, but with what form this new governance will take. On the one hand, some commentators such as Osborne and Gaebler (1992) argue that new governance will be enacted through New Public Management. New Public Management is based on the premise that bureaucracy is no longer capable of providing effective public service and that these provisions should be delivered through greater competition from contracting out, quasi-markets and consumer choice. It is maintained that a new entrepreneurial government should emerge which has the responsibility for making policy decisions (steering) but leaves the service delivery (rowing) to be implemented by private sector, competitive forces. On the other hand, Kooiman (1993) argues that new governance involves managing and operating different kinds of networks which are located across the public policy sphere. It is held that no single actor, public or private has the knowledge, overview or action potential to dominate in a policy area which is based on complex, dynamic interactions and interdependencies. Kooiman believes that governance is the result of the interaction of social and political organisations or bodies,

> Socio-political government is directed at the creation of patterns of interaction in which political and traditional hierarchical governing and social self-organisation are complementary, in which responsibility and accountability for interventions are spread over public and private actors (Kooiman, 1993 p.252).

In recognising this difference of opinion in the understanding of new governance arrangements, Rhodes (1996) outlines characteristics of governance which have been identified by a range of commentators. In new governance Rhodes sees a limited role for government, changing boundaries between the public, private and voluntary sectors, interdependence between organisations and continuing interactions within an interorganisational network. The view that governance will involve the operation of interorganisational networks is also supported by Bryson and Crosby. They note that government can no longer be managed by traditional hierarchical organisations which engage in highly rational expert based planning and decision making. Now the process of government is characterised by 'fluid, somewhat chaotic networks of organisations with overlapping domains and conflicting authorities' (Bryson and Crosby, 1992, p.5).

To effectively manage and operate the new economic, social and political changes which have transformed the world system and order of government, Healey argues a new mechanism of government should be created in which all stakeholders can actively participate in the governmental process and agree on a consensual way forward. Healey emphasises the importance,

First of designing arenas for communication and collaboration which give access to all those who have a stake in an issue: second, finding ways of conducting discussion and shifting decision making power as close as possible to those who will experience and live with the consequences of strategic choices: and third, fostering styles of discussion which allow the different points of view of diverse stakeholders to be opened up and explored (Healey, 1996, p.211).

As one means to adapt to changes in government and the new shared power world, governments at every level have embraced the concept of partnerships. Partnerships are arrangements which envisage the convergence of different actors or sectors of influence to ensure implementation of public policy and the delivery of specific objectives. Bailey states that partnerships represent 'a mobilisation of a co-ordination of interests drawn from one sector in order to prepare and oversee an agreed strategy for a defined area or objective.' (Bailey, 1994, p.293). Partnerships, with their notions of consensual agreement and involvement of other sectors, have become central to the debate over networks and governance. Partnerships have been increasingly seen by government as a new approach to deal with a complex, fragmented and interdependent policy environment. Rhodes argues that partnerships are an ideal mechanism which can bring together organisations in the policy process to build and manage an integrative approach in an interdependent system 'partnerships provide a means of developing strategic direction and co-ordination within a polycentric terrain.' (Rhodes, 1997, xii).

The partnership approach to public policy sees participants at all levels of government coming together with the private, community and voluntary sector to solve common problems and forge a common purpose. Partnerships establish new relationships which imply a change in the nature of governance with the state taking a less pronounced role. Prior comments that the aim of partnerships,

> will be to create a new institutional capacity to achieve specific outcomes, in relation to a shared problem or need by establishing a distinct 'ownership' of that problem and directing specific resources to it (Prior, 1996, p.97).

Therefore, the implementation of the partnership approach has corresponded with recent economic, social and political changes as governments seek to adapt to new governance and a shared power world.

Another reason for the rise of partnerships in public policy is that the approach has gained support from across the political spectrum. Partnerships with their aim of devolving power and increasing responsibility to lower levels, while involving the private sector and reducing the role of the state, have appealed to both the Left and Right of the political spectrum. Partnerships are seen as a politically neutral term as Langton (1983) points out,

> The partnership idea implies drawing on the best strategies that have become associated with liberalism and conservatism in America. For example, partnerships build on the liberal practice of intervention in community life to address a social problem, while building on the conservative preference for drawing on and relating social solutions to the resources and needs of the private sector (cited By De Neufville and Barton, 1987, p.195).

Similarly, Hutchinson (1994) comments that one explanation for the popularity of partnerships is that they can be marketed as a politically neutral term. It is held that partnerships with their connotations of co-operation and sharing appeal to both sectors of the economy; the private sector can promote itself being active on social issues, community groups can achieve access to decision making and the public sector can claim to be facilitating decision making at the local level. In facilitating co-operation between the public and private sector, partnerships are marrying traditional principles of the left and right in the pursuit of one common approach, as Gordon Brown, the then Shadow Minister of the economy, stated,

> It (is) necessary therefore to transcend the old sterile battle between the public and private - between nationalisation on the one hand and the dogma of privatisation on the other, between the idea that government should do everything and the view that government should do nothing... That is why we have to examine how public and private sectors can work together to meet common objectives (Rt. Hon Gordon Brown MP January 1997, cited by Colman 1997).

It is recognised that partnerships are a mechanism which can embrace the two ideological economic and political traditions and tackle the problems of fragmentation, separation and division.

The implementation of the partnership approach is also driven by the pragmatic response of government to deal with the increasing constraints on public resources. From the 1970s governments have been eager to seek new sources of finance and to examine whether partnerships will deliver more with less. By entering into partnership arrangements governments can reduce duplication and lever additional resources from the private, voluntary and community sectors (Lowndes and Skelcher, 1998). Encouraging the participation of voluntary and community groups increases responsibility at the local level and reduces the financial burden on the state. For this reason, the partnership approach has been supported by the US government, as President Clinton and Vice President Al Gore stated in their pre-election manifesto *Putting People First* (1992),

> We can no longer afford to pay more and get less from-our government. The answer for every problem cannot always be another program or more money. It is time to radically change the way government operates - to shift from the top down bureaucracy to entrepreneurial government that empowers citizens and communities to change our country from the bottom up (cited by Murray and Dunn, 1996, p.32).

Furthermore, the growth of partnerships is closely associated with the moves by government to open up local decision making processes. Interest and community / voluntary groups have been actively campaigning for a greater voice and inclusion in the decision making process. In recent years there has been a relative decline in membership of political parties and a concomitant rise in support for local and national pressure groups. This according to Wilson and Charlton has been accompanied by,

> an increasing desire for more involvement in the provision of local services by people from the local community. Individuals and organisations from all sectors are increasingly demanding a voice in defining and implementing the most appropriate responses to many of the challenges facing society (Wilson and Charlton, 1997, pp.11-12).

In the light of poor turnouts at local elections and a rise in the support for community / voluntary groups, local authorities have established partnerships to facilitate community governance and improve service delivery. By involving private and voluntary / community sectors in the decision making process, local authorities aim to develop a consensual decision making model which will strengthen their role. Jezierski points out that public-private partnerships,

> provide a rationale, flexible, voluntary and co-operative alternative decision making structure to augment the local state and the market to 'rehabilitate the civic tradition' (Jezierski, 1990, p.217).

Partnerships have provided voluntary and community groups the opportunity to become more involved with the state and active in the policy process.

The growth of partnerships has also been in response to the increasing complexity of policy issues. Stewart (1996) and Rittel and Webber (1973) refer to these complex problems as 'wicked issues', which can only be addressed by bringing together a range of organisations and interest groups. For example, when tackling social problems in an inner city area, governments must deal with a range of organisations including, local authorities, social services, housing authorities, department of education, the police, local businesses, and community / voluntary groups such as youth groups and organisations for the elderly. In this approach partnerships are created out of necessity and partners are chosen to work together because it is recognised that the issue cannot be effectively addressed without them (Darwin, 1999).

Having reviewed the reasons behind the emergence and pervasiveness of partnerships it is necessary to outline and define what is meant by the term partnership. As discussed in the introduction of this book, partnership is a very loose term and can include a range of different relationships. On this basis it is important to gain an understanding of what is meant by the term partnership by identifying the different types which exist.

The Classification of Partnership Arrangements

Partnership arrangements can be differentiated in a number of ways. Probably one of the most basic classifications is that used by Jacobs, as cited in Hutchinson (1994). Jacobs distinguishes partnerships as being either exclusivist, open to local or national elite, or pluralistic, open to and encouraging every sectional and political interest. Although a simple classification, this seeks to understand the structure of different partnerships. It is pointed out that different structures of partnerships may have implications for the decision making process. Jacobs states that in partnerships, decision making will tend to rest with a forum such as a board of directors,

> who may choose to consult widely with various interested bodies on one issue or a range of issues (as with the pluralist model), or they may choose to use board members as representatives or mere limited interests to achieve a decision (as with the exclusivist model) (cited by Hutchinson, 1994, p.338).

Brown and Wilson (1984), cited by Gray (1989), on the other hand classify partnerships according to their focus,

> Programmatic partnerships involve specific contractual agreements of short duration among limited partners. Developmental partnerships are industry or regional-level efforts that provide group benefits. Systematic partnerships are typically long range and societal in scope (cited by Gray, 1989, p.186).

What is important to distil from Brown and Wilson's classification is that partnerships can vary according to their duration and scope of involvement. In this case partnerships can be seen to range from short term specific contract agreements, involving a small number of partners, to long term agreements which involve a broader community.

Leonardi defines partnerships in relation to their method of programme implementation. Leonardi, cited by Jacobs (1994), refers to vertical and horizontal partnerships. Vertical partnerships are those which operate at different levels, governmental or intersectoral. These arrangements include partnerships between central and local government and partnerships between the public and private sectors. Secondly, Leonardi identifies horizontal partnership arrangements or networks which operate at the same institutional level, governmental or sectoral. Horizontal arrangements, for example, will include partnerships between different governmental departments or between different local authorities. Although Leonardi's categorisation of partnerships maybe basic and does not further assist the understanding of partnerships and their various arrangements, it is a useful method when classifying different types of partnerships across a range of government departments and programmes.

Bailey (1994), however, goes further and attempts to characterise different types of partnerships in a typology based on a number of identified variables (Table 2:1). The variables include the process of mobilisation, that is whether the partnerships are created through a top-down or bottom up process. The second variable relates to the range of partners involved in the balance of power between the sectors. The third variable examines the nature and extent of the remit adopted by the partnership. And the final variable, the area of coverage, refers to the purpose and membership of partnerships. The categories are designed to indicate groupings of similar organisations. Bailey recognises that the fluid and ambiguous nature of partnerships does not make categorisation easy and so there may be examples displaying characteristics which fit into more than one category. It is also acknowledged that in some instances there may be a succession along the categorisation from smaller local initiatives to the larger partnerships.

In this typology Bailey acknowledges the diversity of partnership arrangements ranging from small neighbourhood partnerships between local authorities and community organisations, to sub-regional partnerships involving all sectors to formulate broad strategies for development. Continuing on from this, the OECD has formulated a definition of partnerships which encompasses the variety and diversity of partnerships. Partnerships are defined as,

> Systems of formalised co-operation, grounded in legally binding arrangements or informal understandings, co-operative working relationships, and mutually adopted plans among a number of institutions. They involve agreements on policy and programme objectives and the sharing of responsibility, resources, risks and benefits over a specified period of time (OECD, 1990, p.18).

This gives an overarching definition of the term partnership, outlining practices and principles. From the definition it can be seen that partnerships have a wide remit of functional activities stretching from legally binding arrangements to informal understandings. This diversity of partnership arrangements is also recognised by Bennet and Krebs who state that,

> Partnerships can range from agreement between actors to work towards a common end to agreements for a legal contract, through which specific targets for performance are defined by the contracting parties (cited by Hutchinson, 1994, p.336).

Table 2.1   Bailey's Typology of Partnerships

Type	Mobilisation	Area of coverage	Range of partners	Remit
Development	locally	single site or small area, e.g. a town centre	private developer, housing association plus the local authority	joint development to mutual advantage
Development trust	locally	neighbour-hood	community based with local authority and other reps.	community based regeneration
Joint agreement/ coalition/ company	locally but may be in response to national policy	clearly defined area identified for regeneration	public, private, voluntary	preparation of formal/ informal strategy implementation often through third parties
Promotional	locally, e.g. Chamber of Commerce	district or city-wide	private sector led Sponsored by Chamber of Commerce or development agency	place marketing promotion of growth and investment
Agency	nationally based on legislative powers	urban, sub-regional	public sector sponsored with private sector appointees	terms of reference from sponsoring agency
Strategic	regional/ county/ local	sub-regional	all sectors	determining broad strategy for growth and development

Source: (Bailey, 1994, p.296)

Skelcher *et al* (1996) also comment on this diversity of partnership arrangements and make a distinction between partnerships and networks. It is maintained that partnerships include agreements which are more formal and comprise established relationships, whereas stakeholders, whose relationships are based on more pragmatic and *ad hoc* agreements, are network arrangements,

Partnerships tend to have a formal basis involving such devices as a company structure, partnership board or memorandum of agreement. As a result the partnership has a clear boundary - there is an explicit statement defining who its members are. Because of this, the partnership's composition will be relatively stable and its operation will tend to be formalised through boards, committees, numbers of meetings and agreements over members' rights and obligations (Skelcher *et al*, 1996, p.9).

On the other hand, Skelcher *et al* see networks as the opposite of partnerships containing few rules and procedures, a low degree of formality and a blurred boundary. They argue that networks have boundaries which,

are indistinct - it is not always obvious who is or who is not in a particular network, and one network will often overlap with several others. The composition of networks is changeable since the involvement and activity of members will often vary over time. Finally, networks do not tend to have specific rules and procedures - they have a low level of formality (Skelcher *et al*, 1996, p.8).

It can be seen that Skelcher *et al* view partnerships as including arrangements which are more legally binding with specific targets for performance rather than informal understandings and agreements to work towards a common end.

Prior (1996) underscores this assessment of partnerships by maintaining they are formal, stable relationships. Prior however, goes further and outlines a three fold typology of multi-organisational arrangements consisting of partnerships, consortia and alliances. According to Prior each arrangement is categorised in relation to its separate organisational autonomy. Partnerships are arrangements which have the greatest autonomy over and above the individual participant organisations, and alliances are arrangements in which the participant organisations work together in common areas but most of the autonomy remains with individual organisations rather than the alliance:

Alliances: Formed with the purpose of exerting influence and shaping opinion. They are characterised by a convergence of values between co-operative organisations. The specific aim of the alliance will be to develop ways of acting together to influence outsiders to the network or to influence a third party within the network…Alliances seek to change organisational behaviour but through direct means; they leave existing organisational forms, including the form of the network, unchanged.

Consortia: Concerned with establishing a joint approach to strategy and policy development and with joint decision making. They are characterised by a convergence of policy goals between the partners. Consortium aims will be defined in terms of joint planning and co-ordination of specific projects or programmes, or the use of collective resources in the most efficient and effective ways; or they may be defined in terms of the development of new forms of practice…Consortia seek specific outcomes by tying partners together in formal arrangements to undertake joint action. The consortium will often have a particular identity as a task group, planning team or joint working party but is not constituted as a separate organisational entity…The existing forms of the separate collaboration organisations themselves are, however, left unchanged.

Partnerships: Formed to ensure the implementation or delivery of specific objectives. They are characterised by a convergence of functional interest between partner organisations. The aim of the partnership will be to create a new organisational capacity to achieve specific outcomes, in relation, for example, to a shared problem or need by establishing a distinct 'ownership' of that problem and directing specific resources to it… Partnerships pursue specific goals on behalf of their constituent bodies though a separate organisational form…they imply change in the original organisations, because of the transfer of resources and functions of the new body, and to the network since they constitute a new and autonomous member of it (Prior, 1996, pp.96&97).

In addition, Prior comments that not all of the arrangements will fit easily into one of the three categories,

> The typology does not do justice to the complexity of the network relationships that exist in practice; it will often be the case, for instance, that two organisations are involved in different forms of co-operative relationship simultaneously (Prior, 1996, p.97).

Therefore, it can be seen that Prior views partnerships, alliances and consortia as dynamic, evolving and containing a multiplicity of different interactions which may overlap between the three arrangements.

It appears that there is some confusion as to what exactly are different types of partnership arrangements. The OECD and Bennet and Krebs view partnerships as including arrangements ranging from informal agreements with partners working towards a common end to legally binding formal contracts. On the other hand, Prior and Skelcher *et al* would agree that partnerships are used to characterise formal, legal structures with a large degree of separate autonomy.

Given the fluid and diverse nature of partnership arrangements and the confusion in the literature over classifying partnerships, one useful method of classification is to set them within the context of the multi-organisational continuum. This concept is proposed by Bryson and Crosby who believe that, within a shared power world, a plethora of multi-organisational relationships exist which can be structured or ordered along a continuum in which at one end,

> are organisations that hardly relate to one another, or are adversaries, dealing with a problem domain that extends beyond their capabilities, and at the other end are organisations emerged into a new organisation that contains a new problem domain, pursues shared objectives, and operates co-operatively. In the mid-range are coalitions of organisations that have characteristics of both extremes (Bryson and Crosby, 1992, p.13).

Partnerships, in being varied and diverse arrangements between two or more organisations, can be located within this multi-organisational continuum. Partnerships can be seen to exist within a family of multi-organisational arrangements which can be differentiated in terms of the strength and interconnectedness of the relationships between stakeholders or organisations. What is common among them all is that the organisations are centred on a relationship based approach to problem solving and action which recognises that people and organisations working independently cannot deal effectively with the complexity of issues in a shared power world. As a means to define and characterise different relationships in the continuum, it is helpful to view the different processes which make up the relationship based approach. A number of commentators such as Rogers *et al* (1982), Webb (1991), Gray (1989), Mattessich and Monsey (1992) and Hall *et al* (1977) maintain the continuum is comprised of three main processes, *co-operation, co-ordination* and *collaboration*. To understand and determine at what end of the continuum particular relationships are based it is necessary to define and distinguish these processes.

According to Mattessich and Monsey (1992) *co-operation* is a process which involves a minimal form of dealing between organisations. Co-operation is defined as comprising,

> Informal relationships that exist without any defined mission, structure or planning effort, information is shared as needed and authority is retained by each organisation; there is little risk and both resources and rewards are particular to each participant in the process (Mattessich and Monsey, 1992, p.17).

Similarly, Rogers *et al* (1982) believe that co-operation is a process which is included at the lowest end of the relationship scale. They state that 'co-operation is characterised by informal trade-offs and by attempts to establish reciprocity in the absence of rules.' (cited by Gray, 1989, p.15).

Moving along the continuum it is argued that *co-ordination* is a process which encapsulates a more intense relationship which is characterised by more formal and institutional dealings. Mattessich and Monsey (1992) comment that,

> Co-ordination is typified by more formal relationships and a common understanding of comparable missions, there is some joint planning, division of roles and the establishment of communication channels; Authority still rests within individual organisations, but there is increased risk to all participants. Resources are available to all participants and rewards are mutually acknowledged (Mattessich and Monsey, 1992, p.18).

In tandem with Mattessich and Monsey, Rogers *et al* note the distinction between co-operation and co-ordination as being informal and formal relations. It is held that, 'co-ordination refers to formal institutionalised relationships among existing networks of organisations' (cited by Gray, 1989, p.15). Webb also comments that the process of co-ordination involves a closer more determined and formal relationship than co-operation. Webb argues that co-ordination,

> Implies change and the disturbance of the existing order when it involves the crossing of boundaries between mutually exclusive, competitive or previously unrelated interests and domains. (In the human services) this tends to mean interorganisational and inter-profession boundaries (Webb, 1991, p.231).

Collaboration, on the other hand, is held to involve an even greater interlocking process resulting in a more complete and unified relationship or interaction. Mattessich and Monsey comment that collaboration is identified as a more,

> Durable and persuasive relationship; it brings previously separate organisations into a structure with full commitment to a common mission; the sustainability of these relationships is dependant upon planning and well defined reliable communication channels operating on many levels; authority is determined by the collaboration structures and risk is much greater because each participant contributes reputation and owned resources; the latter are pooled jointly and secured for a longer term effort that is managed by the collaboration structure; product outcomes are shared and more is accomplished jointly than could have individually (Mattessich and Monsey, 1992, p.22).

What is unique about collaboration is that the autonomy is centred on the collaboration and with individual organisations. Huxham (1993) notes that in collaborative arrangements stakeholders develop a meta strategy which is 'jointly owned by the organisations involved and which is super-ordinate to the strategies of the collaborating organisations' (Huxham, 1993, p.23). Collaboration can be distinguished from co-operation and co-ordination in that the meta strategy or collaboration has autonomy over and above the individual stakeholders. In co-operation and co-ordination the individual stakeholders autonomy supersedes the common strategy and multi-organisational relationship. This distinction further points to the view that collaboration is a more formal and unified process and located at the high end of the shared power continuum.

According to Gray (1989) collaboration is seen as an emergent process. Collaboration is thought of as a dynamic, interactive and evolutionary concept which is a more unifying process of interorganisational relationship but which also may include the processes of co-operation and co-ordination. Co-operation and co-ordination are terms used to identify static patterns of interorganisational relations whereas collaboration is a term to which organisations seeking deeper more unifying relationships work towards. As Gray points out,

> collaborations progress from 'under-organised' systems in which individual stakeholders act independently, to more tightly organised relationships characterised by concerted decision making among the

stakeholders....Both co-operation and co-ordination often occur as part of collaboration. The process by which reciprocity is established informally in the absence of rules is as important to collaboration as the formal co-ordination agreements that emerge (Gray, 1989, p.15).

In an attempt to characterise the processes within interorganisational relationships and to show more clearly the division of these processes along a continuum, it will be useful to closely examine Mattessich and Monsey's division of co-operation, co-ordination and collaboration (Table 2.2). Mattessich and Monsey break down the processes into four essential elements: vision and relationships, structure responsibilities and communication, authority and accountability, and resources and rewards. These elements are then used to specifically define the interorganisational continuum and identify the particular processes involved.

Having outlined and assessed the different types of partnership arrangements, attention must now be given to analysing the partnership approach. Examining the strengths and weaknesses of partnerships allows for a greater understanding of partnerships and above all, provides a necessary foundation upon which to construct an evaluation of partnership arrangements in Northern Ireland.

An Analysis of the Strengths of the Partnership Approach

The first advantage of partnerships is that they can create stability in the environment. Due to recent economic, social and political changes, previously referred to in this chapter, organisations now operate in an increasingly turbulent and complex environment. This has left individual organisations unstable and uncertain about their future as they lack the requisite diversity to successfully adapt to ever changing demands. This view is espoused by Damirez who argues that 'the emergence of interrelated, rapid outcomes exceeds the existing organised matching capabilities', rendering the environment, 'increasingly uncertain and unmanageable for the organisation' (cited by Gray, 1989, p.231). It is argued that stakeholders can come together to create a unified organisation which is complex and flexible and capable of adapting quickly to the turbulent environment. Wood and Gray point out that organisations can seek to reduce the pressures and demands of a declining resource base and increased competition by managing, 'interdependencies and gaining control over crucial resource supplies, thus reducing the uncertainty of gaining those supplies' (Wood and Gray, 1991, p.156).

Table 2.2   Mattessich and Monsey's Division of Co-operation, Co-ordination and Collaboration

Essential Elements	Co-operation	Co-ordination	Collaboration
Vision and Relationships	Basis for co-operation is usually between individuals but may be mandated by a third party.	Individual relationships are supported by the organisations they represent.	Commitment of the organisations and their leaders is fully behind their representatives.
	Organisational missions and goals are not taken into account.	Missions and goals of individual organisations are reviewed for compatibility.	Common, new mission and goals are created.
	Interaction is on as needed basis, may last indefinitely.	Interaction is usually around one specific project or task of definable length.	One or more projects are undertaken for longer term results.
Structure, Responsibilities, Communication	Relationships are informal; each organisation functions separately.	Organisations involved take on needed roles, but function relatively independently of each other.	New organisational structure and / or clearly defined and interrelated roles that constitute a formal division of labour are created.
	No joint planning is required.	Some project-specific planning is required.	More comprehensive planning is required that includes developing joint strategies and measuring success in terms of impact on the needs of those served.

Essential Elements	Co-operation	Co-ordination	Collaboration
	Information is conveyed as needed.	Communication roles are established and definite channels are created for interaction.	Beyond communication roles and channels for interaction, many levels of communication are created as clear information is a keystone for success.
Authority and Accountability	Authority rests solely with the individual organisations.	Authority rests with the individual organisations but there is co-ordination among participants.	Authority is determined by the collaboration to balance ownership by the individual organisations with expediency to accomplish purpose.
	Leadership is unilateral and control is central.	Some sharing of leadership and control.	Leadership is dispersed, and control is shared and mutual.
	All authority and accountability rests with the individual organisation which acts independently.	There is some shared risk but most of the authority and accountability falls to individual organisations.	Equal risk is shared by all organisations in the collaboration.
Resources and Rewards	Resources (staff time, Dollars and capabilities) are separate, serving the individual organisations needs.	Resources are acknowledged and can be made available to others for a specific project.	Resources are pooled or jointly secured for a longer-term effort that is managed by the collaborative structure.
		Rewards are mutually Acknowledged.	Organisations share in the products; more is accomplished jointly than could have been individually.

Source: (Mattessich and Monsey, 1992, p.40)

Organisations in a turbulent competitive environment are dependant on other organisations for needed resources and, if they collaborate, resources can be adequately shared, thus placing greater control on the environment. Organisations can come together in a partnership and manage the environment more effectively and efficiently together, as Wood and Gray comment, 'organisations collaborate to achieve legitimacy and to establish a shared understanding of common threats' (Wood and Gray, 1991, p.157). It is held that through partnership, organisations can utilise their own activities to create one organisation to address common problems in a collective way. This approach helps to build a form of stability and reduce the turbulent effects of the external environment.

A further benefit of the partnership approach is synergy. Synergy as noted by Bailey (1994), is centred on the premise that two or more organisations can achieve more by acting together than separately. In this case organisations in collaboration or partnership will tackle a problem with greater ease than if they are acting independently. Gray (1989) refers to this advantage of collaboration as action learning and explains that if organisations act independently they are likely to bring their own preoccupations to problems, restricting the range of possible options. Under the process of collaboration, however, a greater appreciation of the problem is at hand,

> As stakeholders share their individual appreciation about the problem, a more comprehensive understanding of the problem emerges. Thus, collectively the stakeholders can create an appreciation that is rich enough in variety to represent the complexity of the problem itself and robust enough to withstand buffeting from the environment (Gray, 1989, p.239).

Another advantage of partnerships can be explained in relation to the process of transformation. Bailey (1994) comments that the process of transformation reflects the fluid process of decision making within the partnerships and the fact that values and objectives are likely to change as the partnership develops. Bailey states that,

> Each partner is not merely trying to work with the other and find common ground for mutual benefit, each is trying to move the objectives and culture of the other towards their own ideas (Bailey, 1994, p.298).

Under partnership arrangements, organisations have the ability to learn from each other, share experiences and teach partners other processes and procedures. The process of transformation can help to explain the motivation behind the public and private sectors entering partnerships. As Mackintosh points out,

> The private sector is seeking to bring private sector objectives into the public sector, to shake it up, get it to seek more market orientated aims, to work more efficiently in its terms... The public sector, conversely, is trying to push the private sector towards more 'social' and longer term aims, justifying this in precisely the same terms (Mackintosh, 1992, p.216).

Similarly, O'Looney comments that the process of transformation is motivating partnerships. O'Looney states that the public and private sectors are eager to transform and exchange the principles of flexibility and accountability and in particular, the private sector is motivated to make government operate more like business,

> There is movement to bring more accountability into the public sector. As concerns about competitiveness and the environment become more politically salient, the trends in the public sector suggest a movement toward greater flexibility in a number of areas. Concerns about competitiveness, for example, are forcing public sector actors to become more sensitive to the needs of business and more flexible in the way they support and restrict private sector operations (O'Looney, 1992, p.14).

Commentators such as Gray (1989) and Bryson and Crosby (1992) argue that collaboration and partnership will provide new mechanisms under which governments can improve public policy and managers can better organisations. It is explained that in a shared power world, traditional, hierarchical and centralised organisations are no longer capable of formulating and implementing effective policy and that now, collaboration and partnership is the key. This view is supported by Luke who argues that,

> No agency controls the essential elements of a policy making system that is now intergovernmental and intersectoral. The existence, intentions and jurisdictions of other actors substantially reduces functional autonomy and often creates a strong sense of powerlessness... Policy formulation and

implementation require multi-lateral co-operation and shared power across traditional boundaries and jurisdictions (cited by Gray, 1989, p.232).

It is believed that through a collaborative or partnership approach, all relevant actors or stakeholders in the policy process will be involved in developing one common approach, thus creating more effective and co-ordinated policy. Bryson and Crosby comment that,

> Shared power arrangements are typically designed to increase governance and management capacity in this world that is functionally interconnected but structurally divided (Bryson and Crosby, 1992, p.17).

The partnership approach is seen to be a better approach to problem solving as it applies a multi-agency approach to a multidimensional problem. Due to the increasing interconnectedness of the global and local system, problems in the community have become more multidimensional. Wilson and Charlton comment that it is now,

> very difficult to look at an aspect of a community, for example, crime prevention or environment without looking at a much wider range of social issues such as housing, transport, health and education (Wilson and Charlton, 1997, p.12).

With social and economic problems having multiple causes, partnerships which adopt a multi-agency approach, could be seen as the best way of tackling the issue. It is argued that more innovative policies and programmes will result from partnerships as they involve participants who have first hand knowledge of the problems at ground level and include a range of actors who each bring a different perspective to the problem.

Bryson and Crosby also argue that a more effective process of governance will emerge as those within the remit of government will become more empowered and can contribute their own actions and ideas to the policy process. Bryson and Crosby state that for this to occur, leadership within the collaborative arrangements is the key, 'quality leadership can build teams and incorporate and empower other members of groups to be leaders themselves' (Bryson and Crosby, 1992, p.18).

With empowerment established at the lower level of governance, this may encourage participant actors to take responsibility and 'ownership' of certain programmes or policies. Once this is established it is likely that more long term sustainable programmes will be adopted. Mayo supports this view and states that partnerships, 'promote cultures of self help and self sustaining development rather than a culture of dependency' (Mayo, 1997, p.6). By involving a range of organisations and facilitating more responsibility at the lower level, this is a more effective way of ensuring stakeholders at the local community will benefit from government action. Gilchrist states that networking,

> has the potential to transform current inequalities of opportunity because it creates the possibility for information, expertise and influence to flow across organisational and cultural barriers (cited by Skelcher *et al*, 1996, p.25).

Furthermore, by providing greater responsibility at the local level partnerships can improve local democracy. It is argued that empowering traditionally excluded or marginalised groups will give them confidence and purpose to participate in partnership decision making which can complement formal democratic processes such as local government (Wheeler, 1996).

Under the partnership approach the possibilities for greater access to resources will be increased. Wood and Gray (1991) suggest that organisations can act collaboratively, perhaps in a joint venture, and create a plan to unilaterally gain control over vital resource supplies. Bailey (1994) also acknowledges this view of partnership and refers to the concept as budget enlargement. Bailey contends that a common justification for actors entering into partnership arrangements is to seek money, for example,

> a public sector institution with limited resources and a private company seeking subsidy or risk reduction will construct a joint venture dependant on funding from a third party (Bailey, 1994, p.298).

According to Bailey, collaboration to receive extra revenue from central government has become an important role for partnerships. Under this process partnership actors are obviously benefiting from the added resources and increased revenue.

An Analysis of the Weaknesses of the Partnership Approach

One criticism of partnerships is that they increase environmental complexity and turbulence. Pycroft (1996) comments that the use of the partnership approach has significantly changed the local governance process. It is argued that partnerships are being created under numerous strategies and programmes of local economic development and this has created a confusing mix of interlinking and overlapping partnerships and strategic alliances. Bresser, cited by Gray (1989), supports this view and maintains that partnerships create new dependencies, increase environmental complexity and actually reduce participating organisations' control over the environment,

> Collaboration introduces them (organisations) to new bilateral and multi-lateral relationships to which they must attend, it requires them to develop new skills and abandon and reshape old ones..., all of this, even if it reduces environmental complexity and turbulence in some ways, adds to an organisational information load and contributes to increasing complexity and turbulence in other ways (cited by Gray, 1989, p.158).

The view that the partnership approach increases environmental complexity is also supported by Cebulla (1996). Cebulla comments that the *ad hoc* implementation of partnership arrangements establishes a plethora of partnership boards which in turn indicates a lack of co-ordination and a less than unified approach. Cebulla points out that, 'multiple partnership bodies with multiple agencies and programmes will make co-ordination and finding a common vision for ever more complex' (Cebulla, 1996, p.27). Similarly, Peck and Tickell (1995) note the problems of increased environmental complexity with the *ad hoc* arrangement of partnerships. It is held that although the partnership approach may seem sensible at the level of individual initiatives, a mix of partnerships creates fragmentation and complexity, 'the growth of partnerships tends to *exacerbate* those very problems of poor co-ordination and organisational proliferation which the partnership model is supposed to solve' (Peck and Tickell, 1995, p.263).

A second criticism of the partnership approach has been presented by commentators such as Jay (1995), Brindley and Stoker (1988) and Stewart (1994) who argue that partnerships are undemocratic. Stewart points out that the partnership approach has changed the entire nature and system of the traditional process of local politics, meaning that the traditional systems of democratic accountability have been broken down. Stewart states that due to the partnership approach a new system is in place based on the skills of brokerage of support, the mobilisation of interest, the negotiation of mutual position and the orchestration of local stakeholders. Brindley and Stoker in support of this view maintain that the new process of change under partnership, dilutes local accountability as it generates, 'a form of corporatism in which elite groups in the public sector deal directly with private corporate bodies in proverbial 'smoke filled rooms'. This process is intrinsically anti-democratic.' (Brindley and Stoker, 1988, p.8).

Jay (1995) comments that partnerships established for community development and social inclusion are undemocratic as they are unrepresentative of the communities they aim to represent. Jay claims that partnerships,

> Are driven by elite-based bureaucratic priorities not genuine social needs, they are paternalist and inaccurately targeted and more likely to sustain marginalised groups in a state of ingrate semi-detached dependency than to secure entry into full membership of civil society (Jay, 1995, p.16).

Hutchinson is also critical of the democratic value of partnerships, particularly when non elected bodies and self-appointed representatives gain power at the expense of local politicians. It is held that, 'partnerships can play a very significant role in altering the democratic balance of an area with a danger of producing a non-representative imbalance.' (Hutchinson, 1994, p.338).

A further criticism of partnerships is that they are often unable to effectively forge a common position among participant stakeholders. Woodburn (1985) argues that as partnerships combine a wide variety of interests, they are prone to conflict and are thus fragile mechanisms for policy formulation and implementation. Woodburn points out that as partnerships are comprised of representatives from different sectors and professional backgrounds, each participant has a different perspective on how to define any problem. Having different perspectives of a problem creates conflicting objectives and role confusion in the partnerships as there exists,

> different views on the severity of the problem and the urgency with which it should be tackled; different views on the role each organisation has to

play; and different views on how the mechanism of interventionist activity works (Woodburn, 1985, p.10).

In instances where partnerships fail to forge a common purpose Peck and Tickell argue that partnerships, in an attempt to avoid conflict, tend to concentrate on the issues that bind the stakeholders and at times avoid the harsh political questions. In failing to confront the divisive issues partnerships, 'undermine the capacity to achieve results... In operational terms, then, partnerships are hamstrung by the overriding imperative to keep the partners together' (Peck and Tickell, 1995, p.262).

What is important to distil from Peck and Tickell's criticism is that partnerships are hampered by their overall desire to keep the partners together. Partnership operation can be restricted if the stakeholders find it difficult to forge a common purpose, in this case the energy of the partnership is spent making compromise deals and not taking strategic direction. On a similar note, Mackintosh criticises partnerships because they are seen as a formal battleground in which participant actors can voice their grievances. Partnership is difficult to achieve as relations between public and private sectors and central and local government are tense at the national, macro political level of politics. According to Mackintosh what is going on in partnerships, 'is a version of the broader conflict over the future organisation and scope of the public sector' (Mackintosh, 1992, p.221).

A further weakness in the partnership approach has been pointed out by Peck and Tickell (1995) and Martin and Oztel (1996). It is argued that partnerships are very fragile and loose in nature, formulate short term policies and are only in existence to receive external funding. According to Martin and Oztel,

> In the long term, partnerships where agreement on a vague, overall strategy enables partners to access external funding but does not require them to integrate services, is unsustainable (Martin and Oztel, 1996, p.138).

Peck and Tickell (1995) believe that in some cases the entire rationale for partnership formulation is an application for funding from central government or the European Commission, meaning partnerships are held together more by a 'shared concern to bring additional resources to the region than by mutual interest *per se*' and the very looseness of partnership, 'produces policies of the lowest common denominator' (Pick and Tickell, 1995, p.261).

O'Looney (1992) and Hayton and Gray (1996) maintain that partnerships are flawed as they are rarely based on the notion of shared memberships, shared ownership and shared risk. O'Looney claims that partnerships are either dominated by powerful private associations or public sector interests and this leads to problems within the partnerships, 'having partnerships comprised primarily of major players in particular interest areas can lead to the problem of group-think where assumptions are never challenged or explored and innovative thinking is not fostered' (O'Looney, 1992, p.18).

Hayton and Gray (1996) also point out that imbalance in partnerships or public-private companies can lead to failure of the initiative. Hayton and Gray maintain that,

> Private sector influenced public-private companies are so biased against the public sector that any involvement is on very uneven terms... the government's objective of achieving 'a genuine transfer of risk' to the private sector will not be met (Hayton and Gray, 1996, p.87).

Under these circumstances if a genuine transfer of risk cannot be achieved, the public sector is likely to have reservations over allocating full resources and expertise to the partnership. Having examined partnerships and discussed their advantages and disadvantages, an analysis of partnerships can be included within the summary table, 2.3.

The analysis of the partnership approach clearly shows that certain partnerships are not without their problems and difficulties. It is worth repeating that at times the growth of partnership activity has actually increased environmental complexity, fragmentation, organisational and political conflict and created short term policy initiatives; problems which partnerships themselves were created to resolve. These limitations inherent in partnership arrangements, have led to the argument that partnerships are an ineffective approach to public policy formulation and implementation. However, the debate must move on from assessing the advantages and disadvantages of partnerships and stating whether they are intrinsically bad or good. Consideration needs to be given to analysing the performance of partnerships.

Table 2.3   An Analysis of the Advantages and Disadvantages of Partnerships

Advantages of Partnerships	Disadvantages of Partnerships
Partnerships can establish stability in a turbulent environment created by economic, social and political changes. Stakeholders come together to create a unified organisation which is complex, flexible and capable of adapting quickly to a turbulent environment. Stakeholders can address common problems in a collective way.	Partnerships increase environment complexity and turbulence. Partnerships are created under numerous strategies leading to confusing mix of inter-linking and overlapping partnerships and strategic alliances.
Empowerment at the local level will improve local democracy as traditionally excluded groups are given the opportunity to participate in the decision making process.	Partnerships are undemocratic. Partnerships increase the power of self-appointed members of partnership boards vis-à-vis local politicians thus diluting local accountability. Members of community / voluntary sector are unrepresentative of communities they aim to represent.
Stakeholders involved in developing one common approach create a more effective and co-ordinated policy. Partnerships involve participants who have first hand knowledge of the problems at ground level. Partnerships adopt a multi-agency approach to multi-dimensional problems.	Partnerships find it difficult to develop a common approach. Due to the inclusion of a wide variety of interests, partnerships are prone to conflict and are hindered by the need to keep all the partners together.
Involving stakeholders in partnership creates empowerment and ownership which will establish sustainable programmes and a culture of self-help. An inclusive partnership approach also ensures that stakeholders at the local level will benefit from local action.	Partnerships are fragile mechanisms and are unsustainable. Stakeholders come together in partnership largely to gain additional funding.
Synergy. Partner organisations can achieve more acting together then individually through mutual learning and sharing.	Partnerships are dominated by powerful interests which creates conflict and hinders the development of a common approach.

Advantages of Partnerships	Disadvantages of Partnerships
Transformation. Stakeholders in partnerships have the ability to learn from each other, share experiences and teach partners other processes and procedures.	
Stakeholders in partnership can gain control over resources and maximise budgets.	

One of the main problems for policy makers, who have focused on improving the performance of partnership governance, is that there is no one model for success. The reason for this is explained by examining the nature of partnerships themselves. Across a wide range of public policy areas there are many different types of partnerships, they exist for different reasons, create different structures, involve different partners and set themselves different goals. With various government initiatives adopting different kinds of partnerships, each initiative requires a different approach. The problem is compounded even further by the changing environments in which partnerships operate. Similar types of partnerships could be included as part of the same programme but each may be facing different and varying conditions. Given these circumstances, it proves very difficult to apply a uniform definition of what comprises a successful partnership.

Studies undertaken on improving the performance of partnerships have largely concentrated on developing *ex ante* 'how to do it' or 'making partnerships work' guidance manuals, for example, Combat Poverty Agency (1995) and Wilson and Charlton (1997). These focus on steps or procedures for establishing and operating a successful partnership. Though useful for that reason, the manuals offer little insight into the different types of partnership arrangements and the complex contextual conditions in which they operate. It is the aim of this book to study a variety of partnerships with a view to, examining the conditions which affect the performance of partnerships and their value in the emerging public administration system.

In order to approach this aim, the next part of this chapter seeks to highlight and examine the conditions associated with achieving partnership. These conditions will then provide a framework to test the experience of partnership arrangements in Northern Ireland and between Northern Ireland and other jurisdictions. The conditions which affect the performance of partnerships are divided into four subheadings namely

Contextual Conditions, Stakeholder / Organisational Conditions, Decision Making Conditions and Operational Conditions. The chapter concludes by presenting a table summarising the conditions underpinning partnership governance (Table 2.4).

Conditions Influencing the Performance of Partnerships

Contextual Conditions

Contextual issues can be highlighted as being important factors when examining the conditions which facilitate partnership governance. Contextual issues focus on the background or environment in which partnerships operate. First of all, it is argued that partnerships are more likely to succeed if each partner believes that working together will achieve greater benefit than acting individually. Huxham states that it is, 'perhaps a truism to suggest that unless participants see the value in working together over an issue they are unlikely to do so effectively' (Huxham, 1991, p.1041).

If partners believe that working in partnership will improve service delivery or achieve greater economic and operational efficiency, this will motivate each partner and create a favourable partnership environment. Gray commenting on collaborations suggests that it is important for the participant organisations or stakeholders to believe that they must work together to achieve a common goal. It is argued that, 'the recognition by stakeholders that their desired outcomes are inextricably linked to actions of other stakeholders is the fundamental basis for collaboration' (Gray, 1989, p.58).

On a similar note, partnerships need to operate within a contextual environment of understanding and respect. If the partner organisations respect the traditions and values of each other, this is seen as an important factor in determining a successful partnership. As Tilson *et al* argue, 'potential partners need to have a understanding of the cultures within which they operate' (Tilson *et al*, 1997, p.8).

On the other hand, if a partnership is operating against a background of historical and political confrontation this could have a profound impact on the success of the partnership. Historical and political conflict can combine to entrench different groups in the partnership into traditional camps with each seeing the other as the enemy. For instance, community representatives are often accused of adopting an anti business position. Traditional allegiances and animosities can cause tensions and create disputes which lead to the failure of partnership. As Gray comments, 'historical relationships characterised by long-standing adversarial interactions among parties often create insurmountable obstacles to collaboration' (Gray, 1989, p.249).

However, if partnerships operate within an environment which is historically and politically supportive and which has a tradition of civic involvement and inter-organisational collaboration, then the partnerships will be able to use this supportive environment to their advantage. This view is followed by Kagan *et al* who state that, 'a collaboration that is embedded in a historically and politically supportive context is more likely to survive than one that is not' (cited by Mattessich and Monsey, 1992. p.17).

Relationships in which the partner organisations have opposing ideologies can also diminish the spirit of partnership. Different ideologies among organisations create difficulty as the partners are likely to have different priorities, outlooks and goals and communication problems due to the lack of a common language. Under these circumstances, organisations will find it difficult to work together and solve common problems. This view is supported by Rogers *et al* who argue that,

> An ideology that has become entrenched in an organisation and that differs with the ideology of the other organisation can generate conflict, rather than collaboration (Rogers *et al*, 1982, p.64).

In cases where the partners are having difficulties in achieving a collaborative solution and building partnership relationships, Gray (1989) recommends the use of a mediator. It is argued that the convenor or mediator can guide proceedings, assist in solving disputes, build a climate of trust and should have the following characteristics, 'legitimacy, expertise, resources plus authority' (Gray 1989, p.165).

Conditions for economic growth may have a significant influence on achieving partnership governance. In periods of recession when resources are scarce, participant organisations may not be so eager to share resources and work together. Problems for the partnership will arise if partners are not willing to engage in partnership activity and decide to take a more individualist view. Gray argues that,

> A division of resources among many competing for their share is difficult enough, but when allocations require cuts or involve assignment of proportional liabilities, achieving agreement is particularly difficult (Gray, 1989, p.261).

Jezierski notes that the problems of economic decline for a partnership can be exacerbated particularly when representative organisations are answerable to their constituents or primary organisation. It is commented that,

> The consent of an electorate to a partnership is achieved more easily under the conditions of economic growth, whereas decline and restructuring will bring challenges to economic and political elites (Jezierski, 1990, p.219).

It is also argued that geographical proximity between each partner organisation is an important factor in partnership performance. According to Reid and Schmerhorn, co-ordination is made easier if partner organisations are near each other geographically as this allows for informal interactions between key decision makers and communication between staff of the organisations. This would facilitate the recognition of,

> similarities in orientation; similarities in training of staff; possible cross matches between goals and resources; and a dependence upon each other for scarce resources (cited by Rogers *et al*, 1982, p.58).

Geographic proximity assists to facilitate partnership organisation and embed a process of working together. Aldrich maintains that informal contact between organisations, interaction and exchange of information and resources are precursors, 'to the development of overlapping boards and written agreements' (cited by Rogers *et al*, 1982, p.61).

Stakeholder / Organisational Conditions

Having outlined conditions relating to the context or environment in which partnerships operate, attention now turns to reviewing the role of stakeholder organisations.

It could be argued that an unequal balance of power between organisations can lead to the failure of partnerships. In partnerships that vary in power, participant organisations will have a different level of ability meaning some organisations will see others as irrelevant. This may cause disagreement within the partnership leading to conflict and eventual failure. Tilson *et al* point out that inequalities among partner organisations creates difficulties within partnerships. From their study of partnerships established under the Single Regeneration Budget in Great Britain, Tilson *et al* highlight the problems of the voluntary / community sector. Reflecting on their difficulties one representative of the voluntary / community sector stated, 'the more time we spent in partnership meetings the less we could spend in the community... the absence of (these) resources for capacity building and implementation,' therefore, imposes 'a major barrier to effective participation' (Tilson *et al*, 1997, p.11).

Another important issue which must be highlighted is the structure of participant partner organisations. Attempting to define the most appropriate partner organisations has been the one of the most contentious issues among commentators. Rogers *et al* (1982) identify the diversity of opinion in citing the work of Colt who maintains that organisations with highly standardised procedures are better prepared for joint endeavour as they allow for greater leadership, closer supervision and greater accountability. Torrens, cited by Rogers *et al* (1982), also believes that centralised organisations are more able for interorganisational collaboration as an autonomous central office facilitates greater environmental outreach. On the other hand, Rogers *et al* (1982) cite the findings of Aike and Hage who argue that decentralised organisations are better prepared for joint programmes as the organisations are more accessible, operate activities on the ground and are closer to other organisations. Aldrich (1977) supports this view and comments that decentralised organisations in a partnership are more successful as the participant organisations create more linkages, the decision makers are more accountable due to their greater accessibility and visibility, and all organisations have an equal standing within the partnership. Rogers *et al* highlight a problem of centralised organisations in partnerships in that they,

> generally are located far from the area to be co-ordinated, consequently any attempt at a more formalised collaboration may involve poor administrative support and large quantities of red tape (Rogers *et al*, 1982, p.66).

Aside from centralised and decentralised structures, Torm and Vosow discovered that what was more crucial was whether or not the involved organisations are similar in structure. This view is also backed up by Redburn, who believes that greatly dissimilar organisations will have difficulty in planning and implementing joint endeavours as differences incur greater costs due to the problems of, 'different tasks, different modes of operation and priorities, different goals and a lack of functional interdependence of services' (cited by Rogers *et al*, 1982, p.87).

In addition, a partnership is likely to face difficulties if the partner organisations view each other as a threat or perceive that working together will lead to fragmentation of their organisation or a loss of authority (Mattessich and Monsey, 1992; Gray, 1989). Fear of loss of autonomy is particularly true when partners perceive the other organisation to be lower in status and legitimacy or if the organisation fears that lack of resources will generate an inferior exchange position. If a partnership organisation has inadequate resources it may not wish to engage in the partnership as it may be too expensive administratively. Any of these scenarios will cause problems for a partnership as they create suspicion, imbalance and disaffection.

Not only do the differences in size, power, resources and ability of partner organisations cause problems, but difficulties can also emerge when partners join the partnership for different reasons. Some participants become involved in partnerships because it is fundamental to their raison d'être, others may have been persuaded to become involved because of their ability or they have the facilities essential for work of the partnership. In this case, the latter organisation is likely to be much less interested or motivated to work in the partnership (Huxham and Vangen, 1996). If all partner organisations are not pushing equal weight this may be a cause for potential conflict within the partnership.

In terms of the autonomy of the participant organisations, Aldrich (1977) highlights contradictions within the literature by referring to Edner who argues that in partnerships, maintaining the autonomy of individual organisations is crucial for success when divergent values and problem definitions are present in local environments. On the other hand, Aldrich and Pfeffier maintain that an integrated and co-ordinated approach will not evolve if the organisations have independence and autonomy and are free to pursue their own goals.

Finally determination, commitment and stamina among participants is an important condition for facilitating partnership. Huxham and Vangen (1996) comment that collaborations often fail to make progress as the participants are unwilling to pledge their full commitment.

Conflict arises if commitment is not equally spread, with some organisations placing more importance on the collaboration than others. Huxham and Vangen point out that, 'it will take longer than could normally be anticipated and it will be demanding on time and requires persistence to keep trying' (Huxham and Vangen, 1996, p.15).

Decision Making Conditions

Seeking further analysis of the conditions for achieving partnership governance, it is necessary to examine the partnership decision making process. This focuses on the relationships and interactions between organisations and individuals within partnership arrangements.

To develop an effective partnership decision making process, Mattessich and Monsey (1992) argue that it is important to facilitate participation of all individual organisations and ensure consensual agreement. Consensus decision making and participation encourages a common approach and guards against isolating individuals which could lead to tension. Consensus decision making is important for partnerships as it is seen, 'to increase the perceptions of equality of status internally and fair representation externally' (Mattessich and Monsey, 1992, p.42).

On the other hand, McArthur (1995), believes that participatory structures and consensus based style of decision making lengthens the process, making it difficult for the partnership to achieve its aims. As a possible solution to the problem of lengthy decision making, Mattessich and Monsey maintain that the principles of involvement, consultation and participation should be endorsed but that executive power should remain with only a limited number of participants. It is held that,

> Any organisation can only function efficiently and effectively if executive power lies with a relatively small team of representatives. Attempts to create unwieldy bureaucracies that allow every interest group to influence the decision making process are unworkable (Mattessich and Monsey, 1992, p.49).

Following on from participatory and consensual decision making, Mattessich and Monsey argue that in collaborative relationships it is essential that the partnership decision making process is open and informal and provides the opportunity to discuss all issues. Firstly, an open decision making process seeks to encourage participation from all individuals and organisations and helps to build relationships among the partners. Mattessich and Monsey refer to the existence of an informal network and state that for successful partnerships,

> the skill is to use informal networks, links and alliances to build positive relations between different partners, if these informal networks are available to all, then the process will reinforce the values and ethos of the partnership (Mattessich and Monsey, 1992, p.51).

Secondly, allowing individuals and organisations to open up and talk about issues creates a more effective decision making process. Within an open forum partners are permitted to voice their concerns and discuss problematic and contentious issues. Mattessich and Monsey maintain that it is, 'imperative that people look at the differences between the partners and work to overcome them; trying to pretend that different values and outlooks do not exist is felt to be both naive and unhelpful' (Mattessich and Monsey, 1992, p.50).

In addition, Tilson *et al* argue that time is important for a partnership decision making process especially when the voluntary and community sectors are involved, it is held that in certain community partnerships,

> achieving a properly balanced and stable operational capacity for the partnership in the required time is not something which is a precondition, it could not be hurried. The short timescale prevented some partnerships from establishing links with potential partners, especially those from the voluntary / community sector, which meant that they were effectively excluded or included in name only (Tilson *et al*, 1997, p.10).

This view is followed by Hutchinson who comments that a partnership takes a considerable length of time, particularly in developing links with the other organisations and outlining a programme of work. As Hutchinson states,

> Partnerships themselves take time to learn to understand each other's agenda and methods of working, and to reach a stage where in effect they agree or disagree. Partnership requires commitment and sustained joint working, therefore, the investment of time is essential (Hutchinson, 1990, p.341).

Effective communication channels are another condition for facilitating partnership. Huxham and Vangen (1996) draw on the distinction between three different channels and see each as being equally important. The first important communication channel is between the participant organisations in the collaboration. Differences between the organisations' working practices, culture and language can lead to problems in communication and organisational conflict if each organisation takes different interpretations and different outlooks over problems. In this case achieving a common position will be difficult. Therefore, it is essential to establish good communication in which participants can, 'pay careful attention to checking the understanding of each others meaning, as well as language and the need for tolerance' (Huxham and Vangen 1996, p.13). Secondly, communication within the participant organisations is an important part of the partnership decision making process. Huxham and Vangen argue that although it may be time consuming it is essential in terms of gaining, 'trust, commitment, support and resources from the organisations' (Huxham and Vangen, 1996, p.13). And thirdly, communication between the collaboration and the wider community is central to achieving partnership governance as it maintains good relations and a support base for the collaboration. Huxham cites Roberts and Bradley who maintain that, 'the more complex the issue over which collaboration occurs, the greater the need for self reflection by collaborators about the collaborative process' (Huxham, 1993, p.25).

In a somewhat related point, Mattessich and Monsey (1992) hold the view that above all it is the interaction of individuals which makes the partnership decision making process work. It is seen as essential for partnership participants to have the interaction skills of diplomacy, mediation and negotiation. These skills help the partners to be confident in communication, open about problems and differences and how to solve them. It is important that participants who do not possess these skills are trained.

Partnership Operation

A final consideration when discussing the conditions for achieving partnership governance relates to the operation or activities of partnerships.

Wide agreement exists among commentators that partnerships must first develop clear strategies. According to commentators such as Wilson and Charlton (1997), Boyle (1989) and Mattessich and Monsey

(1992), developing a strategy or mission for the partnership is essential as it shapes the development of the initiative in the early stages, defines the scope of activity and provides a constant reminder to everyone of the aims and objectives of the partnership. Developing a strategy at the outset is important, not only in arriving at a common definition of a problem, but also in defining how important each of the problem issues are and which groups of the organisation should participate in solving the problem. It can be seen that developing a strategy or vision at the outset helps to focus the partners and establish processes within the partnership. Mattessich and Monsey recognise the importance of developing a strategy and vision for a partnership in that it establishes, 'better working relations within the partnership and more effective decision making' (Mattessich and Monsey, 1992, p.38). In support of this assessment, Gray (1989) argues that strategic management and developing process issues are fundamental factors for a successful partnership,

> Process issues must be discussed openly, and agreements should be sought on how the group will conduct itself. Drafting and agreeing on ground rules are an essential step in assuring that the parties accept responsibility for the process. Conferring with the parties about what is going to happen next and who is going to do it ensures expectations are not mismatched and that the parties retain ownership of everything that happens (Gray, 1989, p.266).

Huxham and Vangen (1996) comment on the difficulties that participants experience while negotiating the strategy and aims of the collaboration. Collaborations find it difficult to agree on common aims as each actor wishes to pursue an individual agenda and is not willing to compromise. It is argued that a strategy is needed which is formulated into a task orientated or tangible form and not in grandiose terms. It is pointed out that if the strategy and aims have, 'too wide a remit this can be destabilising and if they have too narrow a remit this is unlikely to satisfy all the parties' (Huxham and Vangen, 1996, p.10). This view is followed by Hutchinson who argues that the major problems within partnerships relate broadly to, 'the different agendas which all parties seek to fulfil, difficult priorities and the possibility of conflict between the partner and their parent organisation or body' (Hutchinson, 1994, p.340).

Formulating strategies and procedures helps to develop and design the partnership process. If procedures and processes are not established at the beginning of the partnership this may lead to problems and possible failure of the partnership. At the outset, it is important to operate effective diary management of partnership meetings. At times it is difficult for partnerships to find a mutually convenient time among all partners for meetings; the problem is particularly exacerbated when a number of organisations each give a different priority to the partnership event. This situation leads to a lack of organisation and strategic direction within the partnership which may lead to ultimate failure.

A further example highlighting the importance of establishing rules and procedures is when the partnership becomes established and the participants are seeking to gain credit for success. Ironically, it is usually after the partnership has entered a successful phase that conflict within the partnership can come to the fore. Disagreement and conflict can arise over whom will receive the credit for the success, how employees will be compensated for what they have produced, how future goals will be set and how finances will be organised. O'Looney recognises that conflict can arise after success,

> While failure can lead to undermining of the collaboration, the troubles associated with success tend to be unexpected and therefore more difficult to prepare for or address. Partnerships often create a number of public relations spoils that unfortunately lead sometimes to fights over whom receives credit and subsequently to resentment among partnership members (O'Looney, 1992, p.18).

Therefore, with partnerships clearly outlining a strategy or set of rules concerning success, this will ensure that both additional benefits and risk will be shared equally among partnership stakeholders.

When formulating a strategy Gray (1989), Wilson and Charlton (1997) and Mattessich and Monsey (1992) support the view that partnerships must involve all partners and a wider audience or community into the decision making process. It is believed that greater involvement and participation will create equality within the partnership, ownership of policy formulation and implementation and a more effective decision making process. These qualities are seen as essential to a partnership. Mattessich and Monsey state,

> There is a paramount need to involve not only all the partners but as wide an audience as possible in defining and prioritising the issues, the need for

involvement and participation is the golden thread that binds together successful partnership (Mattessich and Monsey, 1992, p.36).

Table 2.4   A Summary Table Showing the Conditions for Achieving Partnership Governance as set out in the Literature

Contextual Conditions	Stakeholder / Organisational Conditions	Decision Making Conditions	Operational Conditions
Partners must believe that more can be achieved acting together then individually.	An unequal balance of power between organisations can create disputes and eventually lead to conflict.	Consensus decision making and participation in decision making guards against isolating individuals in the decision making process.	Formulation of a strategy shapes the development of the initiative in the early stages, defines the scope of activity and provides a constant reminder of the aims and objectives of the partnership.
Partnerships need to operate within an environment of understanding and respect. In this way partners can understand the cultures in which they operate.	Centralised organisations are more able for partnerships as an autonomous central office facilitates greater environmental outreach.	On the other hand, it is believed that participatory structures and consensus decision making lengthens the process making it difficult for the partnership to achieve its aims.	Partnerships are required to adopt an inclusive planning process as this will facilitate participation and ownership and create a more effective decision making process.
A background of historical and political confrontation will create tensions among the partners and lead to failure of the partnership.	On the other hand, it is argued that decentralised organisations are prepared for partnership as they are more accessible, operate activities on the ground and are closer to other organisations.	An open and informal decision making process will allow the partners to discuss contentious issues and help to build relationships.	Knowledge about the legal duties of partnerships facilitates a smooth operation of the partnership. Knowledge about funding creates access to additional resources.

Contextual Conditions	Stakeholder / Organisational Conditions	Decision Making Conditions	Operational Conditions
Different ideologies among organisations creates difficulty as partners are likely to have different priorities, outlooks and goals.	If partners view each other as a threat they are likely to be reluctant to exchange information and facilitate partnership arrangements.	Time is needed to build relations among the partners, allow them to understand each others agenda and build an inclusive process.	Partnerships require sufficient resources to support their operations.
In different circumstances an independent organisation can be used to settle disputes to build a climate of trust and solve disputes.	Maintaining the autonomy of individual organisations is crucial for success when partners have different values and opinions.	Communication helps to build relations among the partners, break down barriers, build trust and maintain links with the wider community.	Positive publicity facilitates access to resources and establishes wider involvement in the planning process.
A backdrop of economic decline could create problems as partners may not be willing to share resources and work together.	On the other hand, it is argued that a co-ordinated approach will not evolve if organisations are not free to pursue their own goals.	The interaction of individuals is central to the decision making process and so individuals need certain skills of diplomacy, mediation and negotiation.	
Geographical proximity facilitates partnership development as it provides for informal interactions, better communication, and exchange of information and resources.	Commitment is required as all partners need to have full determination and stamina to maintain a partnership process in the long term.		

The importance of involving all the relevant and legitimate key actors at an early stage during collaborative decision making is also noted by Gray. Gray argues that, 'failure to include them in the design stage only invites technical and political difficulties during implementation' (Gray, 1989, p.65).

Tilson *et al* (1997) and Mattessich and Monsey (1992) both believe that knowledge about a wide range of issues from legal duties of partnerships, to information about grant regimes, are important to achieving partnership governance. Knowing the legal duties of partnership creates a smooth operation of the partnership while joint regimes create more opportunity for funding. Tilson *et al* highlight in particular, knowledge about how to access funding from the European Union.

The allocation or accessibility of sufficient funds or resources is also an important condition for the success of partnerships. Mattessich and Monsey note the significance of funding and resources as they state it is important that, 'the collaborative group has an adequate, consistent financial base to support its operations' (Mattessich and Monsey, 1992, p.14).

Mayo (1997) refers to the disastrous effects on partnerships when the programme funding is not renewed or public support withdrawn. Mayo argues that partnerships should be established under long term initiatives and this would provide the participants with sufficient time to develop an 'exit strategy' for their future viability. It is held that, 'partnerships typically need support rather than one-off short term intentions' (Mayo, 1997, p.11).

Finally, Mattessich and Monsey comment that undertaking positive publicity is a condition for partnership success as it, 'can make life easier for partnerships, facilitating access to funds, other resources and wider involvement' (Mattessich and Monsey, 1992, p.56).

Conclusion

Although providing a comprehensive review of the conditions facilitating partnership governance, little insight has been given into the different types of partnership arrangements as each commentator refers to partnership as a general term. However, what is important is that this review has provided a focus for the book based around the four themes of Contextual, Stakeholder / Organisational, Decision Making and Operational Conditions

(Table 2.4) which will be used as a general framework to test the experience of partnership arrangements in Northern Ireland. In the following chapters different types of partnerships, that is those with the different coalition building processes of co-operation, co-ordination and collaboration will be analysed and the conditions associated with performance will be outlined. However, before this, attention will be given in the next chapter to mapping the major public sector partnerships arrangements, in Northern Ireland and between Northern Ireland and other jurisdictions, and selecting the case studies for empirical examination.

3 Public Administration and Partnership Governance in Northern Ireland

Introduction

In Northern Ireland a large number of different types of partnerships have been applied to a wide range of different programmes at different levels of governance. Some commentators such as Cebulla (1996) argue that in certain policy spheres, such as urban regeneration, this has created a complex and confusing picture, leading to the problems of administrative complexity, ineffectiveness and lack of co-ordination. It is the aim of this book to use the complex picture of partnership arrangements in Northern Ireland as a laboratory to select the case studies as a means to examine the conditions which affect the performance of partnerships and their value in a developing public administration system.

Before any research is conducted on partnership arrangements, consideration needs to be given to case study selection. It is the aim of this chapter to map out the terrain of the major partnerships operating in Northern Ireland and to use this map as a basis to select the case studies. To assist this mapping exercise, partnerships will be classified in relation to two variables, the spatial level of operation and the different types of partnership arrangements based on the coalition building processes of co-operation, co-ordination and collaboration. The analysis will be deliberately synoptic with the details of partnership arrangements presented in Appendix 1.

However, in the first instance, it is necessary to understand the system of public administration and partnership governance in Northern Ireland. This will provide a background against which the map of partnership arrangements operating in Northern Ireland can be set. First of all, this chapter seeks to present an overview of the public administration system and then discuss the dynamics behind the emergence of partnerships in Northern Ireland. Secondly, a brief description of partnership governance will be included, followed by the presentation of the conceptual map of partnership arrangements. The chapter will conclude with an outline of the partnership case studies and a discussion of the reasons for their selection.

The Northern Ireland Public Sector Context

Legislative and Executive Arrangements

The present structure of public administration in Northern Ireland has evolved from a failed system of devolution and a continuous period of political and constitutional crisis. The current system of government was established in 1972 when the Northern Ireland Parliament was prorogued and the government suspended after a period of intense political turmoil. The British Government passed the Northern Ireland (Temporary Provisions) Act in 1972 which effectively transferred all executive and legislative powers to Westminster. All legislation for Northern Ireland is now passed at Westminster and takes the form of two measures: 'excepted matters' are enacted by an Act of Parliament and 'reserved' or 'transferred matters' are made by way of Orders in Council.

In terms of the Executive, all decision making and responsibility for policy in Northern Ireland rests with the Secretary of State. The post of Secretary of State was created with the imposition of direct rule, which means the Secretary is a member of cabinet and accountable to Parliament. The Secretary of State has administrative responsibility for the government of Northern Ireland and is directly involved with political and constitutional matters, security policy and broad economic questions (Knox, 1996). The Secretary of State has a team of ministers who are delegated responsibility for the Northern Ireland departments: Agriculture, Economic Development, Environment, Education, Health and Social Services and Finance and Personnel. Each department has its own Permanent Secretary responsible for the conduct of its administration.

Another arm of government associated with the Secretary of State is the Northern Ireland Office (NIO). The NIO has responsibility for political and constitutional matters, security, human rights and justice issues and relations with the Anglo-Irish Secretariat. The NIO is headed by a Permanent Secretary from the home civil service and has a staff who are organised into two divisions, Belfast and London. Those in Belfast advise the Secretary of State on policy matters and staff in London provide the contact between government departments in Northern Ireland and the political and administrative structures in London. The head of the Northern Ireland Civil Service is in overall charge of the Northern Ireland departments but is also accountable to the Secretary of State.

It can be clearly seen that under direct rule the Secretary of State has ultimate executive power in Northern Ireland. This system has been criticised with regard to the weakness of the Secretary of State's accountability to the people of Northern Ireland. One of the major problems with the position of the Secretary of State and the team of Ministers is that they do not have their constituency bases in Northern Ireland, thus dissolving a clear line of accountability. This problem is exacerbated as the different party political structure in Northern Ireland prevents any party from having a direct link to the United Kingdom (UK) Government. This has added to the democratic deficit as Morrow comments,

> The central plank of political representation in liberal democratic societies, the vote, has had little direct influence on the policy content of government in the province (Morrow, 1996, p.148).

In the Executive the problem of democratic accountability is highlighted even further by Morrison and Livingstone. It is held that in the years of direct rule the Northern Ireland Civil Service and the NIO have increased their powers as the Secretary of State spends only a few days of the week in Northern Ireland, meaning the practice of policy making and implementation has been ceded to officials. This has led to a system of governance in which, 'a small number of officials of relative public invisibility has accentuated the idea of government by elite' (Morrison and Livingstone, 1995, p.153).

Local Government

Over the past twenty-five years local government has been operating in Northern Ireland with a small range of functional powers. The (Local Government) Act 1972 was designed to remove deep rooted sectarian bias at the local level by reducing the powers of local authorities in housing, health, education, personal social services and planning. The twenty six district councils are now charged with regulatory executive tasks such as licensing of entertainment and environmental health, leisure provision, street cleaning, refuse collection and the maintenance of cemeteries. To highlight the diminished role of local government in Northern Ireland it is useful to show the level of local government expenditure. In 1986/87, out of a total budget of just over £4.5 billion, local authorities were responsible for spending £109 million or 2% of public expenditure. In 1997/98 the corresponding figures, estimated by the Department of Environment, were £230 million and £8.5 billion, approximately 2.7% of public expenditure (cited by Knox, 1999). This figure is put into perspective even further if it is considered that local authorities in Great Britain spend 30% of total public expenditure (Aughey, 1996). The problem of the democratic deficit in the case of local government is clearly highlighted here.

However, within the last number of years it could be said that the remit or powers of local councils are increasing, namely, in the spheres of local economic development and community relations. Under Article 28 of the Local Government (Miscellaneous Provision) (N.I.) Order 1992, councils have been permitted to spend up to 5p in the pound from rates for the specific purpose of economic development. For the year 1995/96 this has amounted to £9m in total for all the councils (Knox, 1997). Although this may seem minimal, it has increased the role and scope of local councils in stimulating local economic development. Local government has also been funded by the Central Community Relations Unit (CCRU). The CCRU offered councils 75% grant aid for the employment of community relations staff and financial support to implement cross-community activities. Again, local councils view this development as a small but significant extension of their powers.

Quangos, Agencies, Boards and Trusts

While the local authorities have lost power since direct rule, government appointed bodies such as the quangos, agencies, boards and trusts have increased their authority. In an effort to improve central organisational capacity and remove the responsibility for service delivery from the political conflict (Morrison and Livingstone, 1995), reforms of 1971-73 established the Northern Ireland Housing Executive, four area Health Boards, five Education and Library boards and the Police Authority for Northern Ireland. Since 1973 further services have been allocated to appointed bodies, for example, the Industrial Development Board (IDB), responsible for encouraging economic development of the private sector. Boards and trusts, agencies and quangos are all methods of appointed government and it is important to highlight their different functions.

Boards and Trusts

Health boards and trusts are located within the Department of Health and Social Services. In this department important changes have been taking place in recent years to make service provision more efficient, effective and responsive to customers needs by reorganising functions of the department to institute an internal market. To enable this, the four area health boards now operate at the strategic level assessing need and purchasing health and social care for their resident populations from a range of providers, health and social *services* trusts, the voluntary and private sectors (Knox, 1996). Consequently the health and social service trusts are mainly involved with the delivery of services. The trusts are now corporate bodies with the responsibility for the ownership and management of hospitals or facilities previously managed or provided by the health and social boards. The trusts can now contract services to private and voluntary sectors. A total of twenty health and social services trusts have been established since the internal market came into operation in April 1992 (Knox, 1999).

Agencies

A recent development in the public sector in Northern Ireland has been the introduction of the Next Steps Initiative aimed at improving management in the Civil Service. Agencies are government appointed bodies which are solely involved with implementation of government policy. Each agency has a Chief Executive who is responsible for its management and operation and is accountable to the Parliamentary under Secretary of the particular government department. It is the Parliamentary under Secretary, one of the Secretary of State's team of Ministers, who determines the policy and financial framework under which the agency is to operate. It is hoped that by dividing policy operation and implementation this will create greater efficiency and better service for the public. Agencies in Northern Ireland are located across the range of government departments including, the Training and Employment Agency in the Department of Economic Development, the Rate Collection Agency in the Department of Environment, the Social Security Agency in the Department of Health and Social Services and the Compensation Agency in the NIO. In fact twenty four agencies now operate in the Northern Ireland Civil Service accounting for 19,000 civil servants, some 65% of the staff of central government departments and the Northern Ireland Office (Knox, 1999).

Quangos

The term Quango or quasi-autonomous non-governmental organisation is an umbrella term used to classify bodies to which government makes public appointments (Knox, 1996). The use of quangos in the government of Northern Ireland is widespread and according to Weir and Hall, 161 such bodies exist (cited by Meehan, 1997). The main reason why such a large number of bodies exist is due to the lack of local authority power in Northern Ireland. Indeed, Wier and Hall estimate that in 1994-95, £1.56 billion was spent through 8 bodies which they classify as 'extra governmental organisations' meaning they 'fulfil functions carried out by local government in Great Britain' (cited by Meehan, 1997, p.5). The importance of quangos to the government in Northern Ireland is highlighted by their immense spending power. The Education and Library Boards for instance, employ in excess of 16,000 and have an annual budget reaching over £1000 million (Morrison and Livingstone 1995).

Aside from the major service delivery quangos such as the Northern Ireland Housing Executive, the Education and Library Boards and the Local Economic and Development Unit, there are a large number of regulatory quangos. These bodies assist government policy in small, specific areas and have a smaller annual budget. For example, the then Fair employment Commission had an annual budget of £2.95m in 1996 and the then Equal Opportunities Commission £1.5m in 1995 (Meehan, 1997). These bodies have now been merged and replaced by the new Equality Commission. Quangos also exist in the form of government advisory bodies, including the Northern Ireland Economic Council and the Standing Advisory Commission on Human Rights, both created in the 1970s.

There has been widespread criticism among commentators such as Aughey (1996) and Knox (1996) over the role of appointed government bodies in Northern Ireland, in particular their lack of accountability and widespread involvement in service delivery. In Northern Ireland the government department, whose minister is not directly accountable, sets the parameters of operation for the quangos and allocates the necessary funding. This has meant that government departments in Northern Ireland are all powerful, which according to Aughey shifts, the balance of local service provision heavily in favour of the principles of administrative efficiency and bureaucratic expertise and against the principle of local democratic accountability (Aughey, 1996, p.96).

A further problem of democratic accountability follows the introduction of Next Steps Agencies. It is argued that the distinction between Ministerial policy responsibility and Chief Executive operational responsibility has blurred the lines of open accountability. Knox argues that questions have been raised as Ministers have been using this new relationship to, 'create opportunities to safeguard responsibility for policy failures and abdicate control of the agencies' (Knox, 1996, p.14). Therefore, the problems surrounding the accountability of government agencies and quangos, essentially British models of public administration, are exacerbated in the case of Northern Ireland due to its inherent problems of accountability. Knox argues that,

> Northern Ireland is the worst case scenario in which quangos continue to evolve on the back of an administrative system dogged by problems of electoral accountability (Knox, 1996, p.15).

However, despite these criticisms there are arguments in favour of appointed government in Northern Ireland. Appointed government has managed to deliver services in a non sectarian way and against the backdrop of political and constitutional crisis as Morrison and Livingstone point out,

> Quangos may be a successful way of getting the business of government done in Northern Ireland. Services have continued to be delivered and the standard of services in fields such as housing, education and health have improved since 1972. These services appear to have been delivered in a more equitable way over the past 20 years (Morrison and Livingstone, 1995, p.161).

Notwithstanding the changes to the function and operation of government departments with the introduction of quangos and Next Steps Agencies, the public administration in Northern Ireland has also experienced significant change with the adoption of the partnership approach. Within the last ten to fifteen years partnerships have been applied to a wide range of government programmes including, economic development and social exclusion and are reshaping the governance of

Northern Ireland. The next section aims to examine the factors which have facilitated this new dynamic.

Dynamics of Change for Partnership Governance

In Northern Ireland a number of factors have precipitated the rise of the partnership approach and influenced change in the public administration system. These factors have acted together to create a new dynamic for partnership governance. The dynamics of change have emanated from a variety of fields and include, institutional, sectoral and spatial factors. This section analyses each dynamic and their influence on the development of the partnership approach in Northern Ireland and discusses other factors which can build on this momentum and extend partnership governance in future years.

Institutional factors have been one of the most important influences in the momentum for change for partnership governance. In Northern Ireland both the European Commission and the British Government have acted as a dynamic to further the emergence of partnerships. For instance from the mid to late 1980s the European Commission has been actively encouraging innovative local partnerships as a means to deal with economic and social disadvantage. In aiming to tackle problems of long term unemployment, European Commission programmes have favoured a bottom up approach and the involvement of voluntary and community groups in policy formulation and implementation. For example, in a research report, *Local Community and Social Policy: a discussion document,* sponsored by the EU in 1993, it was concluded that, 'polices for local economic development need to be linked to policies for local social and community development, stimulating and facilitating the inhabitants of local communities to play a part in shaping them' (cited by Williamson, 1999, p.15). The European Commission has also been actively promoting the development of local partnerships as a means of encouraging subsidiarity. As a result of these two factors, most of the social and economic development programmes of the European Commission now require the involvement of the local community, usually through participation in partnership arrangements (Williamson, 1999).

In addition, the British Government has also embraced partnerships as a means of gaining access to additional resources and reducing public spending. By developing linkages between the public and private sectors, government has been able to acquire the resources and skills of the private sector to improve service delivery. For example, the Private Finance Initiative is one programme which is designed to deliver higher quality and more cost effective public services in government departments and agencies by facilitating public / private partnership (HM Treasury, 1996).

The voluntary / community sector has also helped to build a new dynamic towards partnership governance. In Northern Ireland voluntary and community groups have sprung up largely in response to the strength of unelected government in Northern Ireland and in the absence of acceptable locally elected representatives (Morrison and Livingstone, 1995). In 1989, there were over 800 active local and community groups in Northern Ireland or approximately one per 2,000 people (Morrow, 1996); more recently, the Northern Ireland Council for Voluntary Action (NICVA) have estimated the combined total of voluntary organisations, community groups and charitable bodies at 5,500 (Hughes *et al*, 1998, p. 226). Increasingly government has been calling on the advice, energy and expertise of these community and voluntary groups in policy formulation and implementation. This was clearly demonstrated with the publication of the *Strategy for the Support of the Voluntary Sector and for Community Development in Northern Ireland* in February 1993. In this document the government set out a commitment to work with voluntary and community groups and outlined principles for how government departments could interact with the sector (Morrison and Livingstone, 1995). In developing partnerships with voluntary and community groups, government can divest itself of public service delivery functions and give consumers greater choice and control over service delivery. Since 1995 government funding to the voluntary sector has exceed £100m per annum, a figure which is close to the expenditure of the district councils (Morrison and Livingstone, 1995).

While aiming to reduce public spending, government has acknowledged the important role voluntary / community groups can play in dealing with complex problems such as urban regeneration. In the early 1990s the limitations of a market led approach to urban regeneration in Belfast started to become apparent and it became clear that government needed to adopt a more innovative community led approach (Birrel and Wilson, 1993; Sweeney and Gaffikin, 1995). As a means to adopt a multi-agency approach to an increasingly complex problem, the focus of the urban regeneration programme Making Belfast Work (MBW) has now shifted and the programme is keen to stress that local communities must be given first priority in the regeneration process. The strategy reflects that, 'the MBW initiative will engage the community at the fullest level in every aspect of policy development' (MBW, 1995, p.10).

The participation of community groups in government programmes can also be seen as part of a wider government effort to bring an end to the community conflict in Northern Ireland. In the early 1990s, government was concerned over the number of communities characterised by disadvantage and opposition to the state (Williamson, 1999). From this basis, policy makers sought to formulate more inclusive, community led partnerships which would address socio-economic problems and involve the politically marginalised. Furthermore, the peace process in recent years has helped to strengthen the dynamic of change in the public sector. Prior to the early 1990s, the government were sceptical and suspicious of funding partnership arrangements which would provide funding to community groups which had associations with paramilitary organisations. In the 1980s government funding and support for some voluntary / community organisations was withdrawn because security and intelligence reports indicated that, according to the then Home Secretary Douglas Hurd,

> they had sufficiently close links with paramilitary organisations as to give rise to a grave risk that to give support to those groups would have the effect of improving the standing, and furthering the aims, of a paramilitary organisation (cited by Williamson, 1999, p.20).

This policy has now been abandoned and as the peace process becomes more established, this allows community and voluntary groups to access partnerships and funding opportunities. Following the paramilitary cease-fires, the emergence of the partnership approach in Northern Ireland has been accelerated by the European Commission with support from the British Government. Under the European Union Special Support Programme for Peace and Reconciliation (EUSSPP&R), District Partnerships have been set up throughout each district council area in Northern Ireland which seek the involvement of the voluntary / community and private sectors, trade unions as a well as statutory organisations.

In addition, in the absence of an elected accountable government, voluntary / community groups have been invited into partnership arrangements to open up the local decision making process. As discussed in the previous section, the Northern Ireland public administration system under direct rule is characterised by serious problems of accountability. However, by involving voluntary / community groups in partnership arrangements, government can facilitate a more inclusive policy process and establish a greater ownership of decisions at the local level. The Strategy for the Support of the Voluntary Sector and for Community Development in Northern Ireland acknowledged that voluntary / community groups should be involved in the formulation of policy in an effort to address the lack of consultation by departments and agencies. The strategy states that government departments in Northern Ireland,

> recognise the important role played by the voluntary sector in the social and economic life of the province where, in the context of Northern Ireland's special circumstances, it provides a forum for reflecting the views and concerns of individuals and communities to government (cited by Morrison and Livingstone, 1995, p.144).

Another development which has added to the momentum of partnership governance has been the recognition by stakeholders that shared spatial problems must be addressed through partnership and working together. The need to deal with common problems has strongly influenced moves by the British and Irish Governments, local authorities and the private sector to address the economic and social problems of the Irish border. For example, in the late 1970s and early 1980s the then EEC, with the British and Irish Governments, commissioned a number of studies on the border region which firmly concluded that the best prospects for tackling the problems of the area lay in greater co-operation. To this end, both the British and Irish Governments, with aid and assistance from the EU, have established cross-border partnership linkages in fields such as economic development, tourism and transport.

In recent years the need to address common spatial problems has extended further than the border region. Common problems and shared opportunities are now considered to exist on an all-island basis which has given further momentum to the partnership approach. From the late 1980s, but particularly the early to mid 1990s, the British and Irish Governments have developed partnership initiatives between departments and agencies. Relationships have been established in a range of areas such as trade (IDB, 1996) and industrial research and development (IRTU, 1995), but all are based on the notion that partnership on an all-island basis will achieve greater synergy.

Business organisations in the North and South of Ireland have also acknowledged the importance of working together and exploiting shared opportunities. In the last number of years the Irish Business and Employers Confederation (IBEC) in the Republic of Ireland and the Confederation of British Industry (CBI) in Northern Ireland have actively promoted the concept of a Dublin to Belfast economic corridor and the development of an integrated island economy (For further discussion on the relationship between IBEC and the CBI see page 127). To support further partnership developments it is argued that greater economic integration will improve trade and competitiveness and create greater accessibility to markets for firms on the island (Coopers and Lybrand and INDECON report for CBI and IBEC, May 1994).

Indeed, moves towards exploiting shared opportunities by working together have been expanded and given further recognition in the National Development Plan (NDP) 2000-2006 of the Republic of Ireland. Chapter 9 in the NDP sets out a framework for co-operation between Northern Ireland and the Republic of Ireland in a number of specific areas including: energy, technological development, transport, environment and education (Ireland, NDP, 1999). Within the context of a national plan this gives greater realisation to the creation of cross-border policy networks in a number of functional areas as envisaged by O'Donnell and Teague (1993).

Therefore, it can be seen that institutional, sectoral and spatial factors have created a dynamic of change which has transformed public administration in Northern Ireland and precipitated the emergence of partnership governance. However, consideration must also be given to future developments which could build on this momentum for change. One of the most influential dynamics in the movement towards partnership governance could come from the 'Good Friday' Agreement. The Agreement has proposed a new system of government which establishes partnership as a key theme in the future governance of Northern Ireland. Under the Agreement a new 108-member Assembly was elected by proportional representation (Single Transferable Vote) on 25th June 1988 under the terms of the 'Good Friday' Agreement to,

> exercise full legislative and executive authority in respect of those matters currently within the responsibility of the six Northern Ireland Government departments, with the possibility of taking on responsibility for other matters (Strand One - The Agreement, paragraph 3:5).

Executive authority will be discharged on behalf of the Assembly by a First Minister and Deputy First Minister and ten ministers with departmental responsibilities. The Office of the First Minister and Deputy First Minister will have an Economic Policy Unit and special responsibility for equality. There will be ten departments which will be shared by Unionist, Nationalist and Republican parties. This will establish a partnership government with the Ulster Unionist Party (UUP) and Social Democratic and Labour Party (SDLP) being allocated three portfolios and the Democratic Unionist Party (DUP) and Sinn Féin (SF), two each. The Departments include: Agriculture and Rural Development; Environment; Regional Development; Education; Higher and Further Education, Training and Employment, Enterprise, Trade and Investment; Culture, Arts and Leisure; Health, Social Services and Public Safety; Finance and Personnel (Irish Times, 19th December 1998, p.6).

Aside from the Assembly and Executive, it is envisaged that the new institutions of government will include a North-South Ministerial Council (NSMC) (Strand Two) and a British-Irish Council or Council of the Isles. In effect, these bodies will develop partnership arrangements in government between Northern Ireland and the Republic of Ireland, and between the Northern Ireland Assembly and Irish Government and the devolved institutions of the British Isles. According to the Agreement a North-South Council is to be established,

> To bring together those executive responsibilities in Northern Ireland and the Irish Government, to develop consultation, co-operation and action within the island of Ireland – including through implementation on an all-island and cross-border basis – on matters of mutual interest within the competence of the Administrations, North and South (Strand Two - The Agreement paragraph 1, p.11).

The Agreement required a 'work programme' on at least twelve matters, six being new implementation bodies, and six being matters for co-operation. The six implementation bodies are: Inland Waterways; Food Safety; Trade and Business Development; Special EU Programmes; Language (Irish and Ulster Scots); Aquaculture and Marine Matters. The Six Areas for co-operation include aspects of: Transport; Agriculture; Education; Health; Environment; Tourism. The NSMC and the cross-border bodies will therefore, provide added momentum to dealing with shared spatial problems and opportunities through partnership and co-operation between the North and South of Ireland.

The British-Irish Council proposed under the Agreement is set to be comprised of the British and Irish Governments, devolved institutions in Northern Ireland, Scotland and Wales, and if appropriate, elsewhere in the United Kingdom, together with representatives of the Isle of Man and the Channel Islands. The British-Irish Council will be established to, 'promote the harmonious and mutually beneficial development of the totality of relationships among the peoples of these islands' (Strand Three – The Agreement paragraph 1, p.11). In this case the concept of a British-Irish Council can further extend the scope of addressing shared spatial problems and create greater synergy. Possible issues for discussion in the British-Irish Council include: transport links; agriculture; environment; culture; health; education; and approaches to EU issues.

In addition, in recognition of the increasing role of the voluntary / community sector in Northern Ireland, the Agreement proposes an independent consultation forum, appointed by the two administrations, representative of civil society, including the social partners and other members with expertise in social, cultural, economic and other issues. The consultation forum could then place the idea of partnership with the voluntary / community sector as a central theme in the new governance arrangements.

Having examined the factors which have precipitated the emergence of the partnership approach in Northern Ireland and discussed prospective directions for future development, attention must now focus on describing the main elements of partnership governance in Northern Ireland. This will provide a necessary backdrop to which the map of major public sector partnership arrangements can be set.

Partnership Governance in Northern Ireland

In Northern Ireland partnerships are becoming pervasive in public administration. Partnerships are located in a wide range of policy areas including, rural development, urban regeneration, health, education and economic and industrial development. This clearly shows that the breath of partnership governance as five government departments, Agriculture, Economic Development, Environment, Education and Health and Social Services are all involved in partnership activity. Within these policy areas the complexity of partnership governance is clearly highlighted. For example, in the city of Belfast, four partnership programmes have been set in place which include, MBW, Laganside Development, the Belfast City Centre Partnership Board and the EU Urban initiative which has established two partnerships in the Shankill and Upper Springfield areas of the city.

Another important feature of partnership governance in Northern Ireland is the range of actors who are involved in partnership arrangements. Across various partnerships, the voluntary / community and private sectors, trade unions, local authorities, government departments and agencies and local councillors all have an important role to play. A significant number of partnerships in Northern Ireland have placed a strong emphasis on facilitating local inclusive or community led partnership arrangements. In the areas of economic development, urban and rural regeneration and health and social care, involvement of the local community has been a central theme. In rural development, for example, the Department of Agriculture for Northern Ireland (DANI) has recognised the need for building the capacity of local communities and has set up area based strategies which aim to develop partnerships comprised of community representatives, local authorities, central government, statutory bodies and the private sector (DANI, 1996). The idea of partnership with the local community and voluntary sector has also permeated the Department of Health and Social Services (DHSS). The DHSS has established community development as an underlying principle with the overall aim of seeking to encourage communities to tackle issues themselves by developing their own skills and knowledge (DHSS, 1997). The DHSS has also contracted out services to the voluntary sector particularly in the areas of elderly care and mental illness (DHSS, 1997).

However, this is not to suggest that partnership governance in Northern Ireland is solely focused on developing inclusive partnerships at the local community level. Partnerships have also been established between government departments and agencies. For example, a partnership relationship between the Department of Education for Northern Ireland (DENI) and the Training and Employment Agency (T&EA) has been developed with the aim of improving education and training skills. Through partnership it is thought that a more co-ordinated and strategic approach will be initiated which will combine the skills and experience of the DENI in education and the T&EA in training (DENI, 1996).

The myriad of partnerships that exist in Northern Ireland would also support the view expressed in the previous section that the European Commission has been influential in establishing partnerships. Across a number of policy areas the Commission has either provided funding or is directly responsible for establishing partnerships through a particular programme. For instance, the Commission has introduced partnerships through the LEADER, Urban and Employment programmes and has contributed funding to partnership arrangements such as that between the Northern Ireland Tourist Board (NITB) and Bord Fáilte (BF). The IFI has also been actively involved in facilitating local community partnerships in rural development, urban / town regeneration and tourism (IFI, 1996).

Another significant aspect of partnership governance in Northern Ireland is the number of partnership arrangements which are organised on an intergovernmental or transjurisdictional basis. Partnerships have principally been developed between central government departments and agencies and local authorities in Northern Ireland and the Republic of Ireland. Cross-border initiatives include a relationship between the Irish Trade Board (ITB) in the South of Ireland and the Industrial Development Board in the North of Ireland to develop trade (IDB, 1996) and partnership between the Industrial Research and Training Unit (IRTU) in Northern Ireland and Enterprise Ireland (formally Forbairt) in the Republic of Ireland (IRTU, 1995) to increase the competitiveness of the Irish industry.

Notwithstanding the numerous cross-border arrangements in Ireland, partnerships have been established with government departments and agencies and local authorities in other jurisdictions. For instance, under the EU programme Ecos-Ouverture, partnerships have been developed between local authorities in Northern Ireland, the EU and Central and Eastern Europe to share experience and skills and create new investment and marketing opportunities. The overall aim of the programme is to assist the development of democracy and the market economy in former Communist bloc countries in Central and Eastern Europe (Murray and Smyth, 1996). Partnership arrangements have also been established between the US Department of Commerce and academia to encourage economic development and promote research activity (IRTU, 1995).

Finally, in reviewing partnership governance in Northern Ireland it is important to mention the variety and diversity of partnerships arrangements which exist. Some partnerships are organised on a loose informal basis, whereas in other partnerships, the relationship between the partners is more formal and institutional. For instance, the relationship between the IDB and the ITB is a loose arrangement with interaction organised on an *ad hoc* basis and with each organisation maintaining its own authority. On the other hand, the MBW programme has established a number of partnership boards in which the partners have clearly defined roles and a common strategy has been formulated.

It can be seen that partnership governance in Northern Ireland is both multifarious and complex with different types of partnership arrangements, involving different partners, operating at different spatial levels and working towards different goals. Consideration must now be given to drawing the conceptual map of partnerships arrangements in Northern Ireland and to use the map as a basis to select partnerships for case study research.

Mapping Partnership Arrangements in Northern Ireland and Case Study Selection

As discussed at the beginning of this chapter, the partnerships are classified in relation to two variables which embrace the diversity and complexity of partnerships, the coalition building processes of co-operation, co-ordination and collaboration and the level of spatial operation, local, sub-region or regional / national. The conceptual map (Figure 3.1) charts the public sector partnership arrangements that exist within Northern Ireland, and between Northern Ireland and other jurisdictions, against the two variables. A detailed description of each partnership arrangement, included in this map, is located in Appendix 1.

Mapping the network of partnerships required extensive secondary data gathering and analysis. The common sources of data have been annual reports and strategy documents collected from government departments, the European Commission, local authorities and community / voluntary organisations. For the mapping exercise, no definitive guide currently exists on the range and types of partnerships involved and 'snowballing' (using existing informants to identify other partnerships who themselves are used as informants) has proved to be a very useful method in locating other partnership initiatives. To supplement the secondary data analysis further information on particular partnership arrangements, when required, was gained through telephone interviews with partnership participants.

Following that, the partnerships were then classified using two variables, the level of spatial operation and coalition building processes. In terms of the coalition building processes, the partnerships were classified using Mattessich and Monsey's division of co-operation, co-ordination and collaboration, as shown in Table 2.2. The multi-organisational continuum is a useful method of classification as it embraces the diversity and variety of different partnership configurations.

Furthermore, the continuum is important as it provides a framework which helps to define the different coalition building processes involved in partnerships by referring to the varying relationships, structures, authority and lines of accountability within them. This makes it easier to identify the coalition building processes and understand the complex relationships that are included in partnership arrangements. When classifying different partnership permutations a general framework creates a standardisation of information and allows for comparability between different partnerships. The framework is based on a number of elements from Mattessich and Monsey's division of co-operation, co-ordination and collaboration, which will become the basis for distinction between the different coalition building processes, and include:

- The partners involved;
- The aims and objectives of the initiative;
- The level to which individual partner organisations and goals become part of the overall strategy of the partnership;
- The basis of interaction and function of the partnership;
- The degree of formality of the partnership;
- The relative independence of each individual organisation;
- The level of joint planning among partners;
- The level of authority of each of the individual organisation in relation to the partnership;
- The duration of programmes established by the partnership.

It was decided to include these factors as they involve all the major criteria which can distinguish the three coalition building processes. All the factors combined directly relate to the structure, strategies and functions of partnerships and to the strength and power of relationships between the participating organisations. Each of the factors included in the framework are also interdependent to understanding the coalition building processes. For example, the degree of formality is directly related to the type of strategy, rules and procedures adopted by the partnership.

Figure 3.1   The Relationship Between Coalition Building Processes and Level of Spatial Operation

	Regional	Sub-Regional	Local
Co-operation	**National / Regional Transjurisdictional** * Industrial Research and Technology Unit - Enterprise Ireland * Industrial Development Board - Irish Trade Board * Industrial Research and Technology Unit - United States Dept. of Trade - Academia # *Northern Ireland Tourist Board - Bord Fáilte*		**Local - Transjurisdictional** * Belfast City Council and Nova Scotia. * Ecos-Ouverture * Co-operation North Local Authority Linkages Project **Local** * Dept of Agriculture for N. Ireland - Community Based Regeneration / Rural Development Network * International Fund for Ireland - CRISP and Urban Development Programmes * Greater Craigavon Partnership * Health and Social Service Trust - local community
Co-ordination	**Regional** * Department of Education for Northern Ireland - Training and Employment Agency * Private Finance Initiative * Industrial Development Board - Northern Ireland Partnership	**Sub-regional - Transjurisdictional** # *Local Authority Cross-Border Networks* **Sub-regional** * Health and Social Services Boards - Voluntary and Community Sectors * Tyrone Economic Development Initiative	**Local** * European Union LEADER 2 Programme * Laganside Development * Fermanagh University Partnership Board * Area Based Strategy Action Groups * Health and Social Service Trusts - Voluntary Sector * Derry Investment Initiative
Collaboration			**Local** * Making Belfast Work * Londonderry Initiative * Portadown 2000 * Belfast and Derry City Centre Partnership Boards * European Union Urban Programme # *District Partnerships for Peace and Reconciliation*

Key: # Indicates Partnerships Selected for Case Study Examination

For the second variable, Northern Ireland was regarded as a region within the UK and partnerships were classified in terms of their level of spatial operation local, sub-regional and regional. *Local level* partnerships were sub-divided into two areas, Local, and Local - Transjurisdictional levels. Local partnerships operate at the local level in Northern Ireland and Local - Transjurisdictional are partnerships operating at the local level in Northern Ireland and at the local level in another national jurisdiction. Partnerships operating at the *Sub-regional level* were mapped out and these were divided into Sub-regional partnerships, and Sub-regional - Transjurisdictional partnerships. Sub-regional partnerships which operate at the sub-regional level within Northern Ireland, and Sub-regional - Transjurisdictional partnerships operate at sub-regional level in Northern Ireland and at the sub-regional level in another national jurisdiction. The *Regional level,* is again sub-divided into two categories of partnerships. Regional - partnerships operate across the region of Northern Ireland and National / Regional - Transjurisdictional includes partnerships which operate throughout Northern Ireland and throughout other national jurisdictions. Table 3.1 summarises the classification used to determine the different levels of spatial operation.

The level of spatial operation was selected to classify partnerships as it also embraces the diversity of partnership arrangements operating at different levels of governance, the local, regional, national or supranational levels.

From analysing the map three representative case studies have been selected to provide detailed information on the conditions which improve the performance of partnerships. In each of the case study data was gathered using a combination of documentation analysis and in-depth interviews with key partnership stakeholders. The selected case studies are as follows:-

(1) The District Partnerships for Peace and Reconciliation established under the European Union Special Support Programme for Peace and Reconciliation in 1995, with a view to maintaining peace and reconciliation following the paramilitary cease-fires of the previous year. The District Partnerships number twenty-six corresponding to each of the district council areas in Northern Ireland and have been allocated a total of almost £46.7 million (14% in the first phase of funding and an increase to 25% or £83.39m for the second phase) to be distributed across four programme priorities, Employment, Urban and Rural Regeneration, Social

Inclusion, Productive Investment and Industrial Development. The District Partnerships in reflecting the interests of the local area, must comprise one third each, local councillors, voluntary / community, business / trade union interests as well as statutory organisations. The primary aim of each of the District Partnerships has been to formulate and implement local action plans detailing social and economic projects to best meet the needs of the programme.

Table 3.1   Classification of the Different Levels of Spatial Operation of Partnerships in Northern Ireland and between Northern Ireland and other Jurisdictions

Local Level	*Local*: partnerships operating at the local level in Northern Ireland
	Local Transjurisdictional: partnerships operating at the local level in Northern Ireland and at the local level in another national jurisdiction
Sub-Regional Level	*Sub-regional*: partnerships which operate at the sub-regional level within Northern Ireland
	Sub-regional – Transjurisdictional: partnerships which operate at sub-regional level in Northern Ireland and at the sub-regional level in another national jurisdiction.
Regional / National level	*Regional*: partnerships operating across the region of Northern Ireland
	National / Regional Transjurisdictional: partnerships which operate throughout Northern Ireland and throughout other national jurisdictions

(2) The Local Authority Cross-Border Networks. These are partnerships which are formed by local authorities working on a cross-border basis to address the economic and social needs of the border region through economic development, tourism and improving the environment. In the late 1970s two Local Authority Networks were established, the East Border Region Committee (EBRC), which is a partnership of Down, Newry and Mourne District Councils and Louth and Monaghan County Councils; and the North West Region Cross-Border Group (NWRCBG), which is a cross-

border partnership of Donegal County Council and Strabane, Derry and Limavady District Councils. It has only been through the INTERREG 1 programme that the two networks finally received money towards a central secretariat. Funding was again awarded under the INTERREG 2 by which time a third network was established. The Irish Central Border Area Network (ICBAN) was set up in 1995 and is a partnership of Omagh, Dungannon, Fermanagh and Armagh District Councils and Sligo, Donegal, Leitrim, Cavan and Monaghan County Councils. Each of the networks have established formal partnership arrangements with committee and executive structures and are currently aiming to involve the voluntary / community sector, private business and the public sector, to develop regional strategies for possible funding under INTERREG 3.

(3) The Northern Ireland Tourist Board (NITB) and Bord Fáilte. A partnership relationship was established in 1995 between the Northern Ireland Tourist Board (NITB) and Bord Fáilte to market the island of Ireland as a tourist destination for overseas visitors. The marketing initiative involves a stepped up marketing and promotional campaigns in key overseas markets. The marketing campaign of the NITB and Bord Fáilte has been funded £6.8 million by the European Union, the International Fund for Ireland and public and private sector contributions. Bord Fáilte and NITB also co-operate on cross-border tourism programmes such as INTERREG and the International Fund for Ireland's Tourism Programme.

Reasons for Case Study Selection

Firstly, with the three case studies each of the important variables are included, for example, the NITB and Bord Fáilte partnership is a co-operative partnership operating at the regional / national level. The Local Authority Cross-Border Networks are co-ordinative partnerships operating at the sub-regional level and the District Partnerships are collaborative arrangements operating at the local level. It is clear that together the selected case studies represent a true spread across the axis of the level of spatial operation and coalition building processes. Table 3.2 shows the spread of the variables.

As well as including variations of the two variables, the case studies reflect the diversity and complexity of partnership arrangements. Each of the partnerships have different structures, involve different partners, have different aims and were established for different reasons. Any research on the performance of partnerships must include a diversity of partnership arrangements.

And finally, the selection of cross-border partnerships is both important and timely given their present volume of operation and possible future role in the governance of Northern Ireland and the island of Ireland in the implementation of the 'Good Friday' Agreement. As discussed, the Agreement (1998) has highlighted cross-border co-operation under Strand Two and proposed the creation of a North-South Ministerial Council and other cross-border bodies, the role and function of which were agreed on the 19th December 1998 (de Bréadún, 1998, p.6).

Table 3.2   **Three Selected Case Studies and the Relationship to the Level of Spatial Operation and Coalition Building Processes**

	Co-operation	Co-ordination	Collaboration
Local			District Partnerships for Peace and Reconciliation
Sub-regional		Local Authority Cross-Border Networks	
Regional	NITB - Bord Fáilte		

It is the aim of the next three chapters to present and analyse these case studies with a view to identifying conditions associated with partnership performance and developing a synthetic model for partnership governance.

4 The District Partnerships for Peace and Reconciliation

Introduction

The cease-fires declared by the Irish Republican Army (IRA) and the Combined Loyalist Military Command (CLMC) in the early autumn of 1994 brought the opportunity of lasting peace to Northern Ireland. Following the cease-fires, the European Commission moved quickly to build on this momentum for peace and adopted the Special Programme for Peace and Reconciliation in Northern Ireland and the border counties of Ireland on the 26th July 1996. The programme was brought forward in the form of a community initiative under the Structural Funds, with the overall aim of reinforcing,

> progress towards a peaceful and stable society and to promote reconciliation by increasing economic development and employment, promoting urban and rural regeneration, developing cross border co-operation and extending social inclusion (Commission of the European Community, 1995).

Total expenditure under the programme for the first three years (1995-97) has amounted to 416 Mecu (£351m) of which 300 Mecu is through the Structural Funds. Financing for the final two years (1997-1999) was agreed in early March 1998 and this amounts to 100 Mecu (£65m) for each year. The European Union has pledged to support projects with up to 75% of the cost, and matching funds for the remainder will come from a variety of sources including the private sector, community / voluntary groups, local authorities and central government. The programme has two strategic objectives:

- To promote the social inclusion of those at the margins of economic and social life;
- To exploit the opportunities and address the needs arising from the peace process in order to boost economic growth and stimulate social and economic regeneration.

To attain these objectives the programme is made up of a series of sub programmes:

1. *Employment*: to promote peace and reconciliation and respond to the opportunities and challenges of peace, by boosting growth and employment and supporting the redirection of redundant skills, as well as reinforcing efforts for the long term unemployed, those most affected by the conflict, the young and by encouraging greater participation by women in the labour force.

2. *Urban and Rural Regeneration*: to promote peace and reconciliation by renewing urban areas affected by multiple deprivation especially by resourcing local residents to tackle the social and environmental needs within their communities: To promote reconciliation in rural areas by encouraging activities which will help to bring the communities in those areas together and by helping to develop the rural economy.

3. *Cross Border Development*: to promote cross-border reconciliation and to exploit the opportunities for increased cross-border development arising from the new situation.

4. *Social Inclusion*: to promote pathways to reconciliation by encouraging grass-roots and cross-community co-operation as well as action to address the specific difficulties faced by vulnerable groups and others at a disadvantage such as victims, children, young people and those previously caught up with violence including prisoners and ex-prisoners.

5. *Productive Investment and Industrial Development*: to promote reconciliation by stimulating private sector investment leading to sustainable employment and development especially in disadvantaged areas.

Delivery Mechanisms

In Northern Ireland the programme is delivered through three main mechanisms:

1. By central government departments or other statutory bodies;

2. By bodies who are independent of government (i.e. Intermediary Funding Bodies such as Northern Ireland Voluntary Trust, Community Relations Council, Co-operation Ireland (formerly Co-operation North) and the Rural Development Council);
3. By District Partnerships formed in each district council area.

District Partnerships in Northern Ireland

The introduction of District Partnerships comes under Sub-Programme 6 of the Special Support Programme and is only applicable to Northern Ireland. Sub - programme 6 seeks,

> To harness the energies and talents of local people in addressing local social and economic needs and promoting peace and reconciliation (DoE, 1995, p.3).

To achieve this aim District Partnerships have been established in each district council area, (Figure 4.1). The partnerships have been allocated a total of almost £46.7 million (14% in the first phase of funding and an increase to 25% of total funding for the second phase) to be distributed on an indicative basis across four programme priorities, Employment 19%, Urban and Rural Regeneration 19%, Social Inclusion 44%, Productive Investment and Industrial Development 18% (DoE, 1995). In order to reflect the needs of their locality, each District Partnership had to be broadly representative of all the main sectoral interests; the partnerships, therefore, comprise one third each of local councillors, voluntary / community representatives and business, and trade union and local statutory interests.

Each District Partnership has been allocated a block of funding which has been distributed on the basis of population and deprivation (Table 4.1). For each District Partnership area 50% of the funding has been allocated on the basis of its percentage share of the total Northern Ireland population, and 50% has been allocated on the basis of its percentage share of the total population of the 10% most deprived census enumeration districts in Northern Ireland. The deprivation census is drawn from the Policy Planning and Research Unit's Occasional Paper No 28 'Relative Deprivation in Northern Ireland' (Robson *et al*, 1994).

Figure 4.1 Distribution of the Twenty Six District Partnerships within Northern Ireland

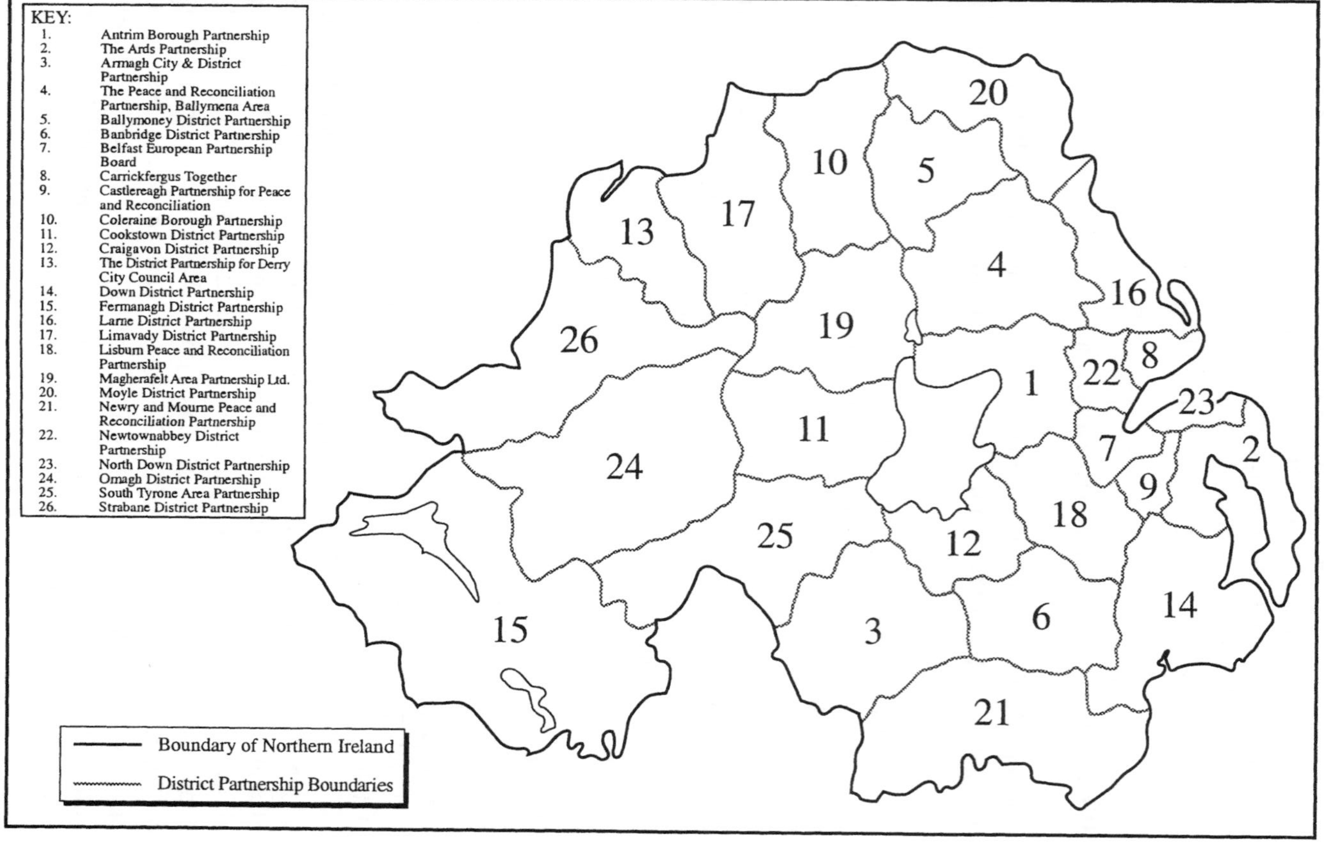

KEY:

1. Antrim Borough Partnership
2. The Ards Partnership
3. Armagh City & District Partnership
4. The Peace and Reconciliation Partnership, Ballymena Area
5. Ballymoney District Partnership
6. Banbridge District Partnership
7. Belfast European Partnership Board
8. Carrickfergus Together
9. Castlereagh Partnership for Peace and Reconciliation
10. Coleraine Borough Partnership
11. Cookstown District Partnership
12. Craigavon District Partnership
13. The District Partnership for Derry City Council Area
14. Down District Partnership
15. Fermanagh District Partnership
16. Larne District Partnership
17. Limavady District Partnership
18. Lisburn Peace and Reconciliation Partnership
19. Magherafelt Area Partnership Ltd.
20. Moyle District Partnership
21. Newry and Mourne Peace and Reconciliation Partnership
22. Newtownabbey District Partnership
23. North Down District Partnership
24. Omagh District Partnership
25. South Tyrone Area Partnership
26. Strabane District Partnership

—— Boundary of Northern Ireland

········ District Partnership Boundaries

Table 4.1   Indicative Partnership Allocations to Council Areas in Phase 1

Council Area	Population	%	Deprivation Index	Allocation Total Per cap £	£'000
Antrim	47, 500	2.91	0.48	593	12
Ards	66, 200	4.06	0.84	857	13
Armagh	52, 400	3.21	1.63	847	16
Ballymena	57, 000	3.49	0.67	729	13
Ballymoney	24, 400	1.5	0.47	344	14
Banbridge	36, 000	2.24	0.39	461	13
Belfast	296, 700	18.18	39.86	10, 157	34
Carrickfergus	34, 500	2.11	0	370	11
Castlereagh	63, 000	3.86	0	676	11
Coleraine	53, 600	3.28	0.7	679	13
Cookstown	30, 900	1.89	3.06	867	28
Craigavon	76, 800	4.71	1.37	1, 063	14
Derry	100, 500	6.16	14.49	3, 614	36
Down	60, 500	3.71	1.02	827	14
Dungannon	46, 200	2.83	3.83	1, 166	25
Fermanagh	54, 800	3.36	2.94	1, 102	20
Larne	29, 800	1.83	0.79	451	15
Limavady	30, 300	1.86	3.35	911	30
Lisburn	104, 100	6.38	4.89	1, 972	19
Magherafelt	36, 300	2.22	1.87	717	20
Moyle	14, 700	0.9	1.19	366	25
Newry and Mourne	81, 700	5.01	6.08	1, 940	24
Newtownabbey	77, 700	4.76	0.98	1, 005	13
North Down	73, 600	4.51	0.18	821	11
Omagh	46, 300	2.84	2.3	899	19
Strabane	35, 700	2.19	6.66	1, 548	43
Total	1, 631, 800	100	100	35, 000	21

By allocating funding in terms of deprivation and population this demonstrates the commitment of the programme to tackle disadvantage. The District Partnerships have the responsibility of formulating a strategy leading to an action plan which will meet the overall objectives of

Employment, Urban and Rural Regeneration, Social Inclusion and Productive Investment, contained in the Sub-programme. The partnerships in their strategies, therefore, seek to achieve a model of regeneration which recognises the need for inclusion and reconciliation as well as economic development. Under the programme the strategies and action plans produced by the District Partnerships have to be approved by the Northern Ireland Partnership Board (NIPB). The NIPB is a central board established as a company limited by guarantee to administer the programme. The NIPB consists of twenty-two individuals, excluding the chairman the Permanent Secretary of the DoE, representing the three main sectoral interests, as outlined below:

(1) Local authorities (8);
(2) Voluntary / Community (7);
(3) Business (3), Trade Union (3) and Rural interests (1).

In addition to approving the action plans and ensuring that they meet the aims of the programme, the NIPB has an executive role to oversee the District Partnerships.

It is hoped that through the partnership approach with its principles of co-operation, building trust, social dialogue, participation and social inclusion, agreement can be built between the Unionist and Nationalist communities in Northern Ireland. It is these same principles of social dialogue and co-operation which helped to foster new relationships and reconcile former enemies at the macro level in Europe and build the European Union (NICVA, 1997).

This chapter seeks to analyse the District Partnerships and identify the factors impacting on partnership performance. The analysis will be structured under four main headings namely Contextual, Stakeholder / Organisational, Decision Making and Operational conditions. In each section important issues concerning the conditions associated with improving partnership performance, which have been raised in the literature, will be tested against the District Partnership experience. However, before that, consideration must be given to carefully selecting a number of District Partnerships for in-depth research.

Selecting District Partnerships for Qualitative Research

The Peace and Reconciliation initiative established twenty six District Partnerships and due to limited time and resources, research could not be conducted on all arrangements. As a result six case studies were selected using key variables or factors. The variables were determined from secondary data analysis, in a review of each District Partnership's strategy documents and action plans, and semi-structured interviews with seven key informants from three District Partnerships, two Intermediary Funding Bodies (IFBs), the European Commission and the NIPB. The list of variables included:

- Geographical spread of partnerships;
- Urban / rural mix;
- Spread of projects supported across the four programme themes;
- Deprivation / TSN indicators, representation across the range or concentration of the 'most deprived' given the centrality of social inclusion to the sub-programme;
- Protestant / Catholic split in the districts;
- Impact of the conflict.

The choice was also informed by advice from the NIPB whose experience in dealing with District Partnerships was invaluable in making the selection. The case studies and reasons for their selection are outlined as follows:-

Armagh
- extensive consultation and information gathering process during strategy and action plan preparation;
- acknowledges acute polarisation at local level.

Belfast
- international recognition as a divided city;
- large scale expenditure;
- innovative action of interfaces and contested spaces.

Castlereagh
- suburban location with outer city estates – targeted approach to TSN;

- strongly unionist, concerned about mutual understanding and sectarianism;
- strong participation by women on the partnership (11 out of 26 members).

Cookstown
- strong and developing partnership processes;
- innovative customer approach with the preparation of application packs;
- demonstrated some integration with other programmes;
- innovative capacity building programme with CRC funding.

Newry and Mourne
- strongly nationalist, strategy analysis of political violence;
- consortium based administration;
- innovative phase 2 action plan, towards a programme approach.

Strabane
- extreme urban and rural disadvantage;
- appointment of joint chairs on the partnership;
- a solid application driven, grant making process.

An Analysis of Contextual Conditions

A Contentious Political Environment

Northern Ireland provides a good example of an environment which has a history of political confrontation. Northern Ireland is a deeply divided society across a number of important issues such as, religious observance, cultural identity and national and political affiliation. What is also important is that these divisions are located against a background of historical confrontation, particularly the last thirty years of inter community conflict. The deep divisions in Northern Ireland have maintained the feelings of distrust, suspicion, fear and anger between the two main communities, Nationalist and Unionist. By looking at the historical and political context of Northern Ireland it would be fair to assume that establishing a local collaborative partnership involving all political affiliations would be destined for failure.

Indeed, in the initial stages of establishing the European Special Support Programme for Peace and Reconciliation (EUSSPP&R) this assumption was becoming clearly manifested. Despite the paramilitary cease-fires of August 1994, October 1994 and June 1997, ending over twenty-five years of inter-community conflict, Northern Ireland has remained a tense and divided region. The first moves to establish District Partnerships across each of the twenty six district council areas, involving all political parties, met with feelings of distrust and suspicion. These feelings were clearly felt by a large body of Unionist politicians who were unwilling to participate in the District Partnerships alongside Sinn Féin party members. The Unionist politicians resented the participation of Sinn Féin whom they saw as being representatives of the IRA who had fought a terrorist campaign against 'their community'. From this position the District Partnerships were seen as a non starter, with the Unionist politicians not committing to the partnerships if Sinn Féin were to be included.

Given this difficult situation, a lot of work was undertaken by the EU officials in trying to 'win' the agreement of the three Northern Ireland MEPs to accept the programme. Despite the difficulties and sensitivities of the programme the three MEPs agreed to the District Partnerships. One interviewee pointed out that the agreement of the three MEPs was vital in establishing the district partnerships; it was stated that, 'Once the political good will was in place, operating the programme was made much easier'.

Considering that the programme was designed by the EU, this also played a significant part in being able to gain acceptance of the District Partnerships from all political parties in Northern Ireland. The EU is regarded as an independent organisation by both Nationalist and Unionist Communities and this made it easier to build trust and gain the support of all political parties. If the programme had been driven by the NIO, this would have raised suspicions and tensions among the political parties and wider community, that the NIO were working to a hidden agenda. In this way the EU acted like a convenor in being able to bring Nationalist and Unionist representatives together and get them to work towards a common goal.

In addition, the willingness of all District Partnership members to work together helped to build and maintain the partnerships. At the time of establishing the District Partnerships there was a strong feeling among board members, that by working together, with all social partners, a collective momentum could be built which could heal some of the division and anger of the past twenty-five years of conflict. One interviewee pointed out that:

> Although partnership members came from different political, religious and social backgrounds, what they had in common was a vested collective interest in tackling the needs of their districts.

This momentum of political good will towards the District Partnerships and the determination to work together, to seek a better conflict free Northern Ireland, was quickly built up after the two paramilitary cease-fires. One interviewee gauged the mood of the District Partnerships extremely well:

> The District Partnerships captured the imagination of the cease-fire era and lots of people entered these arrangements in the hope that things could be slightly different. There was scope to make a contribution to change in Northern Ireland.

Although the cease-fires were a major factor in creating the conditions to build a momentum of political goodwill, the District Partnerships have shown that a willingness to work together, strong political leadership and role of a neutral convenor, which can gain multilateral political support, can override the obstacles to establishing partnerships presented by historical and political confrontation.

Further evidence that a willingness to work together is an important condition for success is highlighted by the return to conflict by the IRA on February 9th 1996 and the tension and conflict surrounding the 'stand-off' by a local lodge of the Orange Order. A stand off ensued at Drumcree Parish Church when the Orange Order was prevented from marching through the mainly Nationalist Garvaghy Road area of Portadown in 1995, 1996, 1998 and 2000. Tension between the two main communities in Northern Ireland also came to the fore when the march was forced down the Garvaghy Road in 1997. Considering that the District Partnerships continued to operate and conduct their business throughout this especially difficult period, shows the strength of the political goodwill which existed among partnership volunteers and its importance to the success of partnerships.

However, this is not to suggest that the partnerships remained unaffected by the continuation of violence and the politically charged atmosphere that surrounds the marching season, particularly at Drumcree. One interviewee states that the return to conflict seriously impacted on the success of the partnership:

> The collapse of the cease-fire and events at Drumcree damaged things considerably. There was a willingness at the start to do a lot more peace and reconciliation work. Where projects were not coming forward that engendered peace and reconciliation principles some partnerships were even thinking about ways to organise festivals, sporting competitions and drama festivals themselves which were cross-community. With a deteriorating political environment, the huge volume of applications and limitations about how far peace and reconciliation could be pushed locally, the momentum was lost.

Although the events of Drumcree and the breakdown of the cease-fire may have affected the partnership process and the operation of the peace and reconciliation initiatives, they did not lead to the failure of the partnerships or a collapse of the programme. It must also be remembered that the District Partnerships operated within a politically competitive atmosphere of three elections (the Forum '96, Westminster '97 and Local Government '97). Throughout these difficult and challenging times the partnerships continued and peace and reconciliation initiatives were still being implemented. There can be little doubt that without the political goodwill on behalf of the District Partnership volunteers the programme would have collapsed due to the rising political tensions. Political good will and the belief that more can be achieved working together than acting individually is important to local collaborative partnerships. If this belief or momentum is strong enough it can override the obstacles presented by historical and political confrontation. This argument is supported and summarised by one interviewee who recalls the tension during the stand off at Drumcree being dampened down by the District Partnership members working together in consensus:

> I believe the events at the time of Drumcree would have been worse if it was not for the good relationships and consensus building atmosphere built by the District Partnership. The consensus and agreement among the local councillors in the partnership managed in some ways to hold the line in the local communities. The board members were in their communities reconciling, thus building a stronger community relations base.

Indeed, District Partnerships have become successful learning environments for partnership representatives. One interviewees experience of the District Partnership highlights the progress that has been made:

> A lot of people around the table that I sit with, I wouldn't have anything to do with in my ordinary life. They come from perspectives that I don't hold or I don't agree with, but we sit around the table and I have had a lot of myths challenged. I never would have sat down with a Sinn Féin councillor, never could have understood what they were trying to do, except be afraid of what they were doing; but listening to them talking about their families and their lives, their backgrounds and things that have happened to them makes it all very different.

An Analysis of Stakeholder / Organisational Conditions

Stakeholder Competition

From the outset the tension and potential conflict between the different sectors in the District Partnerships was very apparent. In the first instance the District Partnerships were part of a programme which artificially brought the different sectors together. All the participants were acting within an enforced working environment or what was termed by one interviewee 'an arranged marriage'.

One of the potential areas of conflict in the District Partnerships was between councillors and the community representatives. Given the strong element of the bottom up approach, the community / voluntary sector was eager to have a strong representation on the partnership boards. The community / voluntary sector members came from a solid grassroots base and had detailed knowledge of their local areas. The councillors on the other hand, were suspicious of the role of the voluntary / community sector as they believed that they, as the only directly elected members of the board, were the true representatives of the community. One interviewee notes the councillors' difficulties with the inclusive nature of the partnerships, particularly those from the Unionist community,

> Generally speaking the Unionist Councillors tend to think that they are representatives of their area, democratically they are, but they didn't have the understanding that the other sectors are equally representative.

The councillors felt their position was under threat from the increasingly confident voluntary / community sector. Furthermore, councillors who sat on Unionist or Nationalist controlled councils found it difficult to deal with challenges from other quarters. The tension between the councillors and the voluntary / community sector had the potential to damage the partnership process and lead to conflict. One interviewee highlighted the difficulties of bringing the councillors into the mould of a partnership process:

> Councillors were seen as trying to stamp their authority on the partnership and to organise everything. When they didn't get their way they engaged in dirty tricks by leaking stories to the press about squabbles in the partnership over one project. The stories were grossly exaggerated and given a political slant. Because the majority party in the council had been unable to exercise control over the partnership they have simply dubbed it 'Republican'.

A Neutral Venue

In order to build a better working environment and to facilitate an effective partnership process it has been good practice for a number of partnerships to attend meetings at a neutral venue. In the first number of months in certain partnerships the voluntary / community sectors felt very uncomfortable attending meetings in the District Council Chambers. One interviewee felt that in the Chamber the community / voluntary sectors were 'the underdogs' in that the meetings were council led and at times involved party politics. If certain members of a partnership feel intimated or undervalued this will lead to the failure of the partnership as not all members will participate in decision making and this may cause disaffection and future conflict. In circumstances where certain members of a partnership board feel uncomfortable, the experience of the District Partnerships has shown that it is good practice to move meetings to a neutral venue. One interviewee states that the gelling of the partnership did not take effect until meetings were held in a neutral venue:

> The shift from the Council Chamber to a neutral venue has created neutral space and prevented councillors from attending to business during partnership meetings. At the neutral venue a strong sense of people getting together has been created with the District Partnership members relating to

one another as individuals, not as individuals within their own attached boxes.

Although it has not been the case for all District Partnerships to move to a neutral venue, neutral venues can be identified as a condition which affects the performance in circumstances in which certain board members feel uncomfortable with the meeting venue.

Stakeholder Priorities

Not only did the voluntary / community sectors and councillors cause concern for future conflict, but the business sector also had problems with the idea of partnership and working together. The business sector found it difficult to adapt to the different culture of partnership and to the themes of the programme. Concepts such as social inclusion, peace and reconciliation and community capacity building were seen as anathema to the business representatives trained to focus on quantifiable inputs, throughputs and outputs. The business sector also found it difficult to give up their voluntary time and thus their attendance on partnership meetings suffered as a result. One local councillor captures the role of the business sector in the partnerships:

> The business sector has difficulties with partnership; the business sector has a different background and want to go to meetings with an agenda and have something completed. Its the nature of their mind and the way it focuses. In the District Partnership there is more discussion, there is more give and take, it is not clear cut. The business sector has difficulty with the District Partnership, especially with terms such as community development.

The coming together of the different sectors into an arranged partnership and the fusion of the different cultures and tensions clearly shows the difficulties and problems involved in partnerships. The District Partnerships have brought a number of main groups mainly elected representatives, public officials, people from business and industry, and community / voluntary group nominees around the partnership table. One interviewee sums up the complexities of the partnership process by stating:

> Community organisations believe that they are instantly accountable to their communities and are in better touch with the feelings of their

communities. The public sector is there to competently deliver a set of services and depoliticise the process. The business sector believes it is the only one able to stand on its own two feet. I don't think the tension is between elected and representative participants but between four divergent cultures.

Commitment

In local collaborations it is important that each member of the participating organisations shows total commitment to the process. In the peace and reconciliation programme the demands on board members have been huge, especially when considering that membership is voluntary. From the start, as the partnerships have been operating against the clock, formulating strategies and action plans and assessing projects, it would have been easy for any of the organisations or board members to simply walk out. However, the District Partnership members showed determination and commitment to the process. One interviewee in describing the experience of working in the partnership clearly shows the commitment of the board members:

> In our case we had to establish a board of over twenty people, all from very diverse backgrounds, who were not used to working together to make decisions within a time-frame which was crazy. Ironically that probably turned out to be our salvation because people had to get on with it. The spirit of partnership was not squandered through inter or intra sectoral personality clashes. It really did put people under pressure. We had over 150 applications; the forms themselves were awful, and we needed twenty days of meetings in the month of November alone. But we did it, and the partnership is justifiably proud of its achievement.

The demands highlighted by the interviewee clearly show the commitment of the District Partnership board members. Commitment was important to ensure that members would work together in a consistent approach, make difficult decisions and move the partnership forward.

An Analysis of the Partnership Decision Making Process

Within partnerships it is essential that each of the participants work together and interact in order to achieve common solutions to problems.

The concept of all the participants gelling and working together in a partnership decision making process is central to the development of a local collaboration. It has already been mentioned that the task of getting each of the different sectors in the District Partnership (voluntary / community, councillors, businesses, statutory and trade union interests) to work together as a group is a difficult one. By analysing the District Partnerships the conditions which facilitate a decision making process can be identified and discussed.

A Participatory Decision Making Process

One condition which has facilitated a partnership process in the District Partnerships, is that each board member has equal participation in the decision making process. In one partnership, for example, it was felt that with the large number of board members the role of certain sectors or individuals could be smothered, become distant from the process and cause disruption in the partnership. In this case an inclusive approach was sought which would involve equal participation from each of the sectors. As one interviewee states:

> You could see the potential for conflict with twenty-one members representing such diverse backgrounds...it was then decided that the only way the District Partnership could work was if all the members participated in the partnership. The District Partnership was structured into three committees to ensure representation of all the sectors, and to look at religious representation within the partnership. It was important that all representatives were part of the decision making process.

Through the committee structure equal representation and participation among the different sectors was ensured and this enabled an environment of trust, understanding and inclusiveness to be fostered. It is also important, however, that fair and equal representation is established among all sectors within each sub-committee.

Despite the initial reservations about the potential conflict between the councillors and the community / voluntary sector and the problems of the business representatives, a dynamic decision making process was enacted. It was refreshing that councillors, once away from the council chambers and the constraints of party lines, became more flexible in their approach and 'opened up' to the partnership environment. One Belfast councillor described the difference in decision making in the City Hall compared with his experience on the partnerships:

> The real benefit is that it forces people to work together on the board. Councillors leave their political baggage in the City Hall and deal with other political parties and community activists, who know the issues in a very focused way. The District Partnership is much less restrictive - these people make up the life of Belfast and I, therefore, have to have a bit more give and take. You are there as an equal partner; if you don't like it you can leave, then your own community is disadvantaged. It is surprising the difference 200 yards can make (a reference from the City Hall to the location of the offices of the Belfast European Partnership Board).

With each of the board members having equal participation in the decision making process, this facilitated an educational process among all sectors. Each of the different sectors have learned from the partnership and from the experiences and skills of the other sectors. This has been particularly true of the voluntary / community sectors who have previously complained about bureaucratic procedures, delays in allocating funding and poor decision making by public bodies. Now with first hand experience of being involved in making decisions, allocating funds to community groups and prioritising projects within a limited budget, a valuable lesson has been learned about the difficulties of dispersing public money. The suspicions of the voluntary / community sectors over the practices of statutory bodies have not been well founded. After their experiences in the partnership, one interviewee remarked:

> The voluntary sector is best characterised by the phrase 'give me'. 'Give me the hammer and the bucket and let me get on with the job'. They were not interested in the process and often regarded funding bodies with disdain and a hindrance to the real work which had to be done. But now the voluntary sector is part of the decision making process. They can ask questions like: 'is this the best hammer; is this the best wood to use; where is it going to be made; who is going to make it; can we design it ourselves' etc? It is the most exciting adult education process that has ever happened in the voluntary sector.

Communication

In the District Partnerships concerns have been raised over the lack of communication. One interviewee commented that a lack of communication was evident in the partnership as a number of board members did not report back to their sectors and discuss partnership issues. By failing in this it could be argued that certain sectors missed the opportunity to share experiences and develop a learning environment. The importance of communication to the partnerships also came to light in the Peace and Reconciliation programme when difficulties arose over the allocation of funding by partnership sub-committees. In some partnerships which divided members into sub-committees, communication broke down. This meant that decisions on funding were taken without the knowledge of the other board members and caused tension in the latter stages as some areas had received more money than others. One interviewee highlights the problem of poor communication:

> Money was allocated in all the sub-committees which were unsure what the other was doing. As a result the District Partnerships gave generously to some areas.

Communication among board members or sub-committees is important to local collaborative partnerships. It is vital that all members are informed of decision making and that a common approach is adopted. If this does not occur members may feel left out of the process and may seek to disrupt or bring down the partnership.

Criticisms concerning the lack of communication also focused on the relationship between the District Partnerships and the NIPB. It was a common complaint that the communication channels between the NIPB and the District Partnerships were poor and this led to feelings of frustration, particularly among partnership members. One interviewee expressed his frustration over the lack of communication with the NIPB by referring to the incident when,

> application forms were not cleared unless the NIPB received further information. Then the District Partnerships passed the information on to the NIPB and the NIPB maintained that it was not enough. The NIPB gave no guidance to the District Partnerships as to what information was required.

It can be seen from this example that good communication helps to foster an effective learning environment and shared experience among participants and within partner organisations. Poor communication can lead to feelings of frustration and even distrust which can break down relations between organisations and individuals and lead to fracturing of the partnership.

Leadership

Leadership in the District Partnership was enacted through the chair of the partnership board. An effective chairman with good leadership skills was seen as being very important to board members, particularly in the early stages, as that person was able to focus the direction of the partnership, settle disputes between individuals and sectors and facilitate a teambuilding environment. One interviewee highlights the importance of leadership by the Chairman,

> A good chairman is one who is prepared to grasp the nettle. If you don't have a good chairman the process of gelling things together is going to be difficult. If you have someone who has an ethical stance on peace and reconciliation that makes things a whole lot easier to raise questions. Once the questions are raised they are easier to tackle.

Another interviewee cites the importance of the chairman, particularly in the first six months of the partnership being established. It was commented that the chairman had strong leadership qualities and was,

> A very capable individual who researched all the documentation, for example, NIPB guidelines. This helped to some extent to control the councillors... the partnership was chaired in the first six months in an efficient, commanding but fair way, this was a crucial time as it set the tone for the District Partnership.

This style of leadership showing efficiency and command can be contrasted by a more consensual style of leadership adopted by other partnerships. In one partnership it was decided to have a joint chair to appease the different sectors. This consensus based leadership was seen to be effective, particularly in stabilising the relationships between the sectors in the initial stages. As one interviewee stated:

> At the start there was suspicion that one or two sectors may have an overriding influence in the partnership. It was decided therefore to establish a joint chair with members from the voluntary / community sector and one from the business sector and that the two chairs have an equal balance of Protestant / Catholic, urban and rural and male and female representatives. It was hoped that the move would gain the confidence of the voluntary / community sector who feared the dominance of the councillors in the partnership. The initial suspicion among the sectors dwindled as gradually the councillors began to take a back seat role.

Different chairs have enacted different styles of leadership. It cannot be determined which style of leadership is the most effective as each individual chair and partnership are particular to different environments and personalities of board members. However, what is important is that good leadership is displayed by the chairman in a style that is most acceptable to the partnership, that the chairman does not take over decision making and that an inclusive approach is undertaken. The leadership role enacted by the chairman has been important in the District Partnerships as they have ensured an inclusive participatory approach for all members and at times raised difficult issues and settled disputes.

An Open Process

For a partnership process to fully develop and to tackle the relevant issues it is vital that a partnership builds an environment in which all issues can be brought forward and discussed. Drawing on evidence from the EUSSPP&R the experience of the District Partnerships shows that discussing contentious issues with all board members is a condition for success. One interviewee points out that the ability of all the members to discuss problems allowed the partnership to continue through the difficult embryonic stages. It is held that:

> The District Partnership emerged from the initial problems as the members were prepared to address the issues. The partnership was trying to be aware of what its weaknesses were and to be up front and honest to ensure no community was excluded.

On the other hand, some partnerships had no structures or mechanisms to talk about the problem issues, particularly sectarianism. In failing to tackle the contentious issues in an open and up front manner, some partnerships evaded the difficult issues concerning peace and reconciliation.

It must be mentioned that in dealing with the problematic issues a number of partnerships developed methods of good practice by adopting the methods of the Community Relations Council (CRC). Omagh District Partnership, for example, organised a training session on community relations in January 1997 attended by fourteen out of a maximum seventeen members. Limavady District Partnership during a two day residential retreat also gained from the assistance of the CRC and discussed the concepts of the glass curtain and single identity work and problems of avoidance. It was important that the District Partnerships set out the problems of the area, understood the concepts of the programme and embedded structures in the partnership to discuss and debate the contentious matters. To avoid the problem was to the ignore the problem. One interviewee recognised the value of the CRC training:

> The CRC trained staff and District Partnership members in community relations matters. This assured that the concept of community relations and sectarianism was not lost in the partnerships and the peace and reconciliation initiative.

Training Partnership Members

In a somewhat related point, it is argued that the training of board members is an important in facilitating a decision making process. It was a frequent comment by interviewees that the board members did not receive the necessary training to prepare for the partnerships. For example, training on how to confront problematic issues such as sectarianism could have been conducted in the first stages of partnership development. One interviewee pointed out that training on group dynamics at the start of the programme would have been useful, as in the beginning, the partnership meetings were very formal and this discouraged the participation of certain voluntary / community members. With training on group dynamics the District Partnership members would have been able to interact with one another from the initial stages and this would have assisted the decision making process.

Local Representation

In the EUSSPP&R it has been a major contention that District Partnerships have included a number of members who are not from the local area. This problem has stemmed from the fact that the community / voluntary sector were nominated to the partnerships by the Northern Ireland Council for Voluntary Action (NICVA), which is a regional organisation. In some cases members of the voluntary / community organisations were not placed with their local district. One interviewee expressed particular concern over the question of nominations and local accountability:

> The voluntary members were nominated by NICVA meaning that local groups did not have a say in their representation. The voluntary members were nominated by a provincial organisation which has a select number of groups affiliated to them. It is, therefore, important to look at the question of accountability and ask, are the members accountable and to whom?

It is important for a local collaboration to be identifiable within the local community and accountable to the local community. Partnership participants need to know the local issues and needs of the area in order to make effective decisions. Secondly, in a collaboration it is vital that relationships are developed and trust built between each of the members. In collaborations the members are committed to a long term strategy, and if trust is established between the members, it is easier for them to reach understanding and address common problems. If a collaboration is comprised of local representatives this provides a more effective local learning environment in which the members will have the opportunity to build relationships and trust; as one interviewee commented:

> The partnership approach works better at the local level where people know each other and have contact on a daily basis; this enables the partnership to build trust and confidence.

Vested Interests

Although it can be argued that it is essential to have a local collaborative partnership constituted with local members, where local members have been on partnerships, concerns have risen over the problem of vested interests. In the EUSSPP&R the board members in the District Partnerships have a profile in the local area which has meant that they are easily contacted by the local community. In this case the accessibility of the board members has established direct accountability. Accountability of individuals although very important in partnerships, has meant that board members have come under pressure from disappointed applicants, concerned as to why their projects have failed to secure funding and why the resources had gone to another community group or sector. One interviewee clearly describes the direct line of accountability of board members:

> There is a councillor representing a rural constituency on our partnership. He recounted that he was driving his tractor down a country lane and met members of the local hall committee who had applied for money for new windows. Because they had been unsuccessful they refused to speak to him for weeks. Now that's local accountability for you !!!

Given this direct line of accountability and pressures on board members, vested interests have become a problem issue in the programme. Practice guidelines were drawn up detailing that members who have an interest must declare and withdraw from discussion. However, members were able to exploit the ambiguity over what constitutes an interest. For example, councillors who have an indirect interest in a particular project were able to secure its approval through bloc scoring with other councillors from the same party. The underlying process of political bargaining involved with vested interests in the District Partnerships was well described by one interviewee:

> Councillors have sat through many of the discussions with clenched teeth. However, when it came to project selection, that's when the political astuteness and experience of the councillors of doing deals and compromising came through. There were done deals before we got to the matrix analysis of project assessment. These reflect local knowledge of the constituencies and, therefore, are not far off the mark.

Problems over the issue of vested interests have not only affected councillors. Voluntary / community members have also been accused of protecting their own projects. It has been claimed that voluntary / community members do not observe the guidelines and according to one statutory representative, 'are more political than the politicians'. Indeed, a common view expressed was that the voluntary / community representatives 'blatantly ignore vested interest protocol and champion projects with which they are known to be associated'. Vested interests have been one of the most problematic issues in the District Partnerships. From this basis it can be seen that the rules in declaring an interest over particular projects should be clearly set out. The ambiguity of vested interest guidelines in the programme have caused confusion and tension which could possibly lead to conflict between board members. It is therefore important for the success of local collaborative partnerships that rules or guidelines on vested interests are clear and observed by all members.

Time and Continuity

From assessing the procedure in the Peace and Reconciliation Programme it would appear that the case of the District Partnerships would support the view that time is required to build relationships, confidence and trust. A common cause of complaint concerning the development of the partnership process was that the voluntary / community representatives, nominated from NICVA, were to be changed after one and half years. This upset the partnerships in that after formulating strategies and assessing projects, members had established relationships and trust and had become familiar with the programme and other members. The problems involved with re-nomination have been recognised as one interviewee explained:

> Continuity is important and from hindsight NICVA would not have changed people after a year and a half. This did seem a reasonable length of time going into the process, but it took the partnerships so long to get going that you could easily argue that appointments should have been for three years.

Moreover, the turnover in District Partnership membership did not solely exist with the voluntary / community sector. The local council elections of 1997 also changed the composition of the partnership boards and its impact on the partnerships is well summarised by another interviewee:

> Turnover of people is good, but what is the point in bringing them in out of the cold and teaching them this process and then as soon as they are up to speed, horse them back out again?

Individual Skills

Finally, it can been argued that, to participate in a partnership board, members must have certain skills. It is held that skills such as debating, negotiating and strategy making are essential as they help individuals to articulate their ideas and help the partnerships to discuss contentious issues. One interviewee, referring to the lack of proper debate on the partnership and to the absence of strategic direction, stated that:

> The District Partnership needs to get the right negotiators, strategists and debaters on board so that members can say no to expectant communities and the District Partnership can focus on quantifiable areas.

There is a strong argument that partnership members require certain skills as they need to understand the aims of the programme and the processes involved in partnership. It is important to the success of a partnership that these qualities are met by each individual participant.

An Analysis of Partnership Operation

A final consideration that must be addressed when assessing the conditions affecting the performance of local collaborative partnerships concerns the operation of a partnership. It is important that operational factors are researched as they refer to the activities of a partnership.

Strategic Development

To assess the importance of local strategies in local collaborative partnerships, it is first of all necessary to review the circumstances under which the District Partnerships formulated their local strategies. The content of the strategies and subsequent action plans were directed in the beginning by the Northern Ireland Partnership Board (NIPB). The NIPB were anxious to ensure that the aims and objectives of the programme would be approached in a systematic and consistent manner. The NIPB published practice guidelines for District Partnerships of which the major considerations were,

(1) To ensure District Partnerships see their role as supporting;

(2) To ensure that the ten per cent most disadvantaged enumeration districts are targeted;

(3) To ensure that a challenging peace vision is incorporated into each strategy;

(4) To ensure that local people are engaged in a meaningful consultation regarding appropriate development themes supportive of peace and reconciliation;

(5) To ensure that a consistent application process is used throughout.

From the outset the role of the NIPB in publishing guidelines can be commended. In the initial stages of the programme the District Partnerships experienced a great deal of uncertainty; the board members had never worked together before and the remit of the partnerships had yet to be mapped out. In this case the NIPB were able to take the lead and set out a programme of operation for the District Partnerships. The NIPB published guidelines setting out steps which the District Partnerships could follow to formulate a focused strategy to reflect local needs and complement the aims of the programme. After this, District Partnerships were more informed about their roles and responsibilities. One interviewee highlights the importance of the NIPB in the programme:

> If you are going to set up twenty-six District Partnerships you must give them their head. Now that means a strategic view has certainly to be taken. The guidance notes in the ring binder were a perfect way to do it. The sentiments were all in there about how you might like to pull the plan together, in terms of the technicalities, headings and so on.

The District Partnerships have shown that established guidelines and rules at the beginning of partnership development are a condition for success. In the initial stages of a collaboration, guidelines and rules are needed to set out a framework of action and to ensure the partnership knows of its role and responsibilities.

It is widely recognised that within the first few months of the District Partnerships each were experiencing certain difficulties. Tensions and suspicions were apparent across a number of sectors, Unionist and Nationalist, councillors and the community / voluntary sector and the Trade Union / business sectors. After being given the task of formulating the strategy the uncertainties of this period are well summed up by one interviewee:

The District Partnerships were tasked with trying to promote something that didn't exist, a vision really. In promoting a vision they also had to work with others whom they may not previously have worked with or considered working with.

However, when the board members sat down to formulating their strategies, it became clear that the strategy helped to focus the attention of the partnership members on making decisions and not on potential conflict and divisions. Formulating strategies in the initial stages of partnership development settled partnership members, helped them to interact and adopt a common approach. In this regard one interviewee explains the importance of the strategies:

> What I didn't buy into was the enormous amount of work as far as the partnership is concerned. This was a big awakening - the pressure, the timetable, the deadlines in regard to preparing strategies and action plans. The whole thing was very difficult, but it was the gelling of the partnership.

The District Partnership strategy documents also contained a mission statement which helped focus the direction of the partnership and the board members towards the goals of the programme. The District Partnership for Derry City Council Area, for example, formulated a strategy which was firmly centred on the local area and people by seeking to heal long standing divisions. The strategy included a mission statement which fully embraces the concerns of Sub programme 6:

> To encourage community interaction and to create opportunities which will lead to social inclusion, reconciliation and employment so that all of its citizens can participate fully in the life of a shared city and district.

Following the mission statement the aims and strategic goals of the partnership were set out: promoting community ownership, reconciliation, a shared city, the empowerment of women and their role in development, accessibility and fostering innovation in the local economy.

A further example of an effective and unique strategy document and mission statement is that formulated by the South Tyrone Area Partnership. The strategy document focuses on what the board members agree is important for the area and a deep appreciation of the power of partnership through an active citizenship working in a common purpose to achieve shared goals. The mission statement seeks,

> To empower and enable the diverse strands which constitute the community of the South Tyrone area in working together towards a more active and equitable society: by building individual and collective confidence, by nurturing inclusion and interaction; by overcoming barriers and respecting diversity; thereby promoting the social, economic, environmental and cultural development of the region and all its citizens, and enhancing the opportunities for peace and reconciliation.

What is important to distil from the South Tyrone Area Partnership Strategy document, as with the Derry strategy, is that not only does the mission statement clearly outline the ethos and aims of the partnerships but that five priority themes or strategic goals are also set out in support of the mission statement. In addition, the South Tyrone Partnership then relates each of the five themes to one of the aims of the Sub - programme 6, social inclusion, employment and productive investment and urban and rural regeneration. The mission statement therefore provides the principal focus for the partnership and sets the parameters of operation. Mission statements were regarded as being very important to the partnerships, as one interviewee stated:

> The District Partnership held a conference in which the mission statement and message of the partnership was presented. This gave the mission and direction of the strategy and helped to lead the future direction for the District Partnership.

It can be seen that developing strategy documents and mission statements are important operational conditions. Not only do they direct the attention of the District Partnerships to certain activities thereby contributing to the gelling process among members, but strategy documents and mission statements also focus aims and objectives and act a constant reminder to participants as to what their goals should be.

In the early stages of partnership development the District Partnerships sought the opportunity to seek the advice of consultants and facilitators. Consultants' advice was not only sought in strategic planning to formulate partnership strategies but also in team building, training and project selection. The role of the consultants and facilitators was felt to be beneficial to the partnerships as they helped to focus members on the significant strategic programme issues, to raise contentious questions and to bring an independent mind and viewpoint to the partnerships.

Despite the value that the consultants brought to the partnerships, problems existed where the consultants took over the role of the board members and formulated an almost independent strategy. This problem occurred in a number of District Partnerships who found it difficult to formulate a strategy within the limited time frame. One interviewee explains the different roles consultants can take and their affect on the strategic planning process:

> We used (a person) to come and act as a facilitator in a couple to sessions and again we came up with the themes etc, working closely with the Board in very much group orientation. There wasn't the problem there might have been in other boards where they were very new and not used to working in that sort of developmental approach so we did have a process by which we arrived at our strategy that I think other areas didn't have the luxury of. They brought in consultants, because of time, again, wrote what they thought, whereas our strategy was grounded in the Board, and we held a few sessions in the community to try and test what people felt.

The dangers of allowing consultants to formulate the partnership strategy are clear. If the decision making role of board members is restricted this may cause frustration and conflict within the partnership. Secondly, consultants may not produce a strategy which is acceptable to the partnership or the local community. Formulating a strategy among all board members creates ownership and ensures the partnership participants will work towards its implementation. Finally, it has already been explained that decision making among board members in the early stages of partnership development creates a favourable working environment and invokes a gelling process among board members. Therefore, if the decision making process is undertaken by consultants the board members will be denied the opportunity to interact and work together.

The experience of the District Partnerships has shown that the effective use of consultants and facilitators are important conditions for improving the performance of local collaborative partnerships. However, it must be ensured that the role of the consultants does not inhibit or overcrowd the role of the board members. The idea of partnership is based on inclusion in the decision making process and if this is restricted the role of partnerships can be questioned. Consultants do have an important role or function to play in partnerships but they should only give assistance and guidance. The role that consultants and facilitators should take was well summed up by one interviewee who stated that, 'consultants should only be brought in to provide a valuable service that can't be provided in house'.

The Strategic Planning Process

In the EUSSPP&R including a wide audience in formulating strategies has been a main consideration for the District Partnerships. Indeed as already mentioned, the NIPB gave direct guidance to partnerships to involve the wider community and to ensure that the 'views of the most marginalised are proactively sought'.

When formulating strategy documents and prioritising needs and issues, the District Partnerships proactively sought the views of wider constituents, particularly the marginalised, who often have less access to community programmes. By adopting a new more inclusive approach the district partnerships aimed to break new ground and to 'make a difference' at the local level.

In relation to the strategic planning process, it is important to refer to the Coopers and Lybrand (1997) mid term review which analysed District Partnership activity. The Coopers and Lybrand study sought to examine the Peace and Reconciliation programme by assessing the extent to which the Programme progressed towards achieving its objectives. In a survey conducted from thirteen out of twenty-six partnerships, Coopers and Lybrand discovered that District Partnerships have used the following methods to seek the views of the wider community:

- Reports in the local media (n =13);
- Advertisements in local media (n =13);
- Leaflets / posters (n =11);
- Invitation for submissions (n =12);
- Public meetings / forums (n =13);
- Word of mouth (n =13); and,
- Direct mailshot information (n =10).

From this Coopers and Lybrand concluded:

> There was evidence of a thorough and consistent approach by the District Partnerships to communicating the plans relating to their establishment (Coopers and Lybrand, 1997, p.B130).

Coopers and Lybrand also reported on the involvement of voluntary and community sectors in the formulation of the strategies. It is stated that District Partnerships interacted with a range of groups including: Unemployed groups; Welfare rights groups; Youth groups; Child care groups; Elderly groups; Women's groups; Travellers groups; Victims of violence; Ex-prisoners groups; and Disabled groups. Again Coopers and Lybrand concluded:

> This would tend to suggest a proactive approach by all the partnerships in working with groups and researching key priorities prior to inviting applications for funding. This is an important finding because it supports the view that District Partnerships have embarked upon a process of out-reach that included various elements in their local communities (Coopers and Lybrand, 1997, p. B134).

The Coopers and Lybrand report clearly shows the ambition and effort of the District Partnerships in seeking to engage as wide an audience as possible. District partnerships used a wide range of methods to seek the views of the most marginalised and were quite successful in doing so.

Fermanagh District Partnership, for example, employed a broad consultation exercise seeking the views of the most marginalised in the county. The scale of the activity and amount of effort given to the consultation is evidence that this District Partnership sought to embrace as wide an audience as possible in the design of its strategy. The consultation was comprised of a number of strands including, media coverage, public meetings, and distributing 1000 questionnaires to community and voluntary organisations, businesses, churches, statutory bodies, councillors, trade unions, community venues and individuals seeking views on how the allocation of £1.5 million should be spent on deserving projects within the District. The Partnership also carried out interviews with locally based representatives of fifteen 'study groups' including women, mentally ill, small farmers, ex offenders, lone parents, long term unemployed, early school leavers, pre school children, elderly, physically disabled, careers, alcohol/drug abusers, prisoners and their families, families displaced from border areas, and the homeless.

By including and engaging a wide constituency the Fermanagh partnership was able to embed its strategy within the grass roots of the local community. Through this approach the local community are not considered to be clients or customers but rather social partners who are also able to take 'ownership' of the strategy. Embracing the wider community in formulating a strategy is important for local collaborations as it is vital that the strategy reflects local needs and that the community can accept the strategy and take ownership of it.

The Importance of Time

After formulating an effective strategy and engaging a wide local constituency, it follows that the strategy and priority themes are implemented. In the case of the District Partnerships there is an argument to suggest that the strategies have not impacted on what the partnerships have funded or implemented. Criticism of the phase 1 action plans emerged stating that there is little correlation between the strategies and projects that have been funded. In the strategy documents the partnerships aimed to fund projects which would address the needs of the most marginalised and make a difference at the local level. However, after reflection of phase 1 it is claimed that the needs of the marginalised have not been met, meaning an implementation gap has developed. The NIPB have commented on the issue of project quality; it is recorded in the minutes of the September 1996 meeting that there is,

> an overall disappointment in the quality of each action plan. Many of the projects therein were from established voluntary organisations with a traditional service ethos, few demonstrated any innovation, there was a lack of any meaningful proposals specifically in relation to peace and reconciliation and there didn't appear to be a groundswell of applications from local groups from the most disadvantaged areas. It was suggested that this lack lustre, risk adverse performance in phase 1 action plans could be explained by the fact that under a very tight deadline District Partnerships have incorporated the safer, high profile, easily approved projects, and that the more innovative, risky and complex projects will feature in phase 2 action plans (DR96G318.EUP p.6).

Furthermore, in a paper tabled to the European Cohesion Forum in Brussels during April 1997 NIPB noted that,

> Most of the projects funded could be classified as worthwhile, however, it is difficult, at this stage, to claim that the District Partnership have brought forward innovative projects that add value and complement existing programmes. This can be explained by the embryonic stage of

development of partnerships, whereby District Partnerships have largely been reactive to applications from worthwhile projects in their area. The challenge is for District Partnerships to develop their capacity to be more strategic, proactive and focused in the future (DR97G167.EUP/DLB).

It is held that District Partnerships, in the early stages, funded the established voluntary and community groups and that the marginalised local groups, who were consulted in the strategies, received little funding and development. In addition, the quality of projects funded are considered to be low quality as they do not specifically tackle the aims of Sub-programme 6.

After reviewing the projects which have been funded under phase 1, the district partnerships have also acknowledged that product outcomes do not meet the priorities of the strategy documents. As one board member commented:

> The applications did not reflect the strategic intentions of the partnership. For example a lot of applications came from playgroups; perhaps the District Partnership made an error in the early stages to give a playgroup a thousand pounds. This was the simple way but then this set a precedent for other applications.

It is important to note that although the criticism is focused on the District Partnerships and their action plans, the partnerships are not faulted for their efforts. The NIPB acknowledges that the quality of projects received may well be a reflection of the short time-scale available to draw down money into the community.

Throughout the programme the District Partnerships have been continuously under pressure to achieve high spending profiles, and following the approval of the strategy documents, to move quickly to assess applications and prepare phase 1 action plans. To highlight the volume of work involved it is noted in the NIPB Annual Report that District Partnerships received 2459 phase 1 applications. By the end of December 1996 most action plans had been approved with Phase 1 allocations reaching £10m spread across 930 projects. The volume of work undertaken is especially notable given that the strategy documents had only been approved by NIPB during the summer months. Given this demanding workload it is not surprising that the partnerships did not have the time to engage their constituencies, improve the nature of the projects or to think strategically. One District Partnership volunteer, after reflection, comments that the time and pressure to spend the money quickly was a failure of the programme as it smothered the importance of the strategy:

> One shortfall or criticism of the programme is that there is no strategic role for the District Partnership. People have always criticised other organisations for delay in getting the money out; in the District Partnership we have got what we asked for and we are now paying the price. We spent the money quickly without having our strategy in place.

Drawing from the experience of the EUSSPP&R, it can be argued that a limited time frame is a condition which can affect the performance of local collaborative partnerships. Partnerships need time to address or correspond to their strategies but when hundreds of applications need to be assessed, partnerships may lose sight of their strategy. This approach could have serious consequences for local collaborative partnerships as a strategy provides the mechanism to focus the objectives and the long term direction of the partnership. If the strategy is not permitted to set the direction, partnerships may lose track of their objectives and focus on short term, *ad hoc* initiatives which do not relate to programme issues. Furthermore, it is important for local collaborative partnerships to implement their strategies as they have been formulated with the aid of the local community as 'social partners'. If the programme output does not correlate to each strategy this may cause disaffection within the local community who may become distant from the partnership and reluctant to work with projects they no longer have ownership of.

The Project and Programme Based Approaches

The disparity between the strategic planning process and programme output can be further explained due to the adoption of an application driven approach. Despite efforts to formulate strategies and identify the needs of each district, the partnerships were largely reactive to making decisions on funding for application forms. Under this approach the quality of projects and programme output were largely at the mercy of the quality of the applications. If applications were not forthcoming from the marginalised areas the partnerships had little scope for operation. As one Project Officer stated:

There are groups in need that are not being assessed, for example, ex-prisoners. It may be the case that they don't want to be involved. There's only so much that can be done and we're always depending on the community groups' interest in accessing our funding.

With the District Partnerships being largely reactive to the quality of applications this would also help to explain why the longer established groups benefited from Phase 1. Larger established groups are well skilled in seeking funding, with their skills and resources they can move quickly in response to new initiatives, perhaps even recycling unsuccessful applications to other organisations.

Therefore the project based approach may not be an ideal mechanism for implementation as it limits local collaborative partnerships from enacting their strategy. Under the project or application based approach the emphasis or onus is placed on the local community to present innovative and original projects. If these projects are not forthcoming and do not include the marginalised community, the operation of the District Partnership is restricted. However, it is important to mention that the project based approach and problems of time are interrelated. Due to time considerations, the partnerships had little opportunity to work proactively with the local community and, therefore, became reactive to assessing projects. The decision to adopt a project based approach was dictated by the operation of the programme. One interviewee sums up the problems of the project based approach and expresses the strong opinion that the experience of the first tranche should not be repeated:

> One thing the District Partnerships have learnt is that the project approach is disastrous in terms of time management. Members have realised that the project approach involves a lot of work for relatively small amounts of money and the other thing is that a lot of the small groups in the area are probably saying that these small bits of money are no good to anybody anyway... If we move to a strategic approach we move from being reactive to being proactive... If there is no difference between a partnership and an IFB then there is no point in us doing it. Not only has NIVT been doing it for longer, they will do it better and cheaper. The District Partnerships need to be out of that game.

Considering that the District Partnerships were still in their embryonic stages when assessing product output in phase 1, it is important to mention that by the phase 2 assessment the partnerships had matured, learned from their mistakes and grown in confidence. They began to review their expenditures under Phase 1. Gaps were identified in the funding provisions and attempts were made to redress the imbalances. For instance, to reduce the implementation gap, the Belfast European Partnership Board acknowledged that in Phase 1 the call for proposals and applications did not meet the expectations of the partnership members and the goals of the initiative. As a result the partnership reflected on these mistakes and revised the strategy, by narrowing the framework of operation. In Phase 2, three priorities were established: interfaces and contested spaces, social inclusion and the encouragement of cross community contact, social economy and employment. This did help the local community groups as it focused the new direction of the partnership and clarified the aims of the programme. In addition, the partnership prepared guidance notes for funding applicants and introduced an example of a model application form to assist community groups in improving the quality of their project submissions. In short, a focused strategy is important to local collaborative partnerships as it more strongly directs the operation of the partnership to very specific aims.

It could be argued, however, that a programme driven approach is an ever more effective way of reducing the implementation gap. By researching into the EUSSPP&R and assessing the experiences of the different District Partnerships, a possible alternative to the application driven approach emerged from the Newry and Mourne Peace and Reconciliation District Partnership. After Phase 1 the Newry and Mourne partnership recognised that a further call for proposals would create another large number of short term or *ad hoc* applications, seeking money for projects not directly related to the strategy of the partnership. As a result, the District Partnership made a decision to focus in on a number of specific themes, thus moving away from the widespread and diverse application based approach. Three working groups were established in November 1996 to meet with the experts and relevant interests groups around the specific themes of employment, people and culture. Sixteen programmes were then drawn up, ten of which would be implemented by delivery agents, with pre-defined budges and targets, selected after an advertising and interview process. For example a programme approach gives the District Partnerships the opportunity to lead the direction of the partnership while allowing the aims to be met by delivery agents who have local knowledge and experience. Thus under the programme approach the views and needs of the most marginalised, who cannot articulate their ideas, are addressed and the District Partnership is given flexibility to focus on strategic issues.

It must be remembered that the Newry and Mourne Peace and Reconciliation Partnership has also recognised the importance of funding projects. A certain amount of money has been set aside for free standing projects to embrace local groups with good ideas who cannot formulate them into a programme. This gives the partnership the required flexibility to focus mainly on a programme approach but leaves the project approach open for innovative projects.

The programme approach has the double advantage of allowing delivery agents to target the specific needs of a local area and to leave the partnership to apply the strategic direction. Under the programme approach there is a stronger correlation between strategic objectives and priorities and product outcomes, thus closing the implementation gap. However, as the Newry and Mourne experience shows it will still be necessary to allow the partnership and the local community enough flexibility to embrace unique, free standing and innovative projects.

Partnership Autonomy and Power

In the Peace and Reconciliation programme the autonomy of the District Partnerships has been a major source of contention. In the programme the partnerships were to be entrusted with local decision making over the allocation of funds. However, in practice the partnerships have argued that the role of the Northern Ireland Partnership Board (NIPB) was heavily prescriptive, setting out guidelines, insisting on financial appraisals and above all approving action plans. This helped to form a perception that the NIPB were only concerned with probity and accountability and restraining the role of the partnerships. One interviewee describes the tension between the District Partnerships and the NIPB:

> There was a schizophrenia about NIPB. There are very well intentioned people in NIPB whose background is in community / socio economic development and they were sending out very positive vibes to District Partnerships about reconciliation and working together. But they were puppets worked from behind by the harder edge civil servant types who are saying 'Yes, but you have got to nail down financial probity, you need to have economic appraisal, there must be monitoring and evaluation'. And the way it has worked out, the harder edge has overwhelmed the softer edge of NIPB. The result is that partnerships are overwhelmed with

bureaucracy which I thought was one of the things we were meant to avoid.

The role of the NIPB has caused frustration for many partnerships who sought their own autonomy to make their own local decisions and implement their own projects and programmes. This perceived power struggle between the NIPB and the District Partnerships has led to frustration, which has been a destructive force in the programme. Local collaborative partnerships need to have a significant degree of autonomy to formulate and implement their own strategy for their local area. If autonomy is not granted the role and operation of the collaboration is then called into question.

On the other hand, it is important to remember that the role of the NIPB in establishing practice guidelines and rules for fledgling partnerships has been praised as a condition for success in the earlier stages of this chapter. It can be seen that the NIPB are placed in a precarious position. The NIPB were given the role of nurturing and monitoring the embryonic District Partnerships. This was a difficult job as different partnerships developed in different ways. Some of the more sophisticated partnerships assumed a decentralised role of local decision making with only occasional guidance and support from the NIPB, whereas other less advanced partnerships invited the NIPB into a more prescriptive role to manage their operations. The role of the NIPB, therefore, becomes confusing especially considering that the NIPB were also a fledgling organisation and who, as one interviewee commented, 'were only one or two pages in front of the District Partnerships'. The NIPB found itself in the position of trying to find a balance between a number of opposing and conflicting tensions, centralisation and devolution; top down prescription and local flexibility; probity of spending and managerial accountability versus risk taking, empowerment and innovation.

The role of the NIPB was, therefore, not an easy one; it was difficult to determine at what stage the District Partnerships were mature and confident enough to embrace full autonomy and responsibility. Setting out guidelines and rules for local collaborative partnerships are equally a condition for success as having the autonomy to formulate and implement strategies. However, what is clear from the District Partnership experience is that the relationship between setting rules and guidelines and allowing autonomy is an evolving one. District Partnerships have shown that local collaborative partnerships need guidelines and rules and that these are important in the embryonic stages of development. However, as District Partnerships become more confident and mature and establish a partnership process, less rule making and more autonomy should be forthcoming.

An Ambitious Programme

In the Peace and Reconciliation programme a common criticism raised by the District Partnerships is that the aims of the programme are too ambitious. District partnerships have argued that their role to improve peace and reconciliation through social inclusion, urban and rural regeneration and employment and productive investment was too broad to achieve any real tangible product outcomes. Certainly the task which set out for the District Partnerships has been phenomenal, especially when considering the partnerships been established for such a short period of time. The ambitious programme set out for the District Partnerships has led to confusion and uncertainty for some partnerships. The themes included in the programme have embraced a wide area of activity and created confusion among the District Partnerships who, unsure of their role, funded a wide range of short term projects. Indeed, one interviewee commented that the partnerships funded community projects which were 'a mile wide and an inch deep'. Following this, questions have arisen concerning the sustainability and added value of certain projects. The ambitions of the programme have hampered the focus and direction of partnerships as they have found it difficult to carve out a niche in which they could make a difference at the local level. It is important for local collaborative partnerships to tackle a number of well defined and focused objectives. In this approach projects and programmes are implemented which combat specific local needs in an effective way and not dispersing small amounts of money across a range of needs.

Considering the ambitions of the programme and the timescales involved, this has placed high demands on board members. Members found that on occasions three to four meetings had to be called each week and that this added too much pressure to individuals committed to the partnerships on a voluntary basis. The commitment of the board members to the partnerships has been outstanding; however, it would not be possible to expect the same level of commitment to be maintained in the long term.

The workload involved with the programme has been too demanding for partnership volunteers. In the initial stages of partnership development it could be expected that the demands on the board members would be high. However, it is unacceptable for the same demands to be expected after the first year. A demanding workload can lead to disillusionment among members and disaffection with the partnership. It is important that local collaborative partnerships have a manageable workload so board members can give their full commitment and attention to the partnership process.

Inter-Organisational Co-operation

With the District Partnerships the experience of working with other partnerships, government departments and agencies has been mixed. In some instances partnerships were largely left to work on their own with little collaborative linkage being adopted. In one partnership, for example, an interviewee noted that the district council's Community Relations Officer did not even sit in an advisory capacity on the partnership. Other partnerships however, have been proactive in this field. Banbridge District Partnership has consulted widely with government departments and agencies to maximise project funding and reduce duplication of effort. Magherafelt Area Partnership Limited has also established collaborative linkages with Area Development Management and the Combat Poverty Agency which manage the Peace and Reconciliation Programme in the border counties of the Republic of Ireland. In this case links have been established between projects in Magherafelt and Monaghan. However, it is acknowledged that across the District Partnerships, contacts and collaborative linkages have not been widely developed. District partnerships found it difficult to deal with government departments and agencies, as one Project Officer remarked:

> I found government departments and agencies to be quite distant I suppose I would contact them if there were projects that I needed to clarify with them... Other than that, that would be about it. The IFB's and the other District Partnerships share information about applications they have received in each round and where there might be overlaps... I can't recall having anything like that with government departments. You know they are fine when you phone them... I've got absolutely no idea who I'm dealing with, where they are, what their remit is. In the IFB's you've got a fairly clear idea about which sub-programmes they are dealing with, the specific measures and all the rest of it. In the programme I haven't seen anything from the government departments. So I'm quite clueless really about them and yes, I should be finding out more about them, but I don't

have the time at the moment to go to them fishing for information. So they are fairly distant really and I don't know how their part in the sub-programme links up with everybody else.

Another interviewee commented that their District Partnership has established contacts and communication with organisations such as LEADER, Area Based Strategy Action Groups (ABSAGs) and the Local Development Officer of the District Council, in which monthly meetings kept each body informed of activity in the area. However, it was pointed out that more work should be done on future projects but that there was a problem with inter-organisational collaboration and trying to complement the different aims of each organisation:

> The District Partnership tried to get LEADER involved in one project but because of their rules and regulations, although they thought it a good project, they couldn't commit because they were not allowed to fund that particular type of project. The problem is that the organisations all have their own sets of rules that we have to abide by; if we are approached by any of the other funders we have to make sure there is a definite peace and reconciliation angle to it to fit our criteria as well.

As with the experience of the government departments and agencies little collaborative contact has developed between the District Partnerships. One interviewee states that:

> I am not aware of any discussion, co-ordination, collaboration between the Boards of any Partnerships in terms of joint training, away days etc. There have been virtually no projects developed between Partnership Boards by Partnership Board members. The secretariats have developed individual contacts - but this is the extent of collaboration. There is no forum for the Boards to share issues and ideas. This has not been encouraged actively and it hasn't happened. There is a need for a forum to speak to NIPB with one voice.

Although some examples of co-operation between District Partnerships and government agencies and departments can be highlighted, the experience of inter-collaborative linkages has been minimal. However, it must be remembered that in the first two years of the programme the partnerships had only been established for a certain period against a demanding workload. Considering that now the District Partnerships have established themselves and become more confident and mature, the opportunities for inter organisational co-operation are now very real. Co-operation with government departments, agencies and other partnerships can improve local collaborations through shared experience, reducing duplication of effort and adopting a more focused approach.

Positive Publicity

In the EUSSPP&R there was widespread agreement among District Partnership members that more publicity for the partnerships is needed. Publicity was seen as being important to the District Partnerships for two main reasons. First of all, it was widely commented that the partnerships needed to raise their profile in the local area to make the local community more aware of the partnership and its aims and more willing to participate in the initiative. One interviewee maintained that it was vital that,

> The District Partnership raises its profile and gets its name linked to projects and make people realise that the money is there for peace and reconciliation. The people of the district will then realise that the process must be inclusive.

A number of partnerships have acknowledged the importance of publicity and have either conducted public relations operations or plan to. One District Partnership for example, organised events which the BBC covered on television and radio to help raise the profile of the partnership. Other district partnerships have planned to organise meetings inside the communities to gauge local feeling and opinion and seek feedback on the work of the partnership.

The second reason why some partnerships believed in the importance of publicity was to show to the public examples of the board members gelling together and working on a consensual basis to implement a project or programme. There is widespread feeling among board members that throughout the programme the media have been selective in their coverage of the partnerships, constantly showing negative images of a small number of issues and events. It is maintained that the District Partnerships need to have a more public role to show the real and complete picture of the partnerships which is more positive. Although the success of the District Partnerships in challenging the media and promoting events has been mixed thus far, the board members realise that in raising the profile of the District Partnerships and celebrating their successes, benefits can be reaped.

Conclusion

From analysing the District Partnerships for Peace and Reconciliation, conclusions can be drawn about the conditions which have a bearing on the performance of local collaborative partnerships. The District Partnerships have shown that local collaborative partnerships can exist and develop within a background of historical and political confrontation if there is enough political good will and a willingness to work together among partnership board members.

The experience of the District Partnerships has demonstrated that commitment from the participating organisations is important in local collaborations. In the District Partnerships the board members showed full commitment to the process by regularly attending meetings and moving the partnership forward, despite a demanding programme.

On the other hand, competition between the voluntary / community sector and local councillors has created tension and conflict which has been detrimental to the District Partnerships. There have been concerns that the councillors, being familiar with partnership and government business, would override the role of the voluntary / community sector. However, in certain cases, it was found that moving the partnership meetings to a neutral venue facilitated a more neutral and comfortable environment and allowed all members to participate in the process. Difficulties have also emerged in the partnerships with the business sector who have different priorities than the themes set out in the programme. They have found it difficult to adapt to the culture of the partnership and their attendance on board meetings has declined which has hindered the partnership process.

To facilitate a decision making process in a local collaboration a number of important conditions can be identified from the lessons of the District Partnerships; equal representation and participation, leadership, open discussion, communication, training, time, accountability, local representation, and clear, established rules on vested interests.

Formulating an effective local strategy is also essential in a local collaborative partnership. Strategies can focus aims and objectives, act as a constant reminder to participants as to what their goals should be and contribute to the gelling process among board members. However, in formulating a strategy collaborative partnerships need guidelines to give them their lead and time to consult local interests and the local community.

Finally, for a local collaboration to effectively operate and implement projects and programmes, it is important that the partnership has autonomy and clear, focused manageable aims. Local collaborative partnerships must have autonomy to make their own decisions and clear manageable aims to ensure that the partnership tackles needs in a focused way thus making a difference at the local level. Local collaborations can also use publicity to promote their successes and invite more participation and collaborate with other partnerships and government departments to share experience and reduce duplication of effort.

5 The Local Authority Cross-Border Networks

Introduction

Three Local Authority Cross-Border Networks are currently operating across the Irish border between Northern Ireland and the Republic of Ireland. In the early to mid 1970s two of the partnerships were established; the East Border Region Committee (EBRC) which is a partnership of Newry and Mourne and Down District Councils and Monaghan and Louth County Councils and the North West Region Cross-Border Group (NWRCBG) which is comprised of Derry, Strabane and Limavady District Councils and Donegal County Council. Being established in the mid to late 1970s, the EBRC and the NWRCBG began to make their first contacts at a time when few cross-border linkages existed at the institutional level. The partnerships were developed by the councils to address the economic and social problems of the border region through greater co-operation and have been promoting and pioneering cross-border development for over twenty years.

In the first ten to fifteen years the EBRC and the NWRCBG existed with funding from their own councils and only managed to achieve a limited degree of success. They implemented a number of small projects, for example, publishing tourism brochures and holding seminars. The two partnerships largely developed as lobbying organisations working with government departments and agencies to develop the border region. It was only under the INTERREG 1 programme that the EBRC and the NWRCBG received funding towards a central secretariat. This money was again awarded under INTERREG 2 and helped establish a third partnership, the Irish Central Border Areas Network (ICBAN) a partnership of Donegal, Sligo, Leitrim, Cavan and Monaghan County Councils in the Republic of Ireland and Omagh, Dungannon, Fermanagh and Armagh District Councils in Northern Ireland. Under INTERREG 2 the three networks have developed into co-ordinative partnerships and are working towards formulating strategic integrated action plans and implementing projects and programmes.

It is the aim of this chapter to highlight the networks as a case study of co-ordinative partnerships operating on a transjurisdictional sub-regional basis. By analysing the local authority networks and outlining their advantages and disadvantages, it is possible to identify the conditions influencing the performance of transjurisdictional co-ordinative partnerships operating at the sub-regional level.

Before the Local Authority Networks are examined, it is first of all necessary to review the history and evolution of cross-border co-operation in Ireland. In Ireland cross-border co-operation is a contentious and sensitive issue and to fully understand the environment in which the networks operate, the history and development of cross-border co-operation must first be outlined. This chapter will, therefore, deal firstly with the evolution of cross-border development in Ireland and secondly, with an analysis of the Local Authority Cross-Border Networks.

Background to Cross-Border Development

Drawing the Emerald Curtain

In the first thirty to forty years after the border was finally confirmed in 1925, few contacts were made at the institutional level between the two governments of Northern Ireland and the Republic of Ireland. In the 1940s and 1950s both states largely developed in isolation as the Free State Government established a strongly Catholic ethos, remained neutral in the Second World War and became an independent Republic in 1949. The Stormont Government on the other hand, was content to limit contact with the rest of the island of Ireland and instead maintain stronger links with Great Britain. Therefore, although few of those involved in creating the Irish border saw it as an international frontier, the Irish border developed as such given the different paths that the governments pursued in the years following 1925. The comments of Major Chichester-Clark in 1971 reflect on the problems created during these years:

> The Border envisaged by the 1920 Act was no major international frontier - no Emerald curtain within these islands. It was others, and not our predecessors, who piled brick upon brick along that wall so that by the end of the day we could scarcely see or comprehend each other (cited by O'Dowd, 1994, p.13).

The divergence of policy approaches in education, health and economic development, had a detrimental effect on the economy of the border region.

People tended to live back to back, with each community looking to its capital city as the centre of activity rather than developing cross-border economic opportunities (Busteed, 1992). The border counties became economically deprived, being characterised by a narrow range of employment opportunities, dominated by small scale farming, high levels of unemployment, under-employment and out migration (O'Dowd *et al*, 1994, p.35).

It was only in areas of immediate common concern that linkages were established, for example, officials from the North and South met regularly to administer and maintain the railway system and to manage a project to regulate drainage in the Erne basin (Stephens and Symons, 1956). Other cross-border links were developed by the two governments in 1952 under the Foyle Fisheries Commission. This was established to regulate and monitor the number of fish in the river, to control water pollution, regulate fishing licences and implement drainage schemes (Foyle Fisheries Commission, 1996).

New Developments in the 1960s

The 1960s could be described as a more progressive period for cross-border co-operation. The first steps towards developing greater North-South co-operation were initiated by Seán Lemass when he was elected Taoiseach in 1959. Lemass negotiated the Anglo Irish Free Trade Agreement (AIFTA) with the British Government in 1965 which sought to set in place a system of tariff reductions which would result in free trade between the two countries by 1975 (Lee 1989). The AIFTA was the first step towards improving North-South economic relations by putting the necessary structures and procedures in place so that open trade could be developed freely within the island. The agreement, therefore, marked a turning point in the decline of the economic significance of the Irish border (House, 1990).

Lemass' economic strategy was also clearly linked to his policy of reconciliation with the Northern Ireland Government which culminated in the talks with the Northern Ireland Prime Minister Terence O'Neill in January 1965. This meeting was a very symbolic one and was the beginning of a political process which sought to change relations between the North and South of Ireland.

The Impact of Civil Distrubances and Community Conflict

Moves towards greater cross-border economic co-operation and political reconciliation between Northern Ireland and the Republic of Ireland were quickly dampened, however, with the outbreak of the 'Troubles' in August 1969. The rise of terrorist violence in the early 1970s created a politically unstable environment and quickly polarised the two main communities in Northern Ireland, Nationalist and Unionist. Against this background the British and Irish governments became concerned with maintaining the security situation rather than developing the economic and political cross-border relationships which had been fostered in the O'Neill and Lemass era (Lyne, 1992).

The Role of the European Community

In 1972 the entry of the UK and the Republic of Ireland into the then European Economic Community (EEC) created a new forum under which cross-border contacts could be rebuilt. The EEC highlighted the socio-economic problems of Northern Ireland and in particular the problems which Northern Ireland and the border region faced by being located on the periphery of Europe. Socio-economic problems were given special attention as it was felt that, 'the desire for peace was closely linked to living conditions and employment' (Moxon-Browne, 1992). Through the Regional Development Fund the EEC, with the British and Irish Governments, commissioned a number of studies to review the problems of peripherality in the border region and to recommend areas for possible co-operation and closer North-South integration.

In 1976 a cross-border communications study was commissioned by the EEC and the British and Irish Governments in the Derry-Donegal area (Figure 5.1). The study concluded that the best prospects for real progress in tackling the problems of the North West border region lay in the direct co-operation between the British and Irish Governments. The study presented a number of recommendations for capital projects and service improvements that could be implemented by government authorities and agencies working on a cross-border basis. The recommendations ranged from harmonisation of road standards for cross-border roads and networks, to improvement of public transport and postal and telecommunications services (Peat, Marwick *et al*, 1977, p.10).

Figure 5.1 Location and general extent of the Londonderry Donegal Cross-Border Communications Study

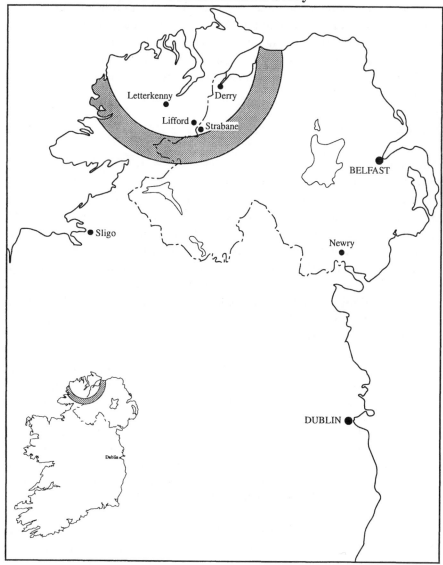

In 1979 another cross-border study was carried out, the Erne Catchment Study, at the behest of the British and Irish Governments and the European Commission under finances from the European Agricultural Guidance and Guarantee Fund (EAGGF). The principal themes of the report were arterial draining and tourism development and the report concluded that the effective management and development of the Erne Catchment area must be conducted on a cross-border basis (also see Chapter 6).

Improving British – Irish Relations

Additionally, the EEC provided a forum under which the British and Irish Governments could discuss and debate matters in relation to Northern Ireland. This helped to develop better relations between Ireland and Britain. Indeed, as early as 1977 meetings between representatives of the two states on the sidelines of the European Council offered a private, multilateral setting for relations between the UK and the Republic. Under the umbrella of the EEC the British and Irish governments could work together in a more co-operative relaxed environment rather than the previous institutionalised formal meetings. The importance of the EEC in assisting deeper British-Irish relations is highlighted by Goodman who states that membership of the EEC had,

> significant effects on British-Irish relations as macro-regional European Union (EU) institutions established a degree of international legitimacy for the Republic's position in the conflict. EU membership enhanced the Republic's international status, and partition became less a symbol of zero sum British nationalism in the face of positive sum Euro regionalism. Indeed, direct political pressure from EU institutions encouraged the emergence of an EC engendered trust between British and Irish governments and provided the practical basis for Anglo-Irish Inter-governmental dialogue on the north (Goodman 1996, p.226).

It was then no coincidence that at the end of the 1970s better British-Irish relationships were established. In 1979 Charles Haughey was elected as Taoiseach and he sought to develop relations directly with the British Government. A communiqué was issued at the end of the Anglo-Irish Summit meeting in May 1980 which stated that both Mr Haughey and Mrs Thatcher, the Prime Minister of Britain, wished to hold regular meetings. This process received institutional expression with the establishment of the Anglo-Irish Interministerial Council in 1981. The Interministerial Council commissioned joint studies covering issues such as possible institutional structures, citizenship rights, security, economic co-operation and measures which would encourage mutual understanding. The studies concluded that further co-operation between the two governments was necessary to develop the Irish border region. Indeed according to the report on the Anglo-Irish Joint Studies of November 1981 it was agreed that,

> steps should be taken at official level with a view to ensuring a harmonious and co-ordinated approach to economic development in the border areas...with specific reference to the question of special EC measures (Anglo-Irish Joint Studies, 1981, p.20).

In 1983 another study was commissioned by the European Community, namely, the Irish Border Areas Study. This study highlighted the socio-economic problems of the entire border region, addressing the local authority areas of Derry, Strabane, Omagh, Fermanagh, Dungannon, Armagh and Newry and Mourne in the North and Donegal, Leitrim, Cavan, Monaghan and Louth in the South of Ireland. The EC through the European Regional Development Fund was concerned with addressing the economic and social difficulties of frontier areas, and to ascertain what could be done to alleviate the particular obstacles to economic development arising out of the existence of the border. The report commented on the border region that,

> These areas...amongst the most economically and socially deprived in Europe, have the additional disadvantage of being cut in half by a frontier that hampers normal economic development (European Economic and Social Committee report on the Irish border areas, 1983).

The study recognised that the highest priority for the border region was the creation of employment and that the development of communication infrastructure, agriculture and industry were priority objectives for the EC.

The Anglo-Irish Agreement

Opportunities for cross-border co-operation were given further recognition with the signing of the Anglo-Irish Agreement in 1985. The Agreement acknowledged that both British and Irish Governments would jointly seek to deal with the conflict in Northern Ireland. This gave the Republic of Ireland a voice in Northern Ireland's affairs by establishing an Intergovernmental Conference, 'concerned with Northern Ireland and with relations between the two parts of Ireland, to deal on a regular basis with political matters, security and related matters, legal matters and the promotion of cross-border co-operation' (Lee, 1989, p.456).

As a means to support the Agreement and to promote more cross-border co-operation, 15 Million ECUs were donated to the International Fund for Ireland. The International Fund for Ireland (IFI) was established by the British and Irish Governments and backed by donations from the EU, the governments of the USA, Canada, Australia and New Zealand. Since its inception in 1986 the IFI has spent around £320 million by supporting projects across a wide spectrum of social and economic activity. Up until September 1995, 544 cross-border and cross community groups were directly assisted by the IFI (International Fund for Ireland, 1996).

Further linkages have also been developed between Northern Ireland and the Republic of Ireland through Co-operation Ireland (formerly known as Co-operation North). Co-operation Ireland was established in 1979 and is voluntary organisation composed of leaders in business, academia, trade unions, the professional bodies and voluntary organisations, who came together to build trust and respect between the North and South of Ireland. Since 1979 Co-operation Ireland has developed cross-border linkages across a wide range of areas which include industry, trade and tourism; youth, education and sport, and social and cultural exchanges. To enhance the development of cross-border trade and business exchanges, Co-operation Ireland has also established a North-South Trade Company to promote trade within the island of Ireland (Co-operation North, 1996).

A Backdrop of Terrorist Violence

By the beginning of the 1990s significant changes were also taking place at the European level to facilitate and promote cross-border trade. The Single European Market was set to be implemented in 1992 with the freeing of border controls on the movement of people, vehicles and goods. However, as a result of terrorist violence, the British Army were operating an increased security presence on the border between Northern Ireland and the Republic of Ireland. The military operations and fortifications then, according to O'Dowd, took precedence over the fresh momentum for cross-border co-operation,

> In times of heightened conflict, notably in the last twenty-five years, the British Army has sought to assert the sovereignty of the UK at the border by establishing fortifications, checkpoints and a systematic policy of road closures. The long struggle over the re-opening and re-closing of the roads reveals the primacy accorded by the British Government to assertion of state sovereignty over the wishes of the local inhabitants and over programmes supported by the same state to improve cross-border infrastructure and communications (O'Dowd, 1994, p.29).

The EU INTERREG Programme

Despite the increasing military presence on the Irish border in the 1980s, cross-border developments were still progressed through the Anglo-Irish Secretariat. The Secretariat provided a basis for formulating areas of joint co-ordination and programmes of expenditure. Co-operation was then formalised at the European Union (EU) level with the introduction of a Commission Initiative, the INTERREG programme, in 1990. The INTERREG programme had an allocation of 1 billion ECU of which 72 million were allocated to Ireland. The programme ran from 1991-1993 and the objectives in the Irish Border Region were,

- To assist border areas North and South, to overcome the development problems associated with under-development and peripherality and to encourage the process of rural regeneration and community development, and
- To encourage cross-border co-operation in order to maximise the growth potential of the area, especially in the lead up to 1992 (INTERREG Programme Document, 1995, p.7).

Although the INTERREG initiative may have further legitimised cross-border co-operation in Ireland, the programme did encounter a number of difficulties and constraints in terms of its formulation and implementation. One of the criticisms of the programme was that there were few projects which were actually implemented on a cross-border basis. The programme tended to focus more on stand alone projects implemented on each side of the border, but were justified as having a developmental effect on the region as a whole. O'Dowd *et al* note that only 38% of projects funded under INTERREG 1 were of a genuinely cross-border nature and within this 38%, 42% of funding was allocated to the Erne-Shannon Canal link, 21% to two forestry projects, 13% to 1 electricity project. This meant that, 'all other cross-border projects amounted to only 24% of the cross-border allocation or just over 9% of the total INTEREG allocation' (O'Dowd *et al*, 1994, p.56).

As a means of improving on the experiences gained from the first INTERREG programme the European Commission introduced a second initiative, INTERREG 2. The INTERREG 2 programme was allocated an increase of funding to 2.9 billion ECU, of which 167 ECU is provided for Ireland, and implemented for the period 1995-1999 (Official Journal of the European Communities, NoC 180165, 1994). The aims of INTERREG 2 still retain the fundamental objectives of addressing the problems of peripherality and promoting the further integration of Europe through cross-border co-operation. However, more emphasis is explicitly placed on subsidiarity and generating partnerships between Member States and regional and local authorities to present proposals for cross-border co-operation (Official Journal of the European Communities, NoC 18060, 1994). Therefore, in an attempt to increase the number of cross-border projects and to involve local and regional actors, the Commission indicated that it considered the presence of a coherent regional and integrated strategy for border areas as a 'single geographic unit', the contribution of the strategy to cross-border co-operation and the degree of involvement of regional and local authorities in the programme.

The INTERREG 2 programme has funded a range of projects which seek to alleviate the problems of peripherality and to promote cross-border co-operation. These projects are distributed among the themes of agriculture/fisheries/forestry, human resource development, environmental protection and regional development.

The EU Special Support Programme for Peace and Reconciliation

Although the INTERREG programme may be the most significant programme in terms of funding, it is also important to mention that other EU initiatives exist which promote cross-border co-operation. For instance in the EU Special Support Programme for Peace and Reconciliation introduced in 1995, one of the sub-programmes is solely devoted to cross-border co-operation. Sub-programme 3 Cross-Border Development was allocated approximately 60 Mecu of which 50% is allocated to the border counties and the other 50% to Northern Ireland with the aim to:

> Provide cross-border reconciliation and to exploit the opportunities for increased cross-border development arising from the new situation. (Coopers and Lybrand, 1997, p.B38).

Since its inception in 1995 Sub-programme 3 has funded a large number of projects, for example, the development of a business forum between two major towns on either side of the border, and the enhancement of mutual understanding between communities through links between schools on either side of the border. The Coopers and Lybrand mid term evaluation report of July 1997 concludes that by the end of December 1996, nearly 40% of the public expenditure allocation to the Sub-programme had already been disbursed to approved projects with the infrastructure measure receiving the highest level of allocation.

Increasing Cross-Border Business Activity

Private business has also recognised the benefits for Ireland as a whole from greater interaction, co-operation and trade on a cross-border basis. Since 1993 the Irish Business Employers Confederation (IBEC) and the Confederation of British Industry (CBI) have been operating a Business Development Programme aimed at increasing the levels of economic and business activity between the North and South of Ireland. IBEC and CBI have actively promoted the development of a Dublin-Belfast economic corridor as a means to improve trade and the economy of the island of Ireland. It has been proposed that Ireland, North and South, should become one integrated island economy in the context of a Single European Market and that this unified economy should be supported by both British and Irish governments and the EU (Coopers and Lybrand and INDECON report for CBI and IBEC, May, 1994).

Regional business has also been willing to develop cross-border linkages. Through the direction of the European Economic Interest Groups (EEIG) which provide a legal framework for cross-border co-operation and with the availability of EU and IFI funds, regional business groups in the border regions of Ireland have come together with the aim of improving cross-border trade and economic development in the region. Business groups have developed along the border region, for instance, the Gap of the North Association which comprises Armagh, Newry, Monaghan and Dundalk Chambers of Commerce, the Lifford-Strabane Development Commission and ECOM involving Derry and Letterkenny Chambers of Commerce.

The Local Authority Cross-Border Networks

The availability of EU funds, in particular the INTERREG programme, has helped to support the Local Authority Cross-Border Networks. In the late 1970s two local authority cross-border networks were established in the Irish border region, the East Border Region Committee (EBRC) which is a partnership of Down, Newry and Mourne District Councils and Louth and Monaghan County Councils and the North West Region Cross-Border Group (NWRCBG) which is a cross-border partnership of Donegal County Council and Strabane, Derry and Limavady District Councils. It has only been through the INTERREG 1 programme that the two networks finally received money towards a Central Secretariat. Funding was again awarded to the Central Secretariats under INTERREG 2 by which time another local authority cross-border network was established, the Irish Central Border Areas Network (ICBAN), which is a partnership of Omagh, Dungannon, Fermanagh and Armagh District Councils and Sligo, Donegal, Leitrim, Cavan and Monaghan County Councils (Figure 5.2).

The two partnerships began to make their first cross-border contacts at a time when few cross-border linkages existed at the institutional level. However, despite the political difficulties the EBRC and the NWRCBG continued to meet on a regular basis and have now developed into co-ordinative partnership structures, formulating strategies, receiving money for a central secretariat and aiming towards developing integrated area plans and the implementation of projects and programmes.

Figure 5.2 Location of the Three Local Authority Cross-Border Networks

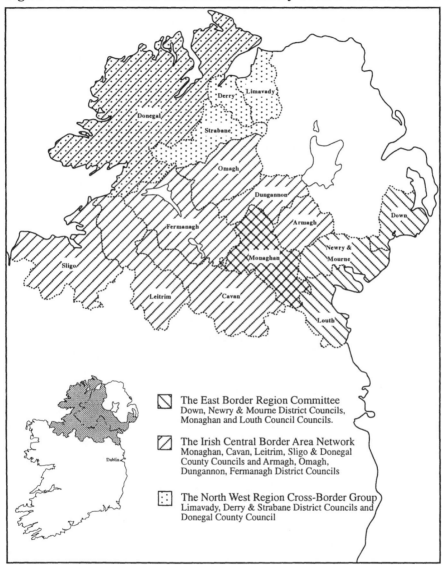

Similarly, although the ICBAN has only been established since 1995, a strategy for the region has been formulated and the partnership is working towards implementing a number of projects and developing an integrated area plan. Therefore, the establishment of the three local authority partnerships shows how cross-border linkages can expand and develop.

It is the aim of this chapter to examine the Local Authority Networks as a case study of a co-ordinative partnerships which operate at the sub-regional transjurisdictional level. By analysing the Networks much can be learned about sub-regional co-ordinative cross-border partnerships; their development can be traced and strengthens and weaknesses identified. The discussion deals with contextual conditions, stakeholder / organisational conditions, decision making conditions and operational conditions.

This chapter mainly seeks to examine the EBRC, however, as a means to support or emphasise arguments and provide additional analysis, the study will also refer to the experience of the NWRCBG and the ICBAN. More attention, in terms of the number of interviews conducted, was focused on the EBRC for two reasons. Firstly, it was decided that the Networks are essentially similar partnerships and that an in-depth study of one would be sufficient to provide a basis for research on the other two. Secondly, the East Border Region Committee was selected for in-depth research as it has been established from the early 1970s but is perceived as not having achieved a significant degree of success. For instance, the network only formulated a regional strategy in 1998 while the North West Region Cross-Border Group had developed their strategy eight years previously. In selecting the most unsuccessful of the two Networks which had been set up from the early 1970s, it was thought that a lot could be learned about partnership problems and the conditions that affect performance. Therefore, the selection of the EBRC would comply with the views of (Stake, 1995&1998) who argues that it is of primary importance for case studies to provide the opportunity to learn.

Contextual Conditions for the Local Authority Cross-Border Networks

A History of Division and Political Conflict

From the partition of Ireland cross-border co-operation has operated within an environment of political confrontation and violence. It has been mentioned in the previous section that due to the violence and political fall out that resulted from partition, both Northern Ireland and the Republic of Ireland developed in isolation. For the first fifty years there was little record of cross-border activity or contact and indeed, a degree of political animosity existed between the two states. After 1925 the Irish Government refused to recognise partition and did not seek to develop cross-border contacts which would legitimise the Irish border. On the other hand, the Stormont Government sought to develop and maintain links with Great Britain and viewed the South of Ireland as a foreign state which had a strong Catholic ethos and a poor economy. As a result of this division the Irish border became symbolically more important; with Northern Irish Nationalists seeing the border as an obstacle to links with Ireland and creating an artificial state, and Unionists regarding the border as an international frontier.

It was against this background that the first moves to develop cross-border partnerships at the local authority level were made by the East Border Region Committee (EBRC) and the North West Region Cross-Border Group (NWRCBG). In the early to mid 1970s due to the political problems, few cross-border contacts had been developed at government level and so it was left to local politicians to develop the first linkages. Individual politicians in the eastern border area began to make initial contacts in the hope that greater co-operation could improve the economic and social problems of the region, and from these individual contacts the EBRC was established. However, to add to the poor political relations between Northern Ireland and the Republic of Ireland, the early 1970s also marked the beginning of the troubles in Northern Ireland. From the inception of the EBRC, the contentious political environment, coupled with a background of increasing sectarian violence, created an extremely difficult, if not impossible, context in which to operate a partnership. Considering that cross-border co-operation was a very sensitive issue at the time, the two governments were reluctant to become involved in partnership development. This left the EBRC without funding and government support which restricted the development of the group. This view is supported by one interviewee from the EBRC who is firmly of the opinion that due to the difficult political climate the government could not back the partnership:

> The EBRC provided a vision of cross-border co-operation and the economic possibilities that followed, but at that time in the 1970s the political environment was dreadful and this created a difficult if not impossible context in which to work. In everything the EBRC tried to do the political dimension got in the way. It was difficult to win the support of the British Government, they were always afraid or reluctant or both to give funding to what would be a formal and institutional cross-border body with a degree of autonomy. The political sensitivities would not allow for it.

As a result of the political sensitivities, the EBRC has also found it difficult to bring Unionist controlled councils into the partnership. Due to its common geographic location the EBRC invited Armagh District Council to the partnership. However, given the political representation of Newry and Mourne and Down District Councils, Armagh refused. It has been difficult for the EBRC to dissolve the perception that the partnership is a Nationalist body. Therefore, operating in a contentious political environment has restricted the EBRC as the partnership failed to expand and bring on board a council which is an important strategic stakeholder in the region.

The political problems of operating a cross-border partnership have also impacted on the success of the NWRCBG. The NWRCBG was established in the mid 1970s and has found it difficult to avoid political matters disrupting partnership business. On a number of occasions politics has caused tension within the group and created a difficult environment for the partnership to operate and develop trust. Indeed, as a direct result of political problems Limavady District Council, who at the time was a Unionist controlled council, left the partnership for a short period.

Operating against a background of violence has placed stresses and strains on the partnerships. The border areas have suffered heavily from the troubles and the violence has created tension and fear, polarising the two communities in the region. This tension and fear have been transferred onto the partnerships and created unease among participants, particularly among Unionist councillors, and directly affected their role on the partnerships. One Unionist representative on the Irish Central Border Area Network (ICBAN) describes his experience:

> It was always one hell of a barrier when you are working on a cross-border basis and then you lifted the paper one morning to find that there was £1 million worth of damage in Armagh or Enniskillen. The troubles created tension and difficulties for Unionists working in cross-border bodies. You always think I am knocking my brains out trying to get funding for a cross-border region and there is £1 million up in smoke under my nose. That took away from your enthusiasm I have to say. As a Unionist Councillor I have always felt that you are climbing a slippery slope, you make progress, you work your tail off and you stick your neck out, and then some terrorist incident happens and you are pulled back down again.

It is without question that the conflict in Northern Ireland and the political sensitivities surrounding cross-border development have impacted on the success of the partnerships. The conflict has made the involvement of the Unionists more difficult by raising tensions, fear and insecurity. On the other hand, if long lasting peace and stability were established, this could create a more supportive and relaxed environment for the partnerships. It was felt that if peace follows the 'Good Friday' Agreement then a more co-operative environment would encourage understanding and help build trust among participants.

What is also important to mention is that a peaceful environment may encourage the participation of Banbridge District Council on the EBRC. In 1996 the EBRC invited Banbridge, a Unionist controlled council, to join the partnership. The council decided to defer the decision and sent representatives in an observatory capacity to identify the advantages and disadvantages of participation. Now with the 'Good Friday' Agreement, which itself includes a cross-border North - South Council, and the opportunity of lasting peace, Banbridge are looking more favourably towards the EBRC.

Despite operating within a difficult political environment the EBRC has managed to forge good working relations among the members. Although not including a Unionist controlled council, Unionist Councillors from Newry and Mourne District and Down District sit on the EBRC and fully participate and encourage the work of the partnership. Good working relationships and an environment of trust and understanding have been developed between Unionist and Nationalist members in the EBRC, as illustrated by the comments of one councillor from Louth County Council:

> In the Good Friday Agreement people will be coming together for the first time in a new cross-border institution. This is something that we have been doing for over twenty years. I know a number of Unionist Councillors that I can sit down and talk to about cross-border development and economic growth. Solid relationships have been built up over the years between councillors. People have got to the stage were they can trust one another.

Indeed, all three local authority cross-border partnerships have managed to develop good working relations among the participants. The question that now must be asked is, how have the cross-border partnerships managed to develop these good relations within such a difficult environment?

The Economic and Social Benefits of Cross-Border Co-operation

There are a number of factors which can explain the reasons behind the development of good working relationships in the cross-border partnerships. First of all, it can be pointed out that by concentrating on economic and social issues and avoiding the wider political problems, a more comfortable and co-operative environment is created. By focusing on less contentious issues, this means that participants can work together on common areas which, in turn, creates more unity. One interviewee from the NWRCBG in support of this argument states that focusing on economic, social and environment issues was the only way to keep the group together:

> The group learned to avoid politics. They have the sense to know that if you go down to politics the whole thing will just explode. It never got on a political level and kept very strictly to things like economic development, non political issues, the small P's. We still need to keep away from the big P's until the big miracle in Northern Ireland happens or it would have the potential of splitting us up. It is not hiding it, we know the differences are there. We just don't allow it to interfere in our relationship.

Working Together

The EBRC, NWRCBG and ICBAN have shown that by concentrating on economic, social and environmental issues partnerships can make progress and can develop good relationships despite the troubles and political confrontation. It is working for the good of the region and tackling common problems that have brought each of the councils and members together, as one member of the EBRC stated:

In the EBRC there is a willingness to work together. No-one forced them to come together. They decided to come together because they saw a need for bettering the economy. For years councils stood with their backs to each other facing Belfast and Dublin. People on the border areas feel isolated from central decision making. But now there is a realisation that by working together things can be achieved, that councils can work together on areas of common concern and everyone can benefit.

It is by coming together to improve the needs of the region that has kept the partners together and fortified the partnership relationship. What is important to learn from the cross-border partnerships is that the belief among partners that they must work together to solve common problems has created the potential to dilute and override the political difficulties.

Potential Access to Funding

It also must be mentioned that in the case of the cross-border partnerships the potential and ability to access funding has assisted in developing and sustaining the partnership relations. Although the EBRC and the NWRCBG have existed for over twenty years without access to resources, other than to fund a secretariat, it is acknowledged that if the councils work together, there is a greater opportunity for accessing previously unavailable resources. According to one member of the NWRCBG, the potential to access resources has been a strong motivation behind the participation of some members of the group:

> Clearly there are people who see cross-border partnerships as a broader base and in the longer term but there are others who are just in it for the money. There is no bigger picture, it is project led money for X, Y and Z. That is their justification for being there, there is no other reason. If the money was not there they would be very much isolated in their own focus just as one district council area. They would not see it as a sub-region.

The decision of Banbridge District Council to participate in the EBRC will be heavily influenced by the potential of gaining more access to funding. Its final decision will be largely based on a balance between the political difficulties of cross-border partnerships on the one hand, and the potential economic and social benefits on other. It is clear that if social and economic benefits were to be forthcoming, participation in the EBRC would be more acceptable, as one member of Banbridge Council acknowledged:

> Banbridge decided to defer decision on full participation. Time was needed to see how the economic development strategy would be implemented and to see if there are any real substantial economic and social benefits that can help improve the Banbridge district. With Banbridge being a Unionist dominated council there is obviously a political dimension which influences decisions that are taken. There are political sensitivities in working in a cross-border organisation with two predominately nationalist councils and two councils from the Republic. However, if economic and social benefits can be gained through membership, then the difficulties concerning the politics could subside.

The Role of the European Union

The role of the EU has been instrumental in developing partnerships and cross-border relations in general. It is believed that the EU, through various legislative measures and in promoting the idea of a Single European Market, has made cross-border co-operation more acceptable and natural. There is also a feeling among the participants of the cross-border partnerships that as Europe progresses the idea of a 'Europe of the Regions', district councils must have a regional or sub-regional perspective. It is thought that as regionalisation is the way forward, district councils must act together if they want to see their areas progress. In this way the EU is seen to be driving ideas forward and giving the participants a need to work in partnership.

It has already been argued in this section that funding is an important factor helping to bring participants together in partnership. However, it is also important to note that participants, who would otherwise feel uncomfortable with cross-border partnerships, felt more at ease with the funding coming from the EU. The EU is regarded in a more positive light by the participants as it is a neutral body, whereas funding from a central government programme would be treated with more suspicion as both central governments would be perceived as having a hidden agenda. In this role the EU has contributed to developing trust and nurturing political sensitivities, as one government interviewee commented on the European INTERREG programme:

With cross-border co-operation the role of the EU helps to ease northern sensitivities. Civil servants, in the North or South, can point out that this is a Brussels programme, it is a cross-border co-operative programme and it is happening all over Europe. It is not a Trojan Horse to a United Ireland. It is normal, natural and makes economic sense and it is happening everywhere.

Finally, the EU was seen as being one reason behind the changing political animosity which existed between Northern Ireland and the Republic of Ireland. By joining the EEC in 1972, this helped the Republic of Ireland break with the past and become more pluralist. One Unionist Councillor sees the changes taking place in Ireland since joining the EEC, influencing his participation on the EBRC:

> The Republic of Ireland Government made it difficult for cross-border co-operation, with de Valera's overbearing Articles Two and Three and his attitude to Northern Ireland, that no one should co-operate with the Northern Ireland Government and those elected members of the Catholic Community should not take part in the elected institutions of Northern Ireland. This caused a fear of being taken over. However, once the Republic joined the EEC a gradual change began to take place. They are now more up-dated, Irish Republicanism is no longer a popular mindset, they are now more pluralist and international. These changes make it more acceptable for cross-border co-operation.

An Initial Informal Relationship

In the ICBAN region the participants have recognised that the political sensitivities in establishing and developing cross-border linkages could have the potential of causing tension and conflict in the partnership. At the time ICBAN was established, Dungannon, Fermanagh and Armagh district councils were Unionist controlled and this left Unionist Councils in a strong position within the partnership. So as not to antagonise the Unionist participants an informal co-operative partnership was adopted. It was felt that an informal approach would develop a greater sense of allegiance and participation among all the members which would help solidify the partnership relations, particularly in the embryonic stages of development. For example, a fixed chairman was not appointed and instead a chairman was selected from each district council where the meetings took place. This meant that Unionist members would have a greater opportunity for becoming chairmen and undertaking influential roles.

Although each of the partnerships have developed good working relations, the political problems surrounding cross-border partnerships are always in the background influencing events. Due to the political sensitivities some Unionist participants are always wary of pressure from other Unionist parties. In elections it may become an issue which could be manipulated, that some Unionist councillors are seen to be actively supporting and promoting deeper links with the South of Ireland. One Unionist Councillor from ICBAN believes that the political problems of participating in a cross-border partnership are never far away:

> People who are trying to take responsibility and trying to make things better always seem to get a kick in the pants. The groups that stand on the sideline and criticise everything can make life very difficult. The best of us have to look over our shoulder and say, 'If I go down this road much further, promoting and participating in ICBAN, will the propagandists do me such harm that I am not going to get elected'.

This interviewee highlights the difficulties for Unionist Councillors participating in cross-border partnerships and shows that operating in a conflicting political environment is always likely to pose problems for partnerships and partnership participants.

Geographical Proximity

In the case of the EBRC, geographical proximity has played a significant role in the development of partnership. This can be linked to the attempt of the partnerships to forge a common sub-regional approach. From the inception of the EBRC questions have been raised over the participation of Monaghan County Council and in particular, Down District Council which is not located on the border. The EBRC has found it difficult to formulate projects which are applicable to the whole region and from which Monaghan and Down councils can gain an equal net benefit. Given the close proximity and common economic and social problems between Newry and Mourne and Louth, these councils have established a central axis within the partnership as they can easily develop common projects and linkages. This has meant that Monaghan Council and Down District have felt peripheral in the EBRC. At times this has created tension when projects are proposed which are beneficial to two or three councils but funding is needed from all four councils, as one interviewee from the EBRC explains:

It seems ludicrous but one of the difficulties of the EBRC is the peripherality. We are trying to overcome peripherality because we are on the extremities of both our countries land masses but there was constantly, and still is, a cry from Down and Monaghan that the EBRC is very much focused on Louth and Newry and Mourne. At times this causes friction within the region. I think this need for everything to benefit the region at the one time has probably hindered the ideas. It is fine for producing brochures promoting economic development to attract investment but there are very few solid projects that you can come up with that are applicable for the whole region.

Stakeholder / Organisational Conditions for the Local Authority Cross-Border Networks

Commitment

In the cross-border networks a commitment to improving the economic and social needs of the region has kept the groups together at times when cross-border development was not fashionable nor profitable. Throughout the years of cross-border co-operation, the councils have shown strong commitment to the partnerships by maintaining good relationships in a difficult political climate and when little support was forthcoming from central government. One member from the EBRC comments that maintaining contacts and relations in a difficult and unsupportive environment illustrates the commitment of each of the partner councils:

> People would say, 'what does the EBRC do?, It is a talking shop' but that was an achievement in itself at the time. People had the interest to keep meeting for fifteen to twenty years with nothing to show for it apart from talking and coming up with ideas which were shot down by the politicians in Belfast and Dublin because they were not interested, did not care or could not get money. Realistically, the chances of developing tourism in the 1970s and 80s were not going to be successful. To me the fact that we kept meeting, developed a big network which is still there is important. People say it was a failure because it did not do anything or achieve anything tangible. I do not think it was a failure. I think the fact that they stuck by it was amazing and showed great fortitude at a time when government was not interested and were even hoping that you would lie down and die very soon.

Now that the developments and contacts have been long established and the European Union is showing encouraging signs of support by funding the central secretariat and regional strategies, more commitment is again required from the participants if the groups are to progress. The three networks are now experiencing a critical stage in their development, moving from organisations largely involved in lobbying central government and producing feasibility studies, to organisations which are facilitators of development in their regions. To make this transformation or progression more commitment is required from the councils and members than ever before. However, questions have been raised whether the full commitment is there among members if the partnerships are to make a leap to the next stage. For example, one member of the EBRC questions the commitment of the partner councils and members who were not prepared to increase funding to the group:

> The big question is whether the councils will be prepared to fund the secretariat and projects if European money was not forthcoming. Looking to the past this is a questionable matter. In the intervening periods between INTERREG 1 and 2 the North West group funded the contribution themselves but the EBRC did not take that decision and decided to wait until further funding would come through from INTERREG. The funding came through very slowly and the momentum of the group was broken up. Whereas the North West group who funded their secretariat were able to continue their work. In the event the NWRCBG were able to receive a rebate from INTERREG anyway. We can point the finger at central government but we can also point the finger at ourselves as we are the members of the body. If we are interested we should be prepared to put our hands in our pockets and produce money.

The Decision Making Process in the Local Authority Cross-Border Networks

In the operation of a partnership it is essential that all the partners work well together and enact an effective decision making process. It is within the decision making process that relationships between the partners are established, a unified approach is adopted and priority actions identified.

An Efficient Decision Making Process

To analyse the partnership decision making process it is first of all necessary to examine the decision making structures within partnerships. The East Border Region Committee is composed of four local authorities who each send six councillors and two officials to the Committee, making a total of thirty-two members. A Foreign Affairs representative from Dublin and a representative of the Central Secretariat in Belfast sit on the board. MPs and TDs are also invited. In previous years, questions have been raised on the size of the board which has over thirty-two representatives on the Committee. This has created a lengthy decision making process and it has proved difficult to manage the partnership. As a means to improve the decision making process, the EBRC has established an Executive comprised of one councillor and one Chief Officer from each local authority and the Project Co-ordinator. The Executive meets once a month or when required, to formulate projects and proposals which are then debated and ratified by a meeting of the full Committee which sits every two months. The Executive being a much smaller body can discuss matters in detail and propose recommendations for debate in the Main Committee (Figure 5.3). This creates a more effective decision making process, with the Executive leading the direction of the group and allowing the Committee to concentrate on debating projects and proposals. The Executive has developed into the engine of the EBRC, driving the partnership forward and has improved the decision making process as one member of the EBRC commented:

> Since the Executive was set up the EBRC has become more effective. The Development Officer and the Executive have developed a good network in the group. They can analyse in detail everything on the agenda and can quickly react to events. Previously, if a Minister or industrialist would visit and certain actions had to be taken, the Development Officer would have to wait until the whole Committee would convene. This delayed the operation of the EBRC and halted the decision making process. But now the Development Officer can consult with the Executive and quick decisions can be taken.

Figure 5.3   Decision Making Structures within the East Border Region Committee

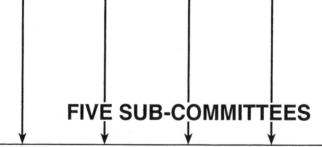

EXECUTIVE

Formulates Policy and Project Proposals. Meets every month or when required.

1 councillor and 1 chief officer from each local authority

MAIN COMMITTEE

Debates and Ratifies Proposals from Executive.

6 councillors and 2 officials from each local authority
1 foreign affairs rep. from Dublin
1 representative from central secretariat
in Belfast. MPs and TDs are also invited

FIVE SUB-COMMITTEES

Feeds Policy and Project Proposals to Executive and Main Committee

1 official and 1 councillor from each local authority.
Representation from public, private
and voluntary/community sectors

The NWRCBG have also found decision making unworkable in the full committee and task teams have been established to improve the process. Task teams are composed of a small number of officials who each formulate projects on specific themes. The recommendations of the task teams are then discussed by the full board (Figure 5.4) Through this procedure, only a small number of members analyse and formulate projects leaving the full committee to concentrate on strategic issues. One member of the NWRCBG was firmly of the opinion that this creates a more efficient and effective decision making process:

> We have developed task teams who work on certain projects. They formulate the fine elements of each project which are then presented to the whole board for discussion, ratification and amendments. It would be impossible if the whole board were to start from scratch and work on the fine elements of each specific project together. But as the basis of the projects are worked up in a task team and then brought to the board, more effective decision making can take place.

It has already been mentioned in the previous section that the strategy of the EBRC has proposed the establishment of similar working groups, called sub-committees. Five sub-committees will be created, composed of one official and one councillor and other representatives of wider community interests: government agencies, private business and the community / voluntary sectors. It has also been proposed that the sub-committees will feed in policy and project proposals to the Executive and the Main Committee for ratification and amendments. In this way the decision making process of the EBRC may become even more efficient and effective, as small thematic groups have a greater focus and allow for greater detail. One member of the EBRC speculates that the thematic groups will be a new driving force and the role of the Executive may weaken:

> The groups will be focusing on one theme or one area and the importance of the Executive may diminish, in that it will not be the driving force as a lot of the ideas and the push for ideas will come out of the thematic groups.

In the EBRC there is a recognition that the partnership is driven by the executive body. There is a tendency that the proposals recommended by the executive will be ratified by the board, the executive sets the agenda

**Figure 5.4 Decision Making Structures within the North West
Region Cross-Border Group**

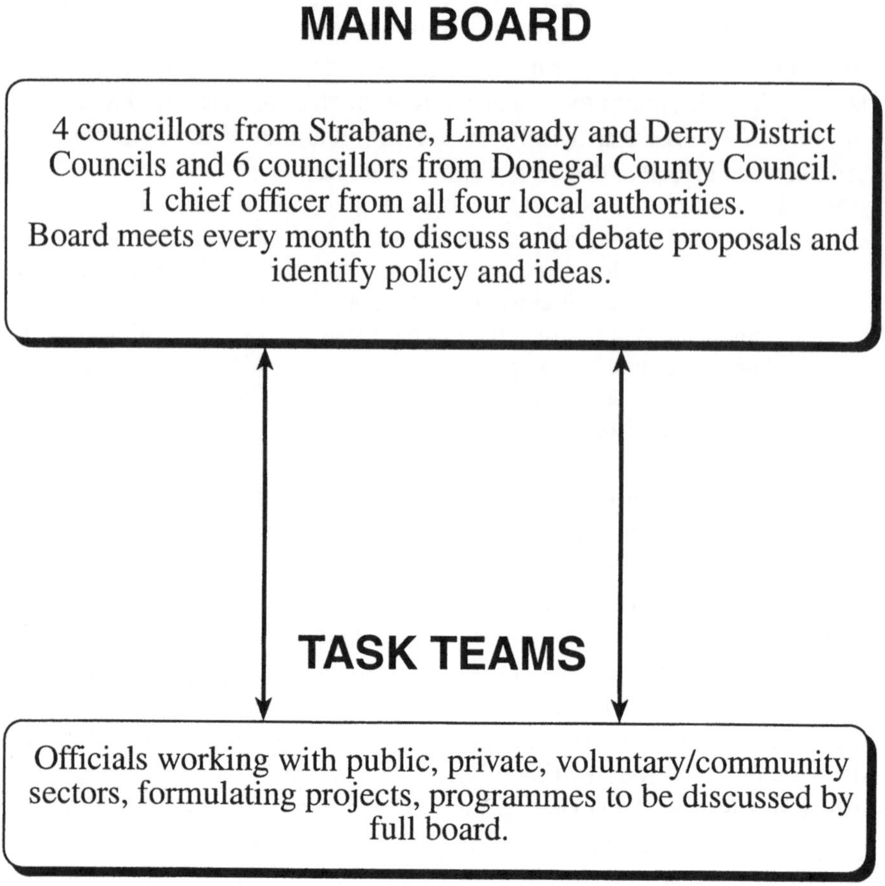

MAIN BOARD

4 councillors from Strabane, Limavady and Derry District
Councils and 6 councillors from Donegal County Council.
1 chief officer from all four local authorities.
Board meets every month to discuss and debate proposals and
identify policy and ideas.

TASK TEAMS

Officials working with public, private, voluntary/community
sectors, formulating projects, programmes to be discussed by
full board.

and is the driving force behind the EBRC. However, within the EBRC there is little tension between the Main Committee and the Executive; each body has it's own respective role which both complements and improves the decision making process. To alleviate the potential cause for tension and conflict the EBRC has established principles and procedures. Although the executive may set the agenda, it is clear procedure that the power of final decision rests with the Main Committee. Without the approval of the committee few actions of great significance can be taken. Furthermore, projects and proposals once passed by the committee have to be ratified by each of the councils. Secondly, the positions held by elected members on the executive are on a rotational basis. Therefore, other councillors are given the opportunity to sit on the executive and this provides a direct link between the two bodies. By maintaining the final decision making power and rotating the councillors on the executive the EBRC has been able to dampen the potential tension.

An Official Led Decision Making Process

However, differences in the power of decision making can be drawn between the officials and councillors. In the EBRC, discussion among all participants is encouraged but it is the support of the officials which carries the most weight. As the officials are the driving force in the partnership some councillors have found it difficult to become fully involved in the process. As a result the attendance of the councillors at partnership meetings is low.

The experience of the EBRC in which decision making power is ultimately held by the officials is also mirrored by the other local authority cross-border partnerships, the NWRCBG and the ICBAN. In the ICBAN two executive bodies have been established, the Strategy Group and the Management Group. The Strategy Group is composed of the Chairmen and Chief Officers of each council who identify agreed strategies and policies. The Management Group is composed of the nine Chief Officers from each local authority and is responsible for the day to day running of the group. Therefore the groups combined have the executive function of the EBRC, setting the agenda and managing current actions. Similarly, the ICBAN main partnership board is called the Network which consists of four elected members and one officer from each local authority, whose role is to discuss and ratify proposals and projects (Figure 5.5).

Figure 5.5   Decision Making Structures within the Irish Central Border Area Network

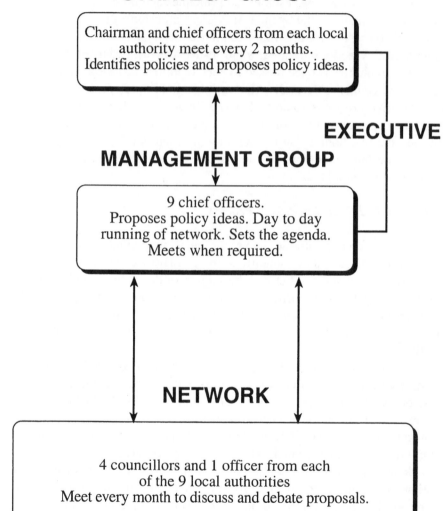

STRATEGY GROUP

Chairman and chief officers from each local authority meet every 2 months.
Identifies policies and proposes policy ideas.

EXECUTIVE

MANAGEMENT GROUP

9 chief officers.
Proposes policy ideas. Day to day running of network. Sets the agenda.
Meets when required.

NETWORK

4 councillors and 1 officer from each of the 9 local authorities
Meet every month to discuss and debate proposals.

In the ICBAN decision making power is not swayed towards the Strategy or Management group to the detriment of the Network but power of decision making, as with the EBRC, is centred with the council officials. This division in decision making power has weakened the role and enthusiasm of the councillors leading to poor attendance at meetings, as one member from ICBAN comments:

> The ICBAN is very much driven by officials. On major issues the officials would drive policy much more so than individual councillors. The elected members do not see ICBAN as a driving force, something which they can engine. If we had a meeting of ICBAN in the morning in Armagh, I could not guarantee that, from this council, there would be more than two councillors out of four present. Local authority members get elected to groups because they take turns to sit on different bodies. If they were elected on to the health board or authority they would be familiar with that but for ICBAN there is a lack of appreciation. They find it difficult to get a hold on it. That is frustrating because more than officials meeting officials you can achieve an awful lot more if the councillors just turn up for meetings and get to know faces and get to talk to each other.

Across the three local authority networks, the officials have the greatest input into the decision making process. Some councillors feel it is not an engine they can drive and attendance in some instances has fallen as a result. In a decision making process it is vital that all participants are included as this creates a more informed and inclusive process. If members feel that they cannot contribute meaningfully to decision making and drive the partnership, they may become disassociated from the process which could lead to disagreement and conflict.

Regular Contact

Organising regular meetings is an issue which has come to light with the cross-border partnerships. In a partnership decision making process it is important that the members get to know one another and develop good relations before difficult decisions have to be taken. In the EBRC it has been the case, for the majority of members, that the only time they get to interact with other participants is during the meetings of the committee. In previous years, meetings of the full board of the EBRC would only take place three times a year and there were few opportunities for the participants to develop good relations and understandings. Moreover the problem was exacerbated by the fact that each councillor was elected on an annual basis which meant a high turnover of members. As a result, partnership participants were not able to develop good relations between each other and found it difficult to keep up to speed with the events ongoing in the committee. This had a detrimental effect on decision making as the participants were not fully informed, as one member of the EBRC reflects:

> In the early days you were elected to the EBRC on an annual basis. Now say a councillor was elected in June to serve on the Committee and just missed that months meeting, the next would have been September and then January or February; you were lucky if you got to two or three meetings per year. By the time you got into the way of it your time was up and then another six councillors were elected. There would have been councillors sitting there who would not have seen the other councillors from one year to the next, and then when people did see each other, they didn't know one another and worse still, they didn't know what was going on. No informed decision making could take place in that sort of environment.

This example of the old practices of the EBRC shows that meetings of a partnership need to operate within short regular timescales. If the meetings are too far apart, members do not get the opportunity to know one another and cannot keep up to speed. This weakens the decision making process as members are not fully informed and cannot contribute meaningfully to the discussion. The meetings of the EBRC now occur every two months for the Main Committee and every month for the Executive which gives the members a better opportunity to develop good relations and establish continuity.

To further emphasise the importance of regular meetings as a condition for success for sub-regional co-ordinate partnerships, the procedures of the ICBAN can be outlined. In the ICBAN the main partnership board, the Network, meets only twice a year. This decision was made to re-emphasise the network approach and make the partnership more acceptable to Unionist Councillors. However, meeting only twice a year has limited the opportunities for the councillors to get to know one another, develop good relationships and enact an effective and informed decision making process.

A Consensual Decision Making Process

Considering that the cross-border partnerships include a mix of different elected representatives and councillors who represent the local area, the partnerships could be described as diverse organisations. To counteract this diversity, there is evidence to suggest that a consensus based approach can bring the partners together as it is an inclusive process in which all participants can air their views. In this way the partnership can move forward together as one organisation. In the NWRCBG there is a strong emphasis on the consensus based approach and for this reason a more effective partnership process has been enacted. One member of the NWRCBG comments that:

> In the full board of the North West group no decision has ever gone to the vote. Everyone has the opportunity to have their say, nothing is agreed unless everyone has agreed, it is a unanimous decision making process. This brings everyone on board, it is an inclusive process and a unifying process.

Although the consensus based approach may have brought success to the NWRCBG by encouraging fair participation and creating a unanimous group approach, questions have been raised that consensus decision making cannot be applied to a partnership which has to make difficult decisions quickly. Currently, the NWRCBG is formulating a strategic action plan which has meant that difficult decisions on the allocation of funds have not been required to date. Having to discuss and decide on funding issues in a consensual way could prove to be a difficult task for the NWRCBG. One interviewee from the NWRCBG is not convinced that consensus decision making is the best approach for the future and presents the following analysis:

> The North West group have not had anything really controversial to decide on. Until you get real money to carry out projects everyone will agree to projects and developments that are aspirational. But regional planning means deciding you cannot have an industrial park in every town. When there is money to implement projects and programmes the decision making process will become more difficult. At the moment you have a sub-group or a task team that deals with formulating projects and these projects are proposed to the full board. In the full board decision making is either unanimous or they decide to defer the decision and talk some

more about it. Now you can see how you could get into a merry-go-round with that process. If you want business done quickly you cannot operate like that. You are going to get to the stage where it is impracticable to defer decisions and a vote must be taken.

Consensus based decision making may not work in instances where decisions have to be made quickly. As the NWRCBG, EBRC and ICBAN progress to implementing projects and programmes, momentum will be quickly built and difficult funding decisions will have to be taken. The consensus based approach is of most benefit to partnerships in the early stages of development to build relations and forge a common approach. However, for operational decisions a quick and more efficient process is needed.

Sub-Regional Representation

In the cross-border partnerships the decision making process is complicated further due to the representation of local councillors. The partnerships operate at the sub-regional level and tensions arise with councillors representing their own local or parochial interests. The tensions between the sub-regional and local viewpoints have made the decision making process very difficult and restricted the scope and development of the networks. One interviewee from the EBRC comments on the difficulties of the group in trying to forge a sub-regional approach in decision making:

> The EBRC cannot involve an anti-objective decision making process because councillors are elected for their own areas. The weakness of the group is that councils are looking at their own local area. It is very difficult to try and work on a regional basis when at times everyone is fighting their own corner. If the press are at a meeting this makes it even more difficult, as councillors want to get their name in the paper so that the people can say, 'Oh great man fighting for us.'

Being composed of local councillors and elected representatives has caused further difficulty and confusion in decision making for the cross-border partnerships. This difficulty is based on the fact that councillors and elected representatives have a number of commitments, they are only part time and are called to sit on other boards as well. Some participants on the cross-border partnerships may be members of the new

Northern Ireland Assembly or Senators and TDs in the Republic of Ireland. In matters of political importance such participants tend to focus on the political issues and not attend the meetings of the partnership. If attendance from councillors is low this makes decision making very difficult as, on their return, some members may not agree with decisions taken in their absence.

Evidence from the cross-border partnerships would suggest that all partners need to be fully involved in the decision making process. If some members find it difficult to become involved, this creates difficulties since they are not committed to decisions that are taken and later seek to re-open the process.

A Central Secretariat

Establishing a full-time secretariat under the INTERREG programme has helped the cross-border networks to act more as one organisation representing one region. Before the introduction of the secretariat, each Chief Officer rotated the administration of the partnership. Under this procedure, the EBRC was organised in a disjointed way by officers whose first priority was to their council business and who could only devote part-time commitment to the EBRC. It became difficult to override the local priorities of the individual councils and forge a common approach. The secretariat, namely the Project Co-ordinator, on the other hand, is organised on a full-time basis and can devote total commitment to promoting the EBRC as one body, binding the partner councils together in a common regional approach. This has given the EBRC more impetus by creating a central information base from which all actions are co-orientated and freeing the Chief Officers from administration, so they can concentrate on policy and project formulation.

The central secretariat for the cross-border partnerships marks a milestone in their development. Prior to the secretariat the groups were organised on a part-time basis by officials whose first loyalty was to promote council interests. Now the secretariat can act as a central co-ordinator pulling the partner councils together and constantly focusing on a regional basis. Although the cross-border partnerships still have tensions associated with building a common approach among councils and officials who focus on the local level, the secretariat has contributed in some way to unifying the partnerships and maintaining attention on the sub-regional level.

The Chairman as a Convenor

In the EBRC since the establishment of the secretariat, the chairman has taken on the added role of working closely with the Project Co-ordinator. Considering that the Main Committee of the EBRC only meets every two months, the chairman has become a point of contact who assists in developing projects and, as an elected member, can agree on something in principle subject to the board agreeing. The chairman acts as another co-ordinator of the organisation promoting the regional view. The importance of the chairman is acknowledged by one member of the EBRC who states that:

> A good chairman just does not confine himself to presiding over the meetings but keeps involved and knows what is going on day to day. The chairman needs to have a good relationship with the whole committee and the Project Co-ordinator. A chairman who just turned up for the meetings and called the next speaker does not contribute an awful lot to the EBRC. If the chairman is in touch with what has been happening and keeps command of the members, then it is not the official who is telling the members what to do. In this way progress and decisions are made much easier and quicker.

What has also been important in the EBRC is that the chair is rotated on an annual basis between each of the partner councils. This is an element of good will which demonstrates that the EBRC is not being administered from Newry, where the secretariat is based, but is focused on a regional basis. Furthermore, considering the role which the chairman has undertaken in the EBRC, the rotating chair has given different members the opportunity to work closely with the Project Co-ordinator in promoting projects and development of the group. This has increased the knowledge of the individual councillors, which has improved the decision making process.

The importance of the chairman can be reinforced by comparing the experience of the ICBAN. It has been explained, in the earlier stages of this chapter, that ICBAN decided not to appoint a permanent chair as it might emphasise the institutional nature of the partnership. However, the organisation of the ICBAN has become more difficult as there is no one single figure who conducts the decision making process and promotes the unity of the whole board.

Partnership Operation of the Local Authority Cross-Border Networks

The final set of matters which must be examined relates to the operation of the partnerships.

Strategic Development

Although the EBRC and the NWRCBG have been in existence for over twenty years it is only recently that the concept of developing a regional strategy has come to the fore. In previous years the local authority networks had been largely concerned with lobbying central government to introduce new policy measures in the border region and with producing tourist brochures. However, in the late 1980s the British and Irish Governments, along with the European Community, commissioned a study of the North West Region. The study included a socio-economic analysis of the problems of the North West Region and identified opportunities for cross-border co-operation and practical action. Two core proposals were made:

- Identifying and building on shared strengthens, in particular those which exist on both sides of the border;
- Overcoming peripherality and creating outward vision.

Nine development themes were presented as an integrated economic strategy for the North West Region for the next decade and include: building on tourist potential; fostering indigenous expertise; encouraging rural development; developing fishing resources; supporting community development; improving access infrastructure; utilising education resources; expanding private services; and, improving the delivery of public services (Coopers and Lybrand, 1990, p.6).

To work towards the development of these themes, the study envisaged that government departments and agencies, local authorities, outside investors, private business, trade unions and the community / voluntary sectors would work together to strengthen the regional economy.

Following the publication of the North West Study, the INTERREG programme was introduced to support trans-frontier co-operation between the European Community member states. In order to attract funding for cross-border co-operation under INTERREG, the NWRCBG then formulated a new development strategy for the region '*A*

Window of Opportunity - Shaping the Future Together' in July 1994, which developed the findings and proposals identified in the earlier North West Study. The Development Programme set out to: 'identify concrete projects whose implementation would accelerate the economic development of the region and reinforce the cross-border aspect to the development.' Two major types of action were envisaged:

(1) Those having a clear cross-border logic within the framework of the cross-border development programme but which would best be implemented by actors within each council area;
(2) Those whose cross-border logic demands both joint planning and joint implementation (NWRCBG Operational Programme, 1995, p.1).

Under the second action an Operational Programme was developed to focus on activities which require joint planning and joint implementation. The programme was presented under INTERREG 2 with the aim of accessing global grant allocations. The programme identified a range of actions which together had a combined strategic aim:

> To enhance the capacity for economic development and to promote directly the economic and social well being of the North West region by jointly implementing actions which made a discernible impact on the cross-border dimension to regional development (NWRCBG Operational Programme, 1995, p.24).

The importance of a regional strategy to sub-regional transjurisdictional co-ordinative partnerships is well represented in the experience of the NWRCBG. Before the formulation of the strategy, the NWRCBG could be described as an unwieldy organisation with no common focus or approach. Each of the partner councils largely concentrated on its own area which confused and complicated the development of the partnership. However, with the formulation of the strategic action plan in 1994, this directed the councils into a more regional focus and they pulled together to work towards the future development of the region, as one interviewee from the NWRCBG recalls:

> In the early days it was superficial commitment among the members. We were all pulling in different directions, we were going to meetings and it was actually more negative than positive, the group was really drifting very badly at that stage. However, from the early 1990s onwards with the

formulation and launch of the strategy things began to change. The strategy identified areas for co-operation which all the member councils could prioritise and work towards. It was the glue that pulled us together.

The development of the strategy marks a watershed in the evolution of the NWRCBG, by focusing the partners on a common approach and prioritising actions which laid the foundations for all future development.

The importance of a regional strategy for a sub-regional co-ordinative partnership is also supported by the case of the EBRC. Prior to the development of the strategy the EBRC had achieved limited success. A number of seminars on topics including land drainage, afforestation and farm diversification were held and a tourism brochure was developed. In the early 1990s a number of small feasibility studies were carried out from which projects were developed, these included: packaging of activity holidays; crafts marketing; and, facilitation of cross-border contacts.

In the formulation and implementation of these projects the opposing views of the member councils came to the fore which emphasised the disjointed approach of the EBRC. The EBRC, like the NWRCBG, could also be described as a disparate organisation with each council area pulling in their own direction. However, the launch of the regional development strategy in March 1998 brought the councils closer together into a more focused approach. Within the regional strategy the aims and specific objectives of the EBRC are now spelled out, detailing tasks for the development of an integrated action plan. This has created a common approach by the partner councils which are working towards its implementation. In the strategy a number of strategic themes were identified for action based upon the detailed socio-analysis of the region and the resultant SWOT analysis. Within each of the themes, key issues and actions have been highlighted. The themes are:

- Tourism;
- Indigenous Business Growth (including inward investment);
- Community Economic Development;
- Human Resource Development (including Education); and,
- Health service provision (This is seen as an issue in its own right but due to the nature of its provision it is not a stand alone theme) (BDO-Stoy Hayward, 1998, p.12).

What also makes the development of regional strategies such an important condition for success for the cross-border partnerships, is that the European Commission have pointed out that, in order to receive any substantial amount of funding for their area, regional strategies and integrated area plans must be developed. Under INTERREG 2 the European Commission are working to give a more devolved function to the local authority partnerships in the form of a block grant, which would allow them certain discretion to spend money. The European Commission and the two national governments have been quick to point out that any cross-border partnership operating on a regional level must have a clear strategic plan outlining specific programmes for action. One interviewee from a government department which administers the INTERREG programme outlines the importance of a regional strategy:

> The only way that the cross-border groups are going to demonstrate that they are capable of developing and maturing, is showing that they are capable of developing an integrated strategic plan. Some of the groups have been in existence of a long time but the progress that has been made, has not been in a strategic fashion. A lot of projects have been duplicated with a lot of people focusing on little areas of their region and not knowing what is going on next door to them.

Although a strategy is of vital importance, the experience of the NWRCBG also shows that formulating a strategy in the initial stages of establishing a cross-border partnership may create problems. It has been explained in this chapter that much political sensitivity surrounds the establishment of the local authority cross-border networks. In the beginning, sections of the Unionist community felt uneasy about developing cross-border contacts given the history and hostility between Northern Ireland and the Republic of Ireland. Within this context, it was felt that establishing the cross-border group and developing good relations between the members was a first priority and that the formulation of a regional strategy could begin at a later date, as one interviewee commented:

> A development strategy was not that terribly important in the early days. If you go back twenty years ago to the mid 1970s cross-border work was not fashionable and there was downright enmity between Nationalist and Unionist populations. For councils thinking of cross-border economic co-operation, what was important in those days was that people kept talking,

dialogue was all important. It was only when the group got more comfortable working together that you had to have a strategy document.

The experience of the NWRCBG demonstrates that it is also important for sub-regional co-ordinative partnerships to develop a strategy which has clear, realisable and manageable aims. The strategies and projects that have been proposed by the partnerships have been too ambitious and for this reason the groups have clashed with central government departments. To highlight the problem of an ambitious strategy one can examine the strategy developed by the NWRCBG. The NWRCBG presented its regional strategy to INTERREG for assessment in 1994 but was refused a global grant. One interviewee from a government department explains the problem surrounding the North West Strategy:

> The North West group submitted a strategy / action plan for funding but the problem with the strategy was that it was effectively a wishlist. It included a number of pet projects some of which did not make economic sense whatsoever. I have been told that the Minister took the strategy document and said, 'That's brilliant I will get back to you on that', but he was never going to get back to anyone on it. At the end of the day you really have a very small region and there is only so much to go around. You will not get twenty million visitors, there is no Disneyland here!!!

When formulating strategies and presenting integrated regional action plans, the local authority networks have had to learn that they are operating within the ambit of national government policy. The INTERREG programme in Ireland is administered by central government departments and agencies in Northern Ireland and the Republic of Ireland who have national policies which take priority. This makes it very difficult for groups like the EBRC or the NWRCBG to formulate an integrated plan for their region which will receive block funding for implementation. The complexities and tensions surrounding block funding for integrated regional strategies is explained by one government member who works on the INTERREG programme.

> You cannot fund an integrated sub-regional plan that covers areas such as tourism, agriculture and economic development as a package. Bureaucracy states that tourist boards have responsibility for spending in the tourism sector, the Department of Agriculture is responsible for the agricultural sector, the Department of the Environment (DoE) for roads, Local Economic Development Unit (LEDU) for small business and Industrial

Development Board (IDB) for big business. That is the way the system works.

Considering the government administrations which operate the INTERREG programme in Ireland and the absence of a government body to assess integrated strategies, it is of no surprise that the North West Strategy did not receive global funding to implement the integrated regional strategy and action plan. The strategy was submitted as an integrated plan but was dissected by the relevant government departments who analysed each section. As a result only specific sections or small parts of the strategy became applicable for funding. The problems of an ambitious strategy seeking global funding from INTERREG are well summarised by one government interviewee whose comments capture the experience of the North West Development Strategy:

> In INTERREG we have up to forty government agencies North and South who assess projects and make executive decisions on where the money goes. This happens at a departmental level and is very centralised in terms of governance North and South. The integrated plan went into INTERREG and the various government departments, but as it went down into the atmosphere towards planet INTERREG it broke up. Because the Northern Ireland Tourist Board (NITB) and Bord Fáilte were looking at the tourism bit, Department of Agriculture were looking at the agricultural section and the Department of the Environment, were in a disaggregated way, looking at discrete bits of an overall plan without seeing the totality of the plan. It became the parts rather than the sum, some elements of the strategy were funded and some were not. It did not survive being put through the mangle grinder of INTERREG.

The experience of the NWRCBG's strategy and action plan clearly shows that sub-regional co-ordinative partnerships must acknowledge that they are operating within a national government system. Strategies cannot be too ambitious and must be developed in accordance with national priorities and policies. First and foremost there is a political jurisdiction to consider and there are competing priorities between government departments and agencies both in the North and South of Ireland.

The Strategic Planning Process

In the formulation and implementation of regional integrated area plans, it is essential that the local authority partnerships involve and include the wider community in the strategic planning process. After the rejection of the North West strategy, questions were raised about how sub-regional cross-border partnerships could formulate and implement strategic integrated action plans. To do this the groups must work with wider interests, government departments, private sector and the voluntary / community sector. With greater involvement and participation in the strategic planning process, local authority wishlists will not be developed but instead the actions will be integrated, relevant to the region and complementary to government policy. One government interviewee explains the required role of the local authority cross-border partnerships:

> The cross-border groups can become a motor to drive a portfolio of projects which they can instigate and manage themselves. They can stimulate this laboratory, information / innovation idea and they can look at means of co-operation with a regional impact, create a policy environment and attract strategic players in their locality. They can lead the catalytic development rather than undertaking the physical management of the projects. Local authorities can embrace issues in a way the Northern Ireland Tourist Board and Bord Fáilte cannot. They are not sector specific, they have the potential to look in a 360 degrees circle. It is difficult to see a cross-border integrated economic strategy being implemented solely by one of the groups but they can be part of the delivery framework, creating, identifying, prioritising and agreeing a delivery mechanism to implement certain projects. They have the potential to direct priorities in an agreed consensual way between various sectoral interests.

In the local authority cross-border networks there is now a recognition that they must work with the wider interests in the community if they are be effective. In the strategy of the EBRC it was proposed that thematic groups should be set up, each dealing with a strategic aim. The thematic groups will be composed of councillors and officials from the EBRC but also members of government departments and agencies, private and voluntary / community sectors who have interest in the particular themes. In the EBRC there is an understanding that the thematic groups are the way forward and not consulting the wider interests was one of the failures of the past. It must also be mentioned that involving the wider interests may help to bring Banbridge District Council into the EBRC. By involving the wider community interests, this could dilute the 'Nationalist political image' of the EBRC and highlight the Committee as working for the social and economic benefit of the region as a whole.

In the strategic planning process the local authority cross-border partnerships have employed consultants to formulate regional strategies. This has caused concern that effective strategies are not being developed because the partnerships do not have ownership of the strategy. One of the values of the cross-border partnerships, is that they operate at the sub-regional level and are composed of local authorities who know the needs of the area. Consultants on the other hand, have no first hand knowledge of the needs of the region. The problem with strategies developed by consultants is explained by one interviewee from a government department which administers the INTERREG programme:

> If I hire a consultant to restructure my current department and come up with a plan for development for the next two years, the consultant is going to ask questions and present something to me in a nicely bound booklet but there is not going to be anything there that I don't already know because he is coming in cold. This is the same with the local authority groups. There is a whole raft of consultants out there who are making a killing. Consultants are like the Oracle of Delphi. They tend to tell you what you want to hear. They know the jargon, they can use all the buzzwords, they can put together a strategy or application that looks like its the business but when you shake it, it just falls apart because there is no substance to it, there is no ownership.

Evidence from the local authority partnerships suggests that employing consultants to formulate a development strategy is not a necessary condition for success. Strategies which are developed by consultants are not always effective, particularly if there is little commitment and ownership among the partners. However, the experience of the cross-border groups has shown that consultants can be employed by co-ordinative partnerships, but only for specific needs which require certain expertise. Government members who are responsible for INTERREG were of the view that local authority groups could employ consultants for data collection or statistical analysis, for example, presenting an outline of disadvantaged areas using statistics. It is only in cases where councils do not have the time or expertise that consultants can meaningfully contribute to the strategic planning process. Therefore the best approach for sub-regional transjurisdictional co-ordinative partnerships is for a balance to be met; partnerships formulate the strategy with each partner working together and consultants can then be employed for statistical analysis in certain areas within the strategic themes.

Having depended on consultants to develop its strategy, the NWRCBG has now only used consultants for their technical expertise to assist in the formulation of a waste management programme. In this approach the ownership of the programme is firmly held by the partnership which means it creates greater ownership and commitment. The consultants can use their technical knowledge to formulate a better programme and save the partnership time. This shows that an effective balance can be met as one member of the NWRCBG explained:

> What I find useful is to employ consultants to facilitate and act almost as a timetable to drive the strategy and programme along. We are all very busy but if you bring in consultants they can help break the problem into stages and deliver a final product but we do the work and feed into the strategy or programme at each stage. There is a lot of merit doing it in-house but having facilitation is more effective. We know the area better than the consultants, we know the needs and problems. We may not have the time to sit and divorce ourselves from the areas but a combination of ourselves working with the development officers and feeding into consultants is effective.

Centralisation versus Regionalisation

In the operation of the Local Authority Networks tension has existed between the Networks operating at the sub-regional level and central government. There is an argument to suggest that the unwillingness of central government to decentralise and allow for greater decision making power has created a limited role for the Networks. The Networks operate within highly centralised systems of government and this has created tension between the partnerships and the government departments in Northern Ireland and the Republic of Ireland. For instance, since the inception of the EBRC various schemes concerning economic development, tourism and agriculture have been formulated and promoted and although Ministers and Officials of the Northern Ireland Office and the Republic of Ireland government have met with the EBRC, no support has been forthcoming. Members of the EBRC have expressed frustration at the attitude of central government which has found that words and soundings of support are never followed by measures and actions.

This led members of the partnership to believe that central government was not interested in the development of sub-regional cross border bodies as it was unwilling to grant autonomy and unshackle its power. Moreover, when money was granted to the EBRC to fund a secretariat there was resentment that central government could still dictate what role the secretariat should undertake. By controlling the secretariat and ordering the delivery of certain studies, this meant the secretariat had little time to develop relations and contacts among the partners which restricted the development of the partnership. One member of the EBRC comments on the difficulties concerning the funding received for the secretariat under INTERREG 1:

> To receive money under INTERREG 1 we applied to central government, the Department of Finance in Dublin and the Department of Finance and Personnel in Belfast who control and still control the INTERREG funding. We were awarded money but we were also given a list of projects to do so that our hands were tied. Time was dictated by having to produce a brochure or do a study and little time was left to network and attend meetings. We asked for money to establish and carry out a regional needs study but we didn't get that. Central government picked and chose difficult topics. It was a packaged based award, they were able to dictate exactly what we got and exactly what we could do.

This interviewee outlines the difficulties experienced by the EBRC in trying to expand and develop. In any new developments undertaken by the EBRC, central government were able to either halt, or dictate the speed of development.

On the other hand, central government has been reluctant to grant funding and greater autonomy as it feels the Networks are not competent enough to administer funds and lead development in the border region. Because the Networks have often developed unrealistic projects, they have not been able to clearly demonstrate to government they can act responsibly and can formulate and implement an integrated strategic plan which will not distort development in the border region.

However, in recent years new developments have taken place which have dampened tension and allowed the Networks and central government to work closer together. Over the last number of years the Networks have acknowledged the importance of a strategy, developing realistic projects and becoming more proactive. With the introduction of the County Enterprise Boards and the introduction of the Special Support Programme for Peace and Reconciliation, both governments in Northern Ireland and the Republic of Ireland are now beginning to see that devolved programmes can be successfully implemented. Therefore, the Networks and central government have been engaged in a two way learning process which has eased frustrations and brought them closer together, as one interviewee from the Department of Finance in Dublin explains:

> The Department of Finance and Personnel at present are a reflection of how the Department of Finance in Dublin was ten to fifteen years ago in terms of the central control we used to have. The other departments were in fear of us because we dictated everything, we held the purse strings and they could not spend without getting our authority. I can see the Department of Finance and Personnel going through the very change that the Department of Finance has experienced, they are on a very similar evolutionary path to us but they are a little bit behind. It is fascinating the way they were evolving and to see the way the peace programme was brought in. The devolution under the peace programme horrified civil servants by the extent of control that was passing down. They could not believe it could operate without being up before the court of auditors. But gradually there was an acceptance that it did seem to be working. I think it is experience and evolution through experience which has changed perceptions. Now, meanwhile, the cross-border bodies are also evolving and becoming more strategic and proactive and we are now more positively disposed towards helping them and getting them going. The frustrating thing is that it seems, looking back, to have been a necessary evolutionary process that all concerned had to go through.

The Project and Programme Approach

Within the last number of years the EBRC and the NWRCBG have been developing projects. However, under INTERREG 2 the partnerships have now turned to the programme approach. The programme approach is the one favoured by central government as it allows for greater impact from a strategy. Both the EBRC and the NWRCBG have established sub-groups working towards developing programmes identified in the strategic themes. By working in the sub-groups, the programme approach will allow the partnerships to bring wider interests on board and to become facilitators for development.

It must be said however, that not all the cross-border partnerships would be in agreement that a programme based approach is the best way forward. The ICBAN are presently working towards the development of a number projects as it feels the need to show a quick, visible impact on the ground so that all partners and community interests can see tangible benefits and outcomes resulting from the partnership. Considering that the ICBAN has only been in existence for a number of years, developing flagship projects will help build the momentum of the group and show that the partnership can implement projects to improve the needs of the region. Once this momentum is built, the group can then work towards developing programmes. One member of the ICBAN argues that flagship projects must be established to prove the value of the partnership:

> Initially the way forward has to be the project approach. ICBAN needs to demonstrate that it can deliver a particular project, even a semi flagship project. This will convince member authorities that it is a worthwhile organisation and they can say, 'If it was not for ICBAN this would not have existed.' We can then use a flagship project to develop a more programmed structure. If ICBAN is perceived as only a talking shop it will begin to lose a lot of hope that was initially there for the group. ICBAN needs to deliver a few projects to realise strong examples of what economic cross-border co-operation can mean so that people can see quick tangible outcomes.

Inter-Partnership Co-operation

Up until recently each of the cross-border partnerships had been working in isolation, formulating strategies and projects for their own particular regions. By working in isolation this caused difficulties for the groups when they came to apply for funding from Europe and central government. As each group focused on its own small region, strategies and projects were proposed which, if implemented, would have duplicated services or drawn funding away from the other border regions. This meant that the groups were acting in competition with each other and not working together for the whole of the border corridor. The cross-border partnerships have now learned from previous mistakes and there is a recognition that they must co-operate together if they are to formulate an effective regional strategy. One member from the NWRCBG comments that when formulating an integrated action plan:

All three groups must act together and have a common purpose, we should not be in the business of out rivalling each other. That does not mean one study for the whole area. There will be three individual plans but there must be a degree of co-ordination between those plans so we are not fighting each other. We need to have an agreed overall framework for the entire border region so we can put the three plans together and they will connect.

By developing co-ordinative linkages, the partnerships in the Irish border region have been able to learn and share in the experiences of other cross-border groups in Europe. In June 1997 the LACE – TAP office was established with funding from the cross-border groups and Co-operation Ireland. LACE-TAP is an action undertaken by the Association of European Border Regions (AEBR) which seeks to provide technical assistance and promotion of cross-border co-operation on internal and external border regions of the EU. The LACE-TAP office has developed linkages between the Local Authority Networks and other similar partnerships in Europe. Cross-border partnerships which operate between France and Germany, Germany and Holland and Holland and Belgium have been in existence for over fifty years and are more advanced than the cross-border partnerships in Ireland. For example, the groups in Europe have control over a pool of funding from which they implement regional strategies. By establishing linkages the cross-border groups in Ireland can learn how the European partnerships have successfully developed their regional strategies and integrated action plans.

There is also a recognition among the cross-border partnerships that by working together at project level greater outcomes can be achieved. For example, the NWRCBG and the ICBAN have developed a joint transportation study for the two regions to highlight infrastructure problems. With both partnerships working together for the joint study, an in-depth analysis of transport needs was carried out covering twelve local authority areas. In this way, the study was able to include transport links throughout the Central and North Western border regions. Indeed, the roads identified for priority were the Sligo to Belfast road link and the Letterkenny - Derry - Omagh - Monaghan - Dublin road. By co-operating together the partnerships could then begin to look at the whole border region and not just the small local council scale.

However, it must be mentioned that the cross-border partnerships have also experienced certain difficulties when trying to introduce co-ordinative measures. As the NWRCBG and the EBRC have been established for a longer period there is a feeling that they are superior to ICBAN which has just recently come together to attract funding. These jealousies and suspicions among the members of the different groups have created a degree of animosity and made linkages difficult to develop. One member of the NWRCBG reflects on the difficulties experienced while trying to establish linkages between the different partnerships:

> Each of the different cross-border groups are at different stages of development, some are more effective than others, some are posturing while others are getting things done. When we seek to work in co-operation there tends to be comments that 'we were the first group'. Instead of talking to Europe as one cross-border area represented by three bodies, some of the politicians have the view that their group should be talking the lead because they were they first ones to start, while the other groups are "Johnny come latelys" who have just jumped on the band wagon to get the INTERREG gravy.

The aim of seeking to establish greater co-operative links is further complicated by the fact that Donegal is a member of the NWRCBG and ICBAN, and Monaghan is a member of ICBAN and the EBRC. Considering that both councils are large counties they are divided, so that North Donegal councillors who have greater economic, geographic and social affinity with Derry and the North West sit on the NWRCBG and South Donegal councillors who have more in common with Enniskillen, Sligo and Omagh are represented on ICBAN. Similarly East Monaghan has greater economic, social and geographic ties with the EBRC and West Monaghan with ICBAN. With Monaghan and Donegal being common to both cross-border partnerships, there is opportunity for these councils to become the link between the bodies and be the driving force for co-ordinative linkages. However, in most cases joint membership of the partnerships has increased parochialism with some members becoming jealous of the dual roles. Jealousies may only be felt by certain members but difficulties in co-ordination among the groups exist. If the cross-border partnerships are to be successful, the jealousies and parochialism must be diluted if effective co-ordinative linkages are to be developed and joint programmes implemented.

Positive Publicity

Members of the EBRC have been unwilling to develop positive publicity about the partnership. There is concern that increasing the publicity of the partnership could be unhelpful as it will raise expectations in the community. It has been difficult for the partnerships to raise their profile within the community as they are not yet seen as groups which can create change and direct development. What is of most concern to the partnerships at this stage is not the backing of the local community, but the support of other development organisations: government agencies, private sector and community economic development groups. It is only when programmes are implemented and funding becomes available that the partnerships will focus on positive publicity. One member from the EBRC states that although few people in the region are aware of the EBRC, developing publicity is not a first priority for the partnership:

> The consultants did a survey and found that a lot of people in the region have not heard of us. It is very difficult when we are meeting and talking and people say, 'Is that the councils yapping again?', but it is only when you are actually achieving things that people sit up and take notice and pay attention. Until the EBRC has the real clout and the capacity to do things and facilitate change, the perception of the public will not change. If you are doing something worthwhile it does not matter if you get public adulation. At this stage it is not the backing of the public that is essential, it is the backing of the other bodies, to come on board into these thematic groups, is what is need.

Conclusion

From analysing the local authority cross-border partnerships, conclusions can be drawn over what conditions have a bearing on the performance of transjurisdictional co-ordinative partnership operating at the sub-regional level. The cross-border partnerships have shown that developing cross-border linkages is a very complex and difficult task. However, this task was complicated even further as the councils have been developing co-ordinative linkages across a border which is politically contested. By operating in a contentious political environment this affected the partnerships by creating tension and unease among the participants.

Despite the difficult political climate, the partnerships did manage to develop good working relationships by working together and focusing on the common problems of economic and social development. By acknowledging a need to work together on common issues, the contentious political environment was prevented from leading to the demise of the partnerships. The groups were also assisted by the EU which set a direction for the cross-border partnerships and provided funding which all participants could readily receive. Finally, for participants which have difficulties being involved in co-ordinative partnerships a more informal approach is favoured in the first tentative years.

Geographic conditions can also be highlighted as an important condition for success, in that sub-regional co-ordinative partnerships need to operate within a clear and distinct region which has common economic and social ties.

In developing a cross-border partnership, the local authority partnerships have demonstrated that the commitment of all member organisations is important. The commitment of all the partner councils ensured that cross-border relations were maintained during very difficult and tense times and further commitment is needed as the networks formulate and implement integrated strategies.

In a co-ordinative partnership it is essential that all participants work well together and enact an effective decision making process. To enable this, it was discovered that a large partnership board will create an unwieldy and unfocused organisation. In such circumstances it is necessary to develop an executive or task teams composed of a smaller number of members. Secondly, all participants should be fully involved in the decision making process or this may cause difficulties with members not being committed to decisions that have been taken without their input. When organising partnership meetings it is important that they are set at regular times as this gives the participants a greater opportunity to develop relations and keep fully informed of events. In addition, it was discovered that a consensus based approach is appropriate in the difficult, initial stages and for making major policy decisions but not for the day to day operations when decisions need to be taken quickly. For sub-regional co-ordinative partnerships it would seem appropriate that the participants should represent the sub-region and not the local or parochial levels. Establishing a central secretariat can however, contribute to promoting the sub-regional perspective. To facilitate an effective partnership decision making process a mediator or chairperson can be identified as having an important role to play.

The development of a regional strategy is a condition influencing performance; however, the strategy must strike a balance between one which is flexible and can adapt to changing circumstances and one which is not too broad and ambitious. In the strategic planning process, the partnerships must involve the wider community interests and thus become a facilitator for development in the sub-region. The strategy needs to be developed by the partners in consultation with wider interests and consultants should only be used for specific needs. When seeking to include other stakeholders, co-ordinative partnerships must be wary of conflicting interests and tensions between different sectors and work to find a way in which all sectors can be involved. The experience of the local authority partnerships however, demonstrates that when developing co-ordinative linkages in a difficult political environment, it is best practice to establish good working relations first before a strategy can be formulated.

Finally, it is important that a partnership has autonomy and power and adopts a proactive strategic approach, seeking to formulate projects and programmes and not acting just as a lobbying organisation. For a sub-regional co-ordinative partnership to effectively operate, a project approach could well be adopted in the initial stages of development and then the partnership could move on to a programme approach when good relationships have been established and a number of projects implemented with clear product outcomes. Developing co-ordinative linkages between partnerships can be identified as important as it reduces duplication and competition, shares experiences and redoubles efforts to produce more effective projects and programme outcomes. The local authority partnerships also need funding to develop projects and programmes and only until actions can be implemented on the ground that developing positive publicity is necessary.

6 The Partnership between the Northern Ireland Tourist Board and Bord Fáilte

Introduction

Cross-border co-operation in tourism involving the Northern Ireland Tourist Board (NITB) and Bord Fáilte (BF) has been on going for over fifteen years. Although the first moves to develop a cross-border partnership were made in the 1960s, it was not until the late 1980s that the boards began to work closer together on tourism projects and the partnership began to take shape. Since the 1980s the level of co-operation has substantially increased due to the existence of a greater number of cross-border programmes and the introduction of a joint marketing initiative to promote the island of Ireland a single tourist destination.

It is the aim of this chapter to highlight the relationship between the NITB and BF as a case study of a co-operative partnership which operates at the Regional / National Transjurisdictional level. By analysing the relationship between the tourist boards, it is possible to more fully interpret the interaction between conditions and performance for Regional / National Transjurisdictional partnerships operating on a co-operative basis.

However, before evaluating the partnership relationship between the tourist boards, it is important to reflect on the recent history of tourism development on the island of Ireland. A discussion of the roles and responsibilities of the tourist boards, recent government approaches to tourism in the North and South of Ireland and the history and development of co-operation, provides the necessary background to the analysis of the relationship.

This chapter is divided two major parts. Firstly, a background to tourism development on the island of Ireland will be presented to be followed by a discussion of the relationship between the two tourist boards with reference to the conditions influencing performance as identified in the literature: contextual, stakeholder / organisational, decision making and operational conditions.

Tourism Development on the Island of Ireland

Roles and Responsibilities of Government in Tourism

From its establishment in 1948 the NITB has been central to the development and promotion of tourism in Northern Ireland, working in conjunction with the DED and the local authorities in a tripartite relationship. The role of the government department (DED since 1982) in tourism has traditionally been focused around administration and funding, providing the annual grant and directives on policy matters to the NITB. The NITB on the other hand, is responsible to the DED, and undertakes the functions of promotion, administration, registration, research and marketing.

In addition, although losing control over issues such as housing and roads after local government re-organisation in 1972 (Knox, 1996), the local authorities (Figure 6.1) have responsibilities for leisure and tourism, which include the attraction of tourists to their areas (through holding special events and other means), the provision of tourism advisory and information services and the upkeep of amenities and services for visitors (Deegan and Dineen, 1997).

Bord Fáilte (BF), the Irish Tourist Board was established under the Tourist Traffic Act 1939 and is the main agency in the Republic of Ireland involved in the promotion and development of Irish Tourism. BF is a semi state agency and is responsible to the Department of Tourism, Sport and Recreation. Bord Fáilte's role is focused on the implementation of government policy which is formulated by the Department. In addition to policy formulation, the Department of Tourism, Sport and Recreation also seeks to facilitate the development of the sector (ITIC, 1998).

In the implementation of national tourism policy BF works in conjunction with the Regional Tourism Organisations. The Regional Tourism Organisations were established by BF in 1964, are now known as Regional Tourism Authorities (RTAs), and are comprised of a wide cross section of members from each region, including members from the industry - hoteliers and travel agents, representatives of local commerce and BF personnel. The RTAs have a general operational function aiming to encourage greater local and regional effort from local authorities and the private sector in tourism development (Pearce 1990, p.138). Therefore, while the RTAs aim to promote a regional tourism product, BF promotes national tourism on their behalf. There are currently seven regional tourism

areas, six of which are the responsibility of the RTAs. Shannon
Development manages the seventh (Figure 6.2).

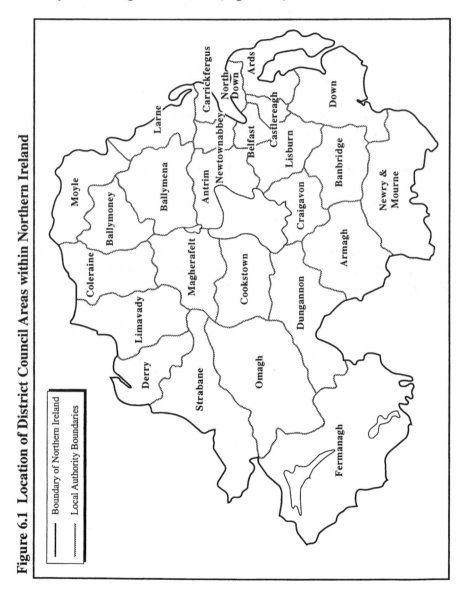

Figure 6.1 Location of District Council Areas within Northern Ireland

—— Boundary of Northern Ireland
········ Local Authority Boundaries

Figure 6.2   Location of the Seven Regional Tourist Authorites in the Republic of Ireland

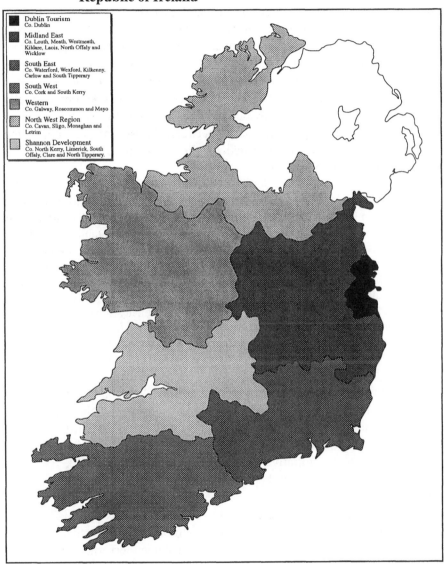

Cross-Border Co-operation in Tourism

In the 1960s tourism in Northern Ireland and the Republic of Ireland showed impressive growth (Deegan and Dineen, 1997) and it was during this period that the first steps towards North-South co-operation were taken. The origins of cross-border co-operation on tourism can be traced back to the meetings between O'Neill and Lemass in 1965/66 when tourism was identified as one area in which co-operation could be mutually beneficial. These meetings provided a whole new impetus to co-operate on tourism and opened up relationships between the two boards. Following the meetings the NITB commented on the potential for greater North - South co-operation in tourism,

> Following on the meeting of the two Prime Ministers and the Minister of Commerce with the Minister of Transport in the Republic, discussions between the board and Bord Fáilte took place in both Dublin and Belfast. These were the first meetings between the two boards and they were held in a most cordial atmosphere. Many facets of joint co-operation were discussed and a practical start had been made towards developing this aim. Capital schemes on and near the border in which both bodies will be concerned are the subject of research. Joint publicity between local bodies arranged by the respective Boards is also contemplated. The Board is fully confident that great benefits will accrue to all concerned from this friendly and practical co-operation (cited by Clarke and O'Cinneide, 1981, p.56).

Previous to this, the two boards had established little or no cross-border contact and in the marketing and promotion of tourism the NITB primarily developed links with the British Travel Association (British Tourist Association (BTA) from 1969). Towards the end of the 1960s, however, co-operative tourism initiatives began to emerge with the NITB, BTA and BF working together on marketing tours abroad to promote holiday tours and packages to the British Isles.

However, just as the tripartite relationship between NITB, BTA and BF began to take shape the civil disturbances in Northern Ireland escalated and were followed by a period of sustained terrorist violence. As a result the NITB began to restrict its overseas marketing and promotional activities. For instance, in 1972 'a low profile was adopted towards press and television coverage as the media seemed more interested in the political situation' (NITB, 1972) and in 1973 'no major advertising was undertaken' (NITB, 1973). The period between 1969-1971 is generally seen as a watershed for tourism in Northern Ireland with tourism numbers falling from 1,080,000 in 1968 to 435,000 in 1972 (Hannigan, 1995). Indeed, the effect of violence on tourism is well illustrated by Lennon (1995) who charts the fall in tourism numbers being directly proportional to the rise in terrorist incidents.

In a similar pattern to Northern Ireland, tourism numbers in the Republic of Ireland in the early 1970s also began to fall. In 1968 tourism visitor numbers reached 1,898,000 but by 1972 had fallen to 1,430,000 (Hannigan, 1995). In the Annual Reports of the early 1970s considerable attention is given to explaining the reasons for the downturn in tourism numbers which include, the devaluation of the dollar, a preference for warm water resorts, business recession in the United States, and high inflation rates (BF, 1972). However, one factor which is continuously cited is the effect of the civil disturbances and the terrorist conflict in Northern Ireland (BF, 1970; 1972).

Tourism in the Border Region

Although the relationship between the two boards did not progress from the position adopted in the late 1960s, at the end of the 1970s however, attention became focused on the tourism potential of the border region. A number of major studies of the border region were commissioned by the British and Irish Governments with funding from the EC which included a number of recommendations for cross-border tourism development. The Londonderry-Donegal Cross-Border Communications Study, published in 1977, led to the setting up of the North West Tourism Co-operative Group, a body representing both tourist boards, working with private and public sector interests in identifying tourism development needs (European Economic and Social Report in Irish border areas, 1983). The Erne Catchment Study of 1979 (Figure 6.3) recommended that co-operation between Bord Fáilte and the Northern Ireland Tourist Board should be enhanced. To this end, the study placed strong emphasis on developing the tourism potential of the region and presented a number of recommendations for tourism development which included: design of the arterial drainage scheme; improvements to the road and telecommunication network; reinstatement of Ballinamore / Ballyconnel canal navigation; increased provisions of hire cruiser bases and jetties; development of craft industry; and, marketing and promotion of the attractions of the catchment as a whole (Brady *et al*, 1979).

Figure 6.3 Location of The Erne Catchment Study Area

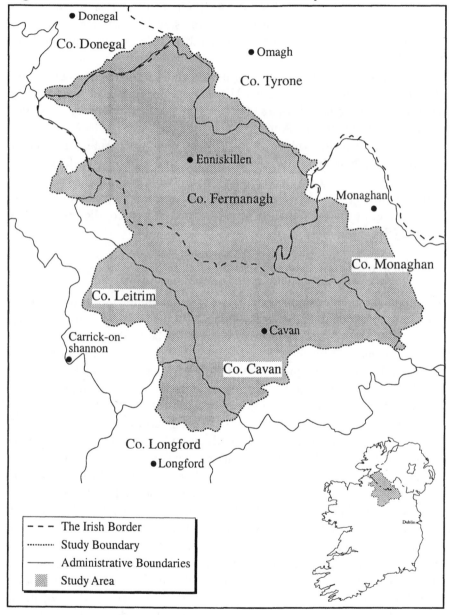

Government Policy Approaches in the 1980s and 1990s

As tourism numbers in Northern Ireland and the Republic gradually began to recover (Hannigan, 1995; Buckley and Klemn, 1993) both governments started to take a stronger interest in tourism and its potential for economic growth. In the 1980s government policy towards tourism became under increased scrutiny in the North and South, largely because tourism was seen as an area offering employment opportunities at a time of economic recession. That period was marked by a decline in mainstay industries and high unemployment in Northern Ireland (Buckley and Klemn, 1993), and a decline in the Southern Irish economy which still had a high dependence of agriculture and with unemployment reaching 20% at the end of the 1980s (Hurely *et al,* 1994).

In the early 1990s greater strategic focus to improve the tourism sector in Northern Ireland was provided with the publication of the DED policy statement '*A View to the Future*', and the Northern Ireland Tourist Board's 1990 Indicative Plan. However, what is also important is that the two initiatives were published at a time when significant amounts of funding were available for tourism. Towards the end of the 1980s and into the early 1990s in particular, tourism received a considerable injection of resources from the International Fund for Ireland (IFI), and from the European Union (EU) under the Operational Programme for Tourism and the INTERREG programme. From 1989 resources allocated to the NITB increased from £5.679m to £11.660m in 1992/3 and to £13.684m in 1995/96 (Wilson, 1993, p.204). In the early 1990s these monies provided for an extensive programme of tourism infrastructure development, funding capital projects, heritage, cultural and interpretation centres and other non-accommodation amenities (Deegan and Dineen, 1997).

In the Republic of Ireland impetus to the development of tourism was provided by the government in 1988 with the publication of ambitious targets for a period of growth, and the publication of the National Development Plan 1989 in preparation for the structural funds allocation from the EU. Under the structural funds significant amounts of resources were committed to tourism development within the Operational Programme for Tourism and, according to Deegan and Dineen (1997), it is estimated that IR£450m was invested in tourist facilities, marketing and training.

Further Cross-Border Co-operation

As well as providing considerable resources for tourism development within Northern Ireland and the Republic of Ireland, the EU and the IFI have also worked to facilitate greater North - South Co-operation. The IFI's Tourism programme is administered jointly by the NITB and BF and its main aim is to increase economic activity in disadvantaged regions through the stimulation of private investment in tourism projects. In the programme, resources have been injected to develop accommodation amenities (marina centres, pony trekking), other tourism amenities (conference, leisure facilities and hotels) and marketing programmes (IFI, 1996).

In the joint marketing scheme the IFI has assisted the two tourist boards to promote the island of Ireland as a single tourist destination. The one island campaign was launched in 1989 and is a joint initiative to promote activity based holidays, for example, golf, angling and heritage and is targeted at the US market. Also in 1989 the IFI provided further cross-border co-operation by funding the sharing of an information desk by NITB and BF in the BTA travel centre in London (BF, 1989).

In 1991 further assistance was given to the border region from the EU with the introduction of the INTERREG programme. The INTERREG programme is divided into five sub-programmes, one of which is tourism. The INTERREG tourism measure is administered on a cross-border basis through an INTERREG working group comprising representatives of NITB, Department of Tourism, Sport and Recreation, BF, Department of Arts Heritage, Gaeltacht and the islands and has the objective to, 'present the border region as a desirable holiday destination and to create an image conducive to inward investment' (Fitzpatrick and McEniff, 1992).

Two INTERREG tourism programmes have been implemented running from 1991-1993 and from 1994 - 1999. Under the second INTERREG programme a total of approximately £13,580,000 has been allocated for tourism, £3,580,000 for Northern Ireland and £10 million for the Republic of Ireland. The INTERREG tourism measure is largely divided into two areas, infrastructure development and marketing. By the mid-term evaluation 37 infrastructure projects and 16 marketing projects were approved some of which include:

- The development of a cross-border cycle trail;
- The development of a cultural activity centre;

- The improvement of tourist information centres;
- Packaging touring holidays particularly targeting incoming tour operators; and
- The development of the Ballinamore-Ballyconnel canal which provides a link between the Shannon and Erne waterways, also funded by the IFI (Browne, 1997).

The EU Special Support Programme for Peace and Reconciliation Programme for Northern Ireland and the Border Counties of Ireland also seeks to develop cross-border co-operation in tourism. Introduced in 1995 the Peace and Reconciliation initiative contains a specific sub-programme for cross-border co-operation. Sub-Programme 3 Cross-Border Development has been allocated 60 MECU and has the aim to:

> Provide cross-border reconciliation and to exploit the opportunities for increased cross-border development arising from the new situation (Coopers and Lybrand, 1997, p.B38).

Under this programme the tourist boards, local authorities and RTAs have been awarded funding to implement cross-border tourism projects.

Marketing the Island of Ireland

In 1994 a second EU programme was introduced which provided for a further increase in resources for tourism. In Northern Ireland the Single Programming Document (SPD) was awarded a total targeted expenditure (EU, public and private sectors) of 165 million ECU and an EU contribution of 75 million ECU, representing increases of 91% and 70%, respectively, over the previous Operational Programme for Tourism 1989-93 (Deegan and Dineen, 1997). Within the SPD a greater diversity of programmes has been allocated funding compared to the Operational Programme 1989-93 with 24.3% of the funds being allocated to marketing and promotion, 22.6% for training in the tourism industry, the provision of accommodation 16.3%, and the conservation of the natural and built environment received 10% of EU funding (Deegan and Dineen, 1997, p.208).

Additional resources for tourism were also allocated to the Operational Programme for Tourism 1994-99 in the Republic of Ireland. However, under this programme a significant increase of funding was allocated to marketing (Deegan and Dineen, 1997), which reflected a concurrent shift in the re-organisation of Bord Fáilte. Following a government review of the tourist board in 1994, it was concluded that the Irish tourist industry in the Republic had expanded and there was no requirement for Bord Fáilte to continue a developmental role. The recommendations of the consultants are presently being implemented and Bord Fáilte's now aims to focus attention on providing supportive and facilitative role, primarily based on marketing and promotion (ITIC, 1998, p.73).

By contrast, considering that tourism in Northern Ireland remains a minor part of the economy and accounts for under 2% of GDP (NITB, 1996/97) compared to 7% in the Republic (BF, 1997), developing tourism infrastructure is still a significant role for the NITB. Despite this, the NITB are also seeking to place greater emphasis on marketing and have set out a new enabling and marketing approach in the most recent Corporate Plan 1998-2001, which requires the board to become more market orientated (NITB 1998a).

Running in tandem with these developments, two major marketing programmes, the Overseas Tourism Marketing Initiative (OTMI) and Tourism Brand Ireland (TBI), were launched in the 1990s to promote the island of Ireland as one destination and facilitate greater North-South co-operation between the tourist boards and within the tourist industry. The OTMI was established in 1993 by the tourism industry to launch a marketing campaign in the US and from 1995 has been extended to include Britain, France and Germany. The OTMI is co-ordinated by BF and is co-funded by the British and Irish Governments, the EU and IFI and in 1997 had a budget of IR£7.3m (OTMI, 1997). Co-operation in tourism between North and South was given further expression in November 1996 with the launch of TBI. TBI is a tourism marketing initiative developed by the two tourism boards to market the island of Ireland as a single tourism destination. In short, therefore, the NITB has three elements in strategic brand awareness. The aim is to develop a 'brand' to position Northern Ireland in appropriate markets as,

- a stand alone destination;
- a sub-brand of 'Britain'; and,
- a sub-brand of 'Ireland' (NITB, 1998a, p.19).

Tourism Growth

During the 1990s both parts of Ireland experienced a period of significant growth in tourism. This growth in tourism numbers was particularly evident in the South of Ireland which recorded the fastest growth in tourism earnings of fifteen prime European destinations in the twelve years up to 1992, with an average annual growth rate of 10% a year (McNulty, 1995). In 1997 overseas tourist visits to Ireland reached five million with tourist expenditure now estimated to be worth £2.1 billion and providing 119,300 jobs (BF, 1997). Tourism in Northern Ireland, on the other hand, remains a minor part of the economy. It accounts for under 2% of GDP compared to 7% in the Republic. However, in the 1990s tourist numbers have been increasing: between 1986-94 the annual average percentage tourism visitor numbers increased by 5.8% (Wilson, 1993), with visitor numbers rising to 1,294,000 in 1994 from 930,000 in 1988 (Hannigan, 1995). In addition, visitor numbers to Northern Ireland have significantly improved from 1994 as tourism benefits from the cease-fires and the peace process. (O'Neill and Fitz, 1996, p.161) By 1996 the tourism visitors to Northern Ireland had reached 1,557,000 and tourism was generating £266 million to the economy (NITB, 1996/97).

After considering the role of government in tourism and the history and development of cross-border co-operation between the NITB and BF, the next number of sections seek to analyse the relationship between the boards with a view to identifying the conditions influencing the performance of Regional / National Transjurisdictional partnerships operating on a co-operative basis.

Contextual Conditions Influencing the Partnership Relationship between the Northern Ireland Tourist Board and Bord Fáilte

A Contentious Political Environment

In the partnership between the NITB and BF, the terrorist violence in Northern Ireland and the political sensitivities surrounding cross-border co-operation have impacted on the success of the relationship. During the 1980s when significant cross-border programmes and initiatives were first developed, feelings of distrust and suspicion over co-operation were held by both tourist boards. Within the NITB political sensitivities emerged in partnering a government agency from the Republic of Ireland, at a time of heightened political tension in Northern Ireland and following a thirty year period of isolationist or back to back development. In these initial stages the NITB was suspicious of cross-border co-operation and wary of the possible political ramifications that may follow, as one representative of a cross-border tourism programme points out:

> In the beginning of cross-border co-operation there were certain sensitivities held within some quarters of the NITB. There were concerns that cross-border co-operation was part of a process which would make the NITB more green. There was distrust and suspicion over the motives of cross-border co-operation, what it meant and where it might lead to?

In contrast to the NITB, the underlying concerns of BF did not rest with the political sensitivities surrounding cross-border co-operation. At first, BF was reluctant to enter into co-operation because by partnering with Northern Ireland, the tourist product in the South could have become associated with terrorist violence. In the 1970s as the increasing violence in Northern Ireland played a significant contribution to the decline in tourism numbers within the Republic of Ireland, BF gradually began to distance itself from the events in the North. It then became difficult for BF in the mid 1980s to engage in co-operation with the NITB when terrorist violence was still ongoing.

With rising violence and high political tension both boards regarded co-operation with suspicion and distrust. Political sensitivities in cross-border co-operation did create obstacles for the partnership but considering that co-operation was in the area of tourism, so much depended on peace and a stable environment. One member of the NITB states that the importance of peace to tourism created more difficulties and obstacles to partnership than the political sensitivities surrounding cross-border co-operation:

> Because Northern Ireland was a tourism wilderness fifteen years ago our partners in the south would have seen us as an albatross around their neck. It is not that we wanted to be a Ulster Defence Institution, in that Northern Ireland will be exclusively promoted. There was a time when that suited our colleagues in the southern industry very much. The southern industry would have been so short sighted in the past as to snub aspects of the northern industry to their short term benefit. For example, you would have some tourist travelling around the South of Ireland coming to Galway

asking, 'Where might I go now?'. Well the last place that they would have advised you to go would be north.

Ongoing terrorist violence and the political sensitivities created feelings of distrust and suspicion and made it difficult for the partnership to develop. Both boards mainly focused on their own priorities with cross-border co-operation receiving minimal attention, even neglect. Steps towards co-operation were initiated but in reality considerable distance remained between the boards. One representative of a cross-border tourism programme describes the relationship between the tourist boards and how it operated in practice:

> Ten to fifteen years ago there was a feeling of mutual suspicion between the tourist boards. At the world travel markets both boards would act like they were poles apart, Bord Fáilte would generally have one massive stand and the Northern Ireland Tourist Board would have a much smaller stand positioned in the far corner. It was like North Korea - South Korea, it was that sort of mentality.

From a position of mutual distrust and suspicion the two tourist boards have maintained and developed the co-operation. Within the last five years, in particular, co-operation has been extended to include a joint marketing programme involving joint stands to promote the island of Ireland. One of the most important events which has changed the nature of the relationship between the tourist boards has undoubtedly been the paramilitary cease-fires and the development of the peace process. The peace process has helped transform the relationship between the boards by creating a more stable political environment which is supportive of cross-border co-operation. Secondly, a greater opportunity now exists to develop and promote tourism in Northern Ireland without the hindrance of civil disturbances comparable to the 1970s. Therefore, with the advent of the cease-fires and the peace process, a major obstacle to partnership development has been removed allowing co-operation to be more open and transparent.

Peace has also facilitated greater co-operation in tourism at the local project level. Under programmes funded by the EU and the IFI, both BF and the NITB have been working together on a cross-border basis to develop tourism in the border region between the district councils in Northern Ireland and the RTAs in the South of Ireland. Before the cease-fires terrorist violence heightened the feelings of distrust and suspicion, but now the peace process has helped to dampen sensitivities and create a supportive political environment. The importance of peace to the development of cross-border projects is well summarised by one representative of the IFI who comments that:

> In the 1980s the atmosphere was not conducive to cross-border co-operation. When you brought the groups together on a cross-border basis each of them would be sniffing each other out like a different species. A number of years ago the Unionists could not even sell the IFI to their constituents and they were reluctant to become fully involved with IFI money. However, since the cease-fire the atmosphere for cross-border co-operation has changed and within a more supportive environment, meaningful contacts and linkages have been established. Now the parties just come together. There is none of this psyching each other out.

It is clear that the cease-fires and the peace process have helped create a more supportive environment for cross-border co-operation in tourism. However, the political environment in which it operates still remains volatile and can create difficulties in developing the partnership relationship, as one interviewee from the Department of Tourism, Sport and Recreation explains:

> It is very frustrating co-operating within a political backdrop in which fear and suspicions can impede on sensible practical co-operation which is beneficial for both parties. For example, the Department and Bord Fáilte developed a strategy document which contained pictures of tourism images such as pubs, restaurants, attractions and so on. But one picture was of a historic castle which happened to be flying a tricolour from one of its towers. We (who developed the brochure / document) did not even notice it, but when presenting the strategy to the Northern Assembly a number of members pointed the flag out, raised the issue and this caused some political tension.

The political environment in Northern Ireland still remains turbulent and operating against this backdrop has restricted the approach of the NITB to partnership. The position of the NITB is a difficult one as it aims to equally reconcile the interests of the Nationalist and Unionist communities and not upset political sensitivities. The NITB has adopted a careful, and an almost reserved approach to cross-border co-operation and this has made it difficult to expand and develop the partnership. One interviewee describes the difficulties faced by NITB and by the partnership as a whole:

The Northern Ireland Tourist Board do not have a clear political line to take as is the case with Bord Fáilte and the Department of Tourism, Sport and Recreation. They run a very different political course, they have to take direction from the British Government and the Northern Ireland Office but at the same time balance themselves between two camps, the Nationalist and Unionist communities. The Northern Ireland Tourist Board have to be a bit more apprehensive and are cagey in the relationship. They have to watch their backs in case of statements from hard-line Unionists that they are selling out and that cross-border co-operation in tourism is going to lead to a United Ireland and Dublin rule.

Moreover, periods of instability in the peace process and sporadic outbreaks of violence in Northern Ireland have caused further problems for the partnership. There are still concerns within BF about co-operating with the NITB and how this may affect tourism numbers in the South of Ireland. For this reason a large section of personnel in BF would still regard co-operation with NITB as a risky venture. Just as the peace process has transformed the relationship, it is true to say that if terrorist violence was to return, this would have a detrimental effect on the partnership, possibly collapsing the joint marketing initiative. One member of BF comments that the development of the partnership hinges on a stable peace and a political settlement in Northern Ireland:

Unquestionably the key is peace. If there is peace everyone is going to benefit, the tourist boards, the tourism industry and the two governments. However, if there is a serious upsurge in violence, a breakdown in the 'Good Friday' Agreement and the bombs start going off in Temple Bar, I would think that the partnership between the Northern Ireland Tourist Board and Fáilte would come under great strain. Ireland can only be sold as one entity and unless there is peace I don't think it will work, because you end up selling a bruised product.

The Role of the EU and the IFI

In the partnership both the EU and IFI have actively pursued greater co-operation between the boards and their respective government departments. The EU and IFI became involved in tourism in the 1980s at a time when political tensions between North and South were high and when both boards had largely pursued back to back development. From the 1980s joint programmes were developed by the EU and IFI, such as the one island campaign, which required both boards to work together on a cross-border basis. In this role the EU and IFI have facilitated partnership by bringing the boards together to work on joint arrangements. One interviewee from the NITB states that:

> The IFI and EU have been critically important to the partnership between NITB and BF. I would give them ten out of ten in every respect. In accounting terms if you were asking what has the additionality been with the input from the IFI and the EU, I would describe that as accelerating the relationship. They got involved at a risky stage and gave us reason to open dialogue and negotiation when previously there was no reason. At that time there was a more competitive framework: I don't need to talk to him.

The IFI and EU can be seen to be facilitating partnership by bringing the tourist boards and departments together to access the potential of co-operation. One member of BF, however, argues that it was the IFI more so than the EU which sought to develop greater co-operation between North and South and actively pursued the role of facilitator:

> The IFI came over and attended meetings and sat looking how the money was spent. The EU approach was - tell us what you want to do and then we will decide whether it is applicable. They would have the broad programme or fund and then you would make propositions from within that. They do not take the same proactive role as the IFI. I have attended quite lengthy meetings in the north where budgets and tourism strategies were discussed and the IFI had a representative explaining their position and taking a substantial interest.

From these interviewees it is evident that the EU, and the IFI in particular, did contribute to facilitating co-operation and accelerating the relationship. It is interesting to note, however, that although being very influential, the IFI did not play a very clear and visible facilitative role. The IFI adopted a backstage approach to cross-border co-operation while at the same time they were working proactively behind the scenes with government departments and agencies promoting partnership. One interviewee from a RTA comments on the low profile but very influential role of the IFI:

> The IFI are an amazing institution, you can't ring them, they don't have a phone number or post office box number. They are almost a secretive organisation and yet they have a lot of influence, organising the tourism programme and bringing the two boards together.

Now that cross-border projects have been maintained and developed, one of the main objectives of the IFI programme has been achieved as a momentum for co-operation has been initiated. Ongoing and deeper co-operation between the boards can be partly regarded as a testament to the influence of the EU and IFI. Indeed, it is a further recognition of the influence of the IFI in facilitating cross-border co-operation that the IFI tourism programme may be discontinued. Furthermore, if the 'Good Friday' Agreement is implemented successfully and peace is maintained, the funders of the IFI may not see the need for further programmes. The following analysis on the influence and future role of the IFI have come from one representative of the NITB:

> The IFI sees its role in facilitating and pump priming co-operation as coming to an end and will probably decide not to give funding to tourism anymore. They have done their bit and it could be time to move off and focus on other areas. Where the IFI get their funding from is equally important. If there is a peaceful environment there may not be an IFI in two years time, so they are obviously looking at an exit strategy for themselves.

The Influence of Government

When analysing the underlying reasons behind the development of the partnership between the NITB and BF it is also interesting to assess the role of the two governments. In the beginning of the relationship between the boards, both governments did not play a very influential or proactive role in working to facilitate greater cross-border co-operation. Broad policy was formulated in both jurisdictions covering aspects of co-operation but no firm or clear direction in partnership was delegated to the boards. Therefore, in the initial stages of the co-operation and until the last number of years, both boards enjoyed a great deal of flexibility. In practice this meant the tourist boards prioritised their own interests giving minimal attention to cross-border arrangements. Under loose direction from government the boards tended to view each other with suspicion and distrust, particularly in relation to marketing. At this stage the relationship was almost maintained on an artificial basis as the partnership was centred on implementing cross-border programmes which provided external funding for co-operation. Without clear direction from government the nature of the relationship is well illustrated by the following comments from one member of Bord Fáilte:

> Up until the last number of years I was not particularly conscious of any edict coming down from the government saying, 'You have got it to the fore in your mind that co-operation is required'. My brief would have been Bord Fáilte keeps it integrity intact and there is no scope for sharing our marketing approach or anything else if it endangers our position as an entity. Everyone could see that if somebody gave you money to spend on a project that was good for everyone and concessions were made. Meetings were set up, we met people and we got on well, but in relation to marketing it was a stone wall exercise. In effect the position was you are not going to become part of our marketing machine. It was done nicely and gently. In some areas there were trade-offs and all the necessary things were put in place to suggest that you were co-operating...but the fundamental was no surrender!!!

Within the broad policy guidelines the role of personalities in the co-operation has been particularly important. Without clear policy direction to the tourist boards, individuals within the organisations enjoyed a great deal of discretion in deciding what shape the co-operation should take. The comments of one member from BF reflect on the flexibility and discretion given to the boards by government in cross-border policy and the role and importance of individuals within the organisations:

> Unless the government's decision is absolutely categorical, personalities are critical. An organisation can do a huge amount to water down a government decision. At that time one of the leading figures in our board was a very strong minded person who had strong views and would almost have avoided greater co-operation at that stage if he felt it was detrimental to his targets. He took the view that he had been given a job to promote tourism with Bord Fáilte and he was going to do it.

Although the two governments may have had a broad commitment towards partnership, in practice this was not actively pursued by the boards. This painted a confusing picture of cross-border co-operation. Government had a broad commitment to partnership and the boards were implementing programmes, but in effect co-operation was given a low priority. Operating cross-border programmes in this situation became very difficult for those at the local project level as they became fully exposed to this confusing leadership.

However, within the last number of years both governments have taken a more proactive role in facilitating greater co-operation and providing focus and direction to the boards. Cross-border co-operation is now seen as part of a wider government strategy in Britain and Ireland to support the peace process and a political settlement. Political will and clear government policy has, in the last number of years, helped to facilitate greater co-operation and give strong unambiguous direction to the boards that co-operation is required. Under this situation any overriding concerns about co-operation have been set aside as partnership is now a priority government policy. There is now a clear government commitment to partnership and this has filtered down to the tourist boards and individuals within the organisations. The new era of co-operation in tourism is captured by the following comments of one member from the Department of Tourism, Sport and Recreation:

> In co-operation some members of Bord Fáilte would be wary of the Northern Ireland Tourist Boards association with the troubles in Northern Ireland, Drumcree, Omagh and the possible random attacks by dissidents. However, the government have embraced co-operation and it is now part of an agenda to deliver the peace process, and the government have moved Bord Fáilte into line on this issue. Reservations on co-operation with the Northern Ireland Tourist Board are now seen in a wider context of securing peace and stability in Ireland.

Similar comments were expressed by another interview working on a cross-border tourism project who stated that government involvement has given a new impetus to the partnerships and provided greater direction for the boards:

> Basically what the two governments have done is to kick ass and said, 'Right, in the field of tourism we expect co-operation.' So there has been a blanket commitment from both governments who have said to the tourist boards go and deliver it, this is new policy. Some members of the Northern Ireland Tourist Board or Bord Fáilte may have certain reservations about co-operation but the boards cannot turn around and question that or give any sort of rational argument; it has been handed down. Even if someone wanted to go unilateral they would not be allowed to do it anymore. Politically, Stormont, Westminster and the Dáil would not accept it.

These interviewees outline the importance of government political will in supporting and directing greater partnership between the boards. The interviewees also reflect on the reservations among members of the tourist boards and the strong approach adopted by the two governments in directing and facilitating greater co-operation. Under this directive approach from government, interviewees from the NITB and BF expressed concerns, particularly in the beginning of the peace process, that tourism was being used as a 'political football' and that the boards were being taken 'hostage to fortune'. In recent years, however, there is now an acceptance that tourism is part of a wider government agenda to facilitate and support the peace process and, within a new political agreement, change is inevitable. A common reflection on this development is given by one interviewee:

> There is a history of co-operation between the institutions and they are starting the new phase ahead of everyone. The boards should celebrate that they can contribute to the new institutional arrangements within the context of the peace process and that tourism is a pathfinder to cross-border co-operation which highlights practical, sensible commercial co-operation which is mutually advantageous and reinforcing on both sides of the border. Tourism can demonstrate to both parts of Ireland that co-operation can be successful and tourism can be seen as a role model of cross-border partnership and integration.

Although the governments have injected fresh impetus into cross-border co-operation and provided greater direction to the boards, not all government intervention has been supportive and facilitative. It must be remembered that, despite the peace process, cross-border partnerships are still operating within a tense political environment and as a result, governments need to adopt a sensitive approach. The need for a careful and sensitive approach can be highlighted by reflecting on one incident when a Government Minister from the South of Ireland changed the new tourism logo under the TBI initiative, agreed by both boards, by enlarging the size of the shamrock motif. This intervention caused considerable controversy, upset political sensitivities and created difficulties for developing an effective partnership relationship. The importance of sensitive government involvement in partnership when operating within a complex political environment are captured by the comments of one interviewee from the NITB:

Storms in a tea cup can occur. We are a nation fixated with symbols and emblems. A very clumsy approach where politically, tourism can be offered as an example of how co-operation should not happen, was on the symbol for Brand Ireland. That logo entered the political debate and was interfered with by the Minister in the Republic of Ireland and caused an absolute rumpus because we had an example of cross-border co-operation agreed at operational level. The Minister then said, 'I don't like this I am going to have it changed' and did have it changed without the appreciation that he was becoming involved in what was agreed on a cross-border basis. It is a logo, but changing it caused some people great offence. That was the tourist board almost trying to make more Irish an institution that was the NITB. That is an example of where political involvement can be a little negative and shows an element of where you have to be streetwise in co-operation.

Additional Funding

In the relationship between the NITB and BF the potential access to funding and resources has acted to facilitate greater co-operation and partnership development. The EU and IFI have not only acted as convenors between the partnership boards but, in providing extra partnership resources, have also created greater incentive for co-operation. Indeed, it was the potential to access more financial resources for tourism which helped to facilitate co-operation, particularly in the early stages, and develop the partnership. The financial incentives in-built into co-operative programmes provided the necessary lure for the boards to enter into partnership, as one member of BF states:

> The EU and IFI were crucially important in the development of the partnership. Our budget was certainly being curtailed in the south so we would have got into bed with anybody if there was money to be gained from it. The trade off was always we will share and work co-operatively but we will not do anymore than we have to, to get the money. In fact the money was the only thing that brought us together in the early stages.

In the initial stages of co-operation the ability to access more resources from the EU and the IFI helped to bring the tourist boards together to work in cross-border programmes. The availability of funding has also contributed to maintaining the relationship as the EU and IFI programmes have continued to facilitate and fund co-operation on cross-border programmes.

Working Together

In the relationship between the NITB and BF there is a recognition that co-operation is mutually beneficial. Given that both boards are to gain from partnership, this has driven the partnership forward and acts like a reinforcement in all aspects of co-operation.

It has been mentioned earlier in this chapter that certain quarters within the NITB were concerned about the political implications of co-operating on a cross-border basis. However, there was also an immediate recognition by the NITB that co-operating with BF would bring added economic and commercial benefits to Northern Ireland. Co-operating with BF improves the promotion and marketing of the island which will attract a greater number of tourists to Ireland who can then travel into Northern Ireland. Increasing the tourism potential of Northern Ireland allowed the NITB to take a pragmatic decision to co-operate based on economic and commercial benefits which override any political considerations. The importance of mutual benefit in the partnership is captured by one interviewee from the NITB:

> Strategically and tactically the Northern Ireland Tourist Board has always adopted the position that our primary objective is to get the best return and profitability in the tourism industry. In this approach you forget about partnerships and politics and you look commercially and economically at how you improve the wealth of the Northern Ireland tourism industry. In terms of NITB's marketing material it is patently and unapologetically on a brand Ireland basis, getting long haul customers to come to our backyard who will be attracted by the Cliffs of Moher, Ring of Kerry and the Giants Causeway. It does not matter in terms of the visuals they are getting as long as we are attracting them to Ireland. We (NITB) then benefit from the spread of those tourists in Ireland.

It can be seen that, by co-operating together and marketing tourism products and attractions, more tourists will be encouraged to visit Ireland, both the North and South. This mutual benefit has encouraged both boards to co-operate and has provided a supportive partnership environment. In the tourist boards there is also a recognition that in the global tourism market Ireland is one country and that the NITB and BF are essentially selling the same product. Therefore, by co-operating to jointly market the island of Ireland the tourist boards are reacting to market realities and reducing the costs of duplication.

However, it is true to say that marketing the island has experienced difficulties in that it not been well received by tourism interests throughout Ireland. Concerns have been voiced by tourism interests in the south of Ireland who feel that the joint marketing programme may encourage tourists to travel further north. Tourist interests largely based in the extreme south are anxious about co-operating in marketing as they feel this may upset the traditional pattern of tourists who travel between Dublin or Shannon and visit the South West. However, although concerns may exist over the perceived threat to tourism in the traditional parts of Ireland, there is an acceptance that with co-operation the numbers visiting Ireland can be maximised which will benefit all tourism interests throughout the island. As the tourism numbers increase, it is then up to each region to attract tourists to its area.

In addition, although there are concerns marketing the island of Ireland could push the tourists further north, tourism interests in the border region would welcome a shift in the traditional tourism pattern in Ireland. Those in the border region are very supportive of the marketing campaign and in this respect are allied to the interests of the NITB.

Finally, in discussion over the concerns of a possible shift in the traditional tourism travel patterns in Ireland, it must be remembered that the tourist boards have very little influence in deciding where the tourist visits. Both the NITB and BF would largely see their role as encouraging the highest numbers of tourists to visit Ireland and after that there is an acceptance that each area is in competition.

Pressure from the Tourist Industry

In acknowledgement of the mutual advantages for the tourist boards in co-operation and of the benefits for tourism in Ireland, the tourist industry throughout Ireland has been fully supportive of cross-border partnership. Indeed, as the two governments have played a direct role in the development of the partnership, the tourist industry can also be seen to have encouraged and, in certain cases, pressurised the tourist boards to extend co-operation. The role of the tourist industry in facilitating co-operation may certainly not have been as direct and influential as that of government or even the EU or IFI, but in being supportive of partnership and willing to see more co-operation, the private sector has encouraged the boards to work closer together.

Organisational / Stakeholder Conditions Influencing the Partnership between the Northern Ireland Tourist Board and Bord Fáilte

A Dominant Partner

Over the last twenty years the south of Ireland has been attracting a larger number of tourists and receiving a greater amount of overseas tourism expenditure than Northern Ireland. Therefore as BF in the Republic of Ireland promote a much larger and more productive industry than NITB in the north of Ireland, BF in theory can be regarded as a stronger partner. This imbalance has been reflected in the relationship between the tourist boards and created obstacles in the implementation of joint programmes.

Although the boards are working together to market the island of Ireland it is has been difficult to promote and develop this programme on a practical basis. In Northern Ireland the tourism infrastructure is not as well developed and this causes problems for tour operators who want to package and promote the whole island, but cannot include the North due to the limited accommodation facilities. In this case the boards are co-operating on a joint marketing initiative but Northern Ireland cannot co-operate on a equal basis and facilitate tourists in holiday packages. There is a growing anxiety in the South of Ireland over the capacity of the northern tourism industry to deliver on quality standards and deal effectively with an increase in tourism numbers.

The imbalance in strength in the relationship between the two boards has also heightened the sensitivities of the NITB over cross-border co-operation. Despite the peace process, tensions still remain in that some members of the NITB at times feel that they are being overshadowed by BF, the larger, more dominant partner. One representative of a cross-border project reflects on the imbalances between the two boards and the tensions that largely come to the fore in the world travel markets:

> I have seen conflict between the boards in shows in Europe. On the Tourism Brand Ireland stand for instance, Bord Fáilte have more personnel in Europe and the Northern Ireland Tourist Board have a skeleton staff, so it works out that on the stand Bord Fáilte may have four or five representatives and the Northern Ireland Tourist Board only one. In these situations tensions may arise with the Northern Ireland Tourist Board representative who will say that they felt swallowed up as Bord Fáilte were calling the shots and it was like a 4th Division team playing a Premiership team in the FA Cup.

However, as one means to deal with the imbalance between the organisations, the NITB and northern tourism interests have been given favourable representation in decision making structures and exposure in joint marketing programmes. In relation to decision making structures it is recognised that difficulties and conflict may arise if northern representatives are made to feel an inferior partner in the co-operative process. Therefore, partnership has tended to be more successful in instances where the partners are given equal representation. One example, where equal representation of members is seen as successful, is the joint committee known as Ireland Waterways, which promotes the Shannon-Erne Waterway. Although the Irish Boat Rental Association (IBRA) in the Republic of Ireland has eleven members and 650 boats and the Erne Charter Boat Association (ECBA) in the north of Ireland has around six members and 140 boats, Ireland Waterways is composed of an equal number of representatives from both associations. This is a case of a larger more dominant organisation which has given equal representation and decision making power to their northern counterparts. Although it was not a conscious decision by Ireland Waterways (which includes a representative each from NITB and BF) to allow for equal representation, this has contributed to allaying fears of dominance and helped to build an effective partnership process, as one interviewee commented:

> In any examples of cross-border co-operation that I have seen on paper and in reality the north always proportionally does better, it is usually on a 50:50 basis. From a northern perspective regardless of your political allegiance or political outlook, if you are in Northern Ireland you would say to yourself, am I going to be swallowed up here?, am I going to loose my identity and be rail roaded? If you have these fears then going into a cross-border relationship for the first time where someone offers you equal recognition or exposure helps to allay any apprehensions or suspicions you may have.

Allowing for better representation for northern tourism interests has also been conducted at the island of Ireland level between the tourist boards. In the marketing of Ireland in programmes such as TBI and OTMI, it is held that Northern Ireland has received a favourable amount of publicity and promotion when compared to funding contributions. By receiving a disproportional level of publicity this has helped to allay fears of the NITB that the identity of Northern Ireland tourism may be compromised and diluted in an all-Ireland marketing campaign.

However, within this programme concerns have been raised in the south of Ireland over the funding allocated by the NITB and the amount of publicity which Northern Ireland receives. This disproportional amount of publicity allowed for under the programme has led to disagreements over funding and created tensions between the boards, as one interviewee explains:

> Overseas Tourism Marketing Initiative was extended to include the Northern Ireland Tourist Board in 1995. The Northern Ireland Tourist Board contribute directly to the Overseas Tourism Marketing Initiative, though it has to be said not a great deal. At times this causes tensions and difficulties within the partnership. The Department of Tourism, Sport and Recreation in the Republic of Ireland have largely funded most of the programmes Tourism Brand Ireland, Overseas Tourism Marketing Initiative and the Domestic Marketing Campaign with Northern Ireland receiving a disproportional amount of promotional coverage and advertisements when compared to financial contributions.

Considering that the NITB could be seen as the weaker partner, the joint Trimble / Mallon statement on matters for North-South co-operation indicates that the dissemination of information in overseas markets must be conducted in a balanced and comprehensive nature to reflect the diverse traditions, cultures and identities on the island of Ireland (Trimble / Mallon Statement, 1998). Although it is uncertain as to how this statement would be implemented in practice, it certainly seems to suggest that Northern Ireland tourism and the NITB will receive strong representation. However, one interviewee from the Department of Tourism, Sport and Recreation is of the opinion that greater representation for Northern Ireland tourism must be matched by more funding contributions:

> In relation to the new North-South body calls have been made that the North and South are to be equally represented. If equal representation is established in terms of control of the new institution and equal representation in terms of balance and diversity of traditions, North and South, is to be fulfilled, there is a feeling that this will have to be matched or met with equal funding contributions and staffing.

Although tensions have also existed in relation to the imbalance between the boards in that BF could be perceived as being the dominant partner, tourism interests in the south of Ireland also have benefits to gain from co-operating with the NITB. Within Northern Ireland good tourist products and attractions do exist and being able to market them as one package will benefit BF as more tourists will be attracted to the island of Ireland. The value of being able to include the tourist products and attractions of Northern Ireland within an all-Ireland package is illustrated by the comments of one interviewee from the Department of Tourism, Sport and Recreation:

> The TBI adds the strengths of the tourism product of all-Ireland. There are advantages in including the products of Northern Ireland, for example, the Giant's Causeway for one is a very important tourist icon and there are not many icons in Ireland. The Giants Causeway is synonymous with Ireland and being able to promote it in one package will bring tourists to all of Ireland. The peace process and being able to include Northern Ireland's golf courses are also positive advantages for BF.

Co-operative Competition

Although the tourist boards are working together in partnership, the NITB and BF have found it difficult to co-operate while they still see each other as competitors. In certain areas of co-operation competitive tensions have created feelings of suspicion and distrust and inhibited the development of the partnership. One area in which competition between the boards has raised difficulties is in the joint marketing of the island of Ireland. In practice the tourist boards have co-operated well together when marketing Ireland in the global markets in America, Australia or the continent. However, in the home market tensions have come to the fore between individuals who wish to promote either the North or South of Ireland and who essentially see the tourist boards to be in competition. The views of one interviewee from the NITB reflect on the difficulties of operating the partnership in the home markets:

> In the Foreign markets for example in Sydney, California or New York we work hand-in-glove with BF and the main objective is to get the tourists to Ireland. In the market personalities come into the equation and there are markets where our overseas staff have a perfect relationship with BF and that is the situation in the majority of cases. But there are some markets where there is a bit of friction, competition and jealously and that is something which we have to watch, but it is human nature and we cannot overcome that entirely. The basic scenario is that the further away from

> home you get people the easier it is to present a united front. Once you
> come into the home markets we have a competitive approach. In the
> British market BF have their list of operators and the NITB have their list
> and partnership is not that apparent.

This interview shows that working together in an environment of
competition and where the organisations perceive each other as a threat can
create difficulties. In the relationship between the tourist boards,
competition has in some cases accentuated the feelings of distrust and
suspicion and created obstacles to partnership development. BF and the
NITB are mindful that they are in competition and that this can distort the
focus of the partnership as the boards feel they have to carefully monitor
the movements of the other.

Competitive tensions between tourism interests in the North and
South of Ireland have also come to the fore at the local level and created
difficulties in developing cross-border tourism projects. In the early days of
co-operation in the mid 1980s, tensions were evident when tourism
interests were concerned that cross-border projects may lead to a decline in
tourist numbers in their area. Tourism interests in the South of Ireland (BF,
RTA's and the industry) were reluctant to work towards the development
of certain cross-border tourism projects in the 1980s because they felt this
may encourage tourists to travel into Northern Ireland. As tourism interests
in the South of Ireland perceived the North as a threat to their industry, this
created a difficult environment to develop cross-border projects.

In co-operation tensions and conflicts have been raised between
the boards which have caused problems in the development and operation
of the partnership. It must be recognised that the tourist boards are
different organisations operating in different jurisdictions, which to date
have been working together on a loose co-operative basis. Under this
relationship the boards have had a considerable degree of autonomy to
work towards their own interests. However, it is argued that if a more
formal partnership or integrative structure was established, this may create
further problems of competition between the North and South of Ireland.
The following analysis on the potential for increased tension and conflict if
one tourist board was established has come from one interviewee from the
NITB:

> Now the two tourist boards are separate and we can do our own thing and
> look after the interests of our own but if the relationship is based more on

integration, hard decisions will have to be made. For example, on what side of the border might a new hotel be built? and in what part of Ireland will a tour operator organise a package? There are similarities in the cross-border relationship between the tourist boards and the Industrial Development Board and the Industrial Development Authority who are competing for incoming business.

Different Organisational Cultures

Cultural differences are reflected in the approaches to the management and administration of funds and this has caused tensions between tourism interests North and South. In the NITB there is a strict approach towards the management and regulation of funds, to strongly abide by accounting principles, whereas in BF the attitude is more relaxed. The approach of the NITB to funding has caused considerable frustration with tourism interests in the south of Ireland and created difficulties when developing cross-border projects. One interviewee from an RTA reflects on his experience of co-operating with NITB and comments that the cultural differences between north and south are difficult to reconcile, if not impossible:

> I was a member of a board which was a Company Limited by Guarantee charged with implementing a cross-border tourism project which was 50% owned by Bord Fáilte and 50% by Northern Ireland Tourist Board. But the Northern Ireland Tourist Board could not get their heads administratively around giving us the grants in time without creating a million questions, they had no capacity to be pragmatic. Our experience of trying to draw down money was just phenomenal and this caused frustrations and tensions within the company. Even on the day when we were handing over the company in crisp condition the person in the Northern Ireland Tourist Board, who administered our grants, sent word that there was a fax machine that could have been subject to a grant, which in the event was not. But the question was, where was the fax machine? and nothing about the fact that we were closing down a cross-border company and that it was a shame. But that absolutely typifies the approach of the Northern Ireland Tourist Board, they frighten me in terms of their bureaucratic red tape. In my experience you cannot merge the gungo-ho-ness of Bord Fáilte, and Bord Fáilte in southern terms is recognised as not being very gungo-ho at all, with the over zealousness of Northern Ireland Tourist Board.

Different Partner Priorities

In the partnership between the NITB and BF, both boards have different priorities in the type of tourist products or attractions they wish to see developed and promoted. Therefore, when the boards work together to discuss the development of projects common agreement cannot always be found. For this reason certain cross-border projects are not established or maintained as they do not have the support of both boards. Due to the different priorities of the tourist boards some cross-border projects have had to be discontinued as one interviewee from a RTA recalls:

> One of the reasons why the Christian Heritage Promotions project had to close was that on the Northern Ireland Tourist Boards scale of priorities that sort of cultural tourism was so far down the list they were not worried about it at all. Bord Fáilte, on the other hand, maybe because the south of Ireland is a much bigger geographic area or has a more developed tourism product, would tend to cherish all the products equally and maintain diversity. Northern Ireland Tourist Board have a clear view of what they are going to spend their money on and nothing else. The project needed the support of both boards and as a consequence it collapsed.

Following on from this argument, cross-border co-operation is made even more complex given that the tourist boards are currently at different stages of development. It has been discussed in the previous section that as tourism in the South of Ireland has reached a certain stage of maturity, the role of BF should now be refined to a marketing organisation. On other hand, although the recent Corporate Plan 1998-2001 envisages NITB operating only as a marketing organisation, tourism in Northern Ireland has yet to reach maturity and as a result the NITB still maintains a significant development function. The difference in tourism life cycles has created difficulties for the tourism boards in finding areas of common cause. This view is supported by one interviewee who comments that:

> The different life cycles of development make partnership very difficult to operate in practice. In Northern Ireland major investment is required and more money is needed to generate the tourism product and tourism development. Tourism in the south of Ireland is on a different life cycle with major tourism investments being undertaken in the last ten to fifteen years. The tourism needs in the south are very different. In this case it is difficult to develop needs on a co-operative basis and develop greater

commonality. Indeed, because of the different life cycles there is an argument to suggest that the current loose relationship should remain and that more integration is not feasible.

The Partnership Decision Making Process in the Relationship between the Northern Ireland Tourist Board and Bord Fáilte

A Formal Decision Making Process

In the initial stages of the relationship between the NITB and BF tensions between the two organisations made it very difficult for an open and effective partnership process to be developed. These tensions were focused around the problem of competition, in that both organisations found it difficult to develop partnership at a time when they both perceived each other as a threat. Coupled to this, tensions were heightened as BF did not wish to develop partnership with the NITB as they believed association with the troubles would effect tourism numbers in the South of Ireland. Within this environment the decision making process became very difficult as the tensions and suspicions between the boards permeated down to individuals at cross-border meetings. The views of one interviewee from BF reflect on the negotiating positions in the decision making process and the attitudes of the boards to co-operation at that time:

> The fundamental issue in the partnership, as I would have seen it, was economic and I took a very strong view on this, that these were two separate economic entities. In relation to the benefits of tourism which related to the growth of GDP, employment and balance of payments, Northern Ireland was a competitor as far as I was concerned. So I took a very strong view at that stage that we were not going to make it easier for any competitor to steal our business and I presume NITB would have felt the same way and there would be no hard feelings about that.

In the initial stages of co-operation decision making between the boards was mainly conducted in committees composed of members of the board and senior executives from both organisations who met only three or four times a year. As the relationship between the boards was clouded in tension, members of the organisations found it difficult to engage in an open and effective decision making process. One member from BF recalls that although representatives from each board met at the committee stage, the decision making process was really artificial in nature:

> In the initial stages of co-operation the tourist boards largely ignored each other. In the south we did not have any interest at all in what the Northern Ireland Tourist Board were doing. We occasionally had contact with people from the north. I remember the Chief Executive of the Northern Ireland Tourist Board coming to the south years ago and he went around a tour of the country fishing and we enjoyed surges up to the north. But by in large there was really no discussion in terms of, what are you doing?, are there any mechanisms where we can benefit in what you are doing and vice-a-versa? And really for years that was the case.

This interviewee highlights the difficulties in facilitating a partnership decision making process when each of the partners perceive each other as a threat. In such cases although personal relationships may be developed between the partners, the decision making process is artificial as individuals are not willing to fully engage in open discussion. At the committee level the decision making process between members of BF and the NITB was conducted on a formal and structured basis, meetings were very focused and had a clear agenda which each board strictly adhered to. In this approach decision making became static, leaving little opportunity to exchange information and share experience. As a result, limited progress was made and the partnership could not develop.

At the local project level, between members of district council, RTAs, representative of BF and the NITB who administered the INTERREG and IFI programmes and local tourism interests, the partnership process has also tended to be based on a structured and formal basis. Political sensitivities surrounding cross-border co-operation have impacted on the co-operation and made it difficult for partnership relationships to be developed. One member of a cross-border project describes the problems that have been faced when trying to establish a decision making process and develop partnership relationships in a sensitive political environment:

> I am amazed at how stiff the representatives from some tourism organisations at the local and regional level are when they engage on a cross-border basis. But it is only now that I am beginning to think that it was probably because it was their first cross-border contact. That rigidity then comes through in the decision making process when making a

contribution towards the design and implementation of a project. If you are intellectually constipated you are not going to deliver your best and the projects will be retarded.

In cross-border projects one way to address the problems of political sensitivities and the tensions surrounding the imbalance between partners is to allow for equality and parity between north and south. It has been discussed earlier in this chapter, that giving equal representation to northern tourism interests has helped to dampen the political sensitivities of cross-border co-operation and allay fears that northern tourism interests will be not be over shadowed by the larger, more dominant southern industry. In the INTERREG programme, for instance, joint committees have been established between an equal number of government representatives to provide a balanced decision making process. Furthermore, certain safeguards have also been set in place to ensure that projects are fairly and equally developed between north and south.

However, one of the problems with this approach is that it creates a very formal and structured decision making process which restricts the development of personal relations and open discussion. In the INTERREG programme formality in decision making has hindered the development of a cross-border partnership process, as the comments of one interviewee indicate:

> INTERREG is a government body, the application forms for INTERREG go to the Department of Finance and then are distributed to all the representative departments who deal with them in a North-South INTERREG Intergovernmental Tourism Committee. But INTERREG gives lip service to the idea of cross-border co-operation and the development of a partnership process and building personal relationships. They have this joint budget so they don't get into each others hair and it is really a case of we have our money and you have yours.

The problem with trying to achieve equal representation in the management of cross-border projects is that it can be strictly applied in too many circumstances. In these instances parity in representation can hinder the partnership decision making process as it emphasises rigidity and formality, not allowing partners to engage on a personal, informal and open basis.

Seeking to achieve parity in cross-border relationships, however, is not only the intention of the tourist boards. Some funding programmes, for example the IFI, stipulate a preference for parity in cross-border arrangements. However, one representative of the IFI expresses similar sentiments that parity in relationships and decision making creates formality and rigidity, restricting further partnership development:

> One of the criticisms that I would have of the IFI programme is that it focuses too much in establishing parallel relationships. That you must have two groups from the north meeting two groups from the south or three officials from the north and three officials from the south. Under this approach the opportunity for synergy is limited.

When co-operation in tourism is undertaken at the project level between district councils in the North of Ireland and RTAs in the South, there is a need to adopt a careful and nurtured approach. At the project level the role of personalities and personal relationships become more important as individuals undertake cross-border contact almost on a daily basis. Therefore, political tensions and feelings of distrust and suspicion between individuals can have an immediate and detrimental impact on the partnership. When political sensitivities between individuals are critical to the success of a co-operation, it is important that individuals process the necessary language skills. By using the proper language this helps to avoid raising political tensions and allows for greater personal relationships to be established between members, as one representative of a RTA explains:

> Growing a cross-border partnership takes incredible people skills and incredible patience and far more time than people believe. It is about language skills, it is about semantics, it is about calling an initiative a project and not a programme. For reconciliation I don't think we have the language or the feeling for it. If I met six representatives from Fermanagh on a tourism delegation I am not sure that I am properly attuned into what can make them comfortable and to have a proper meeting of minds. It takes language skills to deal with all the sensitivities and nuances of cross-border relationships.

Moves Towards a More Open and Informal Process

Within the last number of years however, the decision making process has been re-invigorated and there is now more opportunity for members from each of the boards to meaningfully engage. With the cease-fires, government involvement in the peace process and the development of a joint marketing programme, decision making is open and conducted at all levels between the boards, not just at committee level. What has been important in the last number of years is that more urgency has been applied to the partnership and this has been transferred to the decision making process. Now the issue in decision making is to find a solution, not to protect priorities and this has given both the partners and the process greater energy.

In a similar vein, greater urgency has also been applied to the partnership decision making process at the project level. Over the last number of years as more tourism projects have been developed by the boards this has given the process greater energy and drive. Through a period of working closer together on a greater number of projects, with a limited number of personnel, the partnership process at project level is also becoming more open and fluid. Better relationships have now been established which are facilitating a more effective decision making process and greater synergy. The comments of one interviewee reflect on this new, transformed decision making process:

> The structured and ordered process has been changing almost out of necessity because the number of people working in the boards are diminishing. Therefore, there are fewer people who can hop into a car and go to a meeting. What is happening behind the scenes is that because the number of people involved on a professional level in tourism on both sides of the border is relatively small, personal relationships are developing to such an extent that people are picking up the phone and if there is a problem to be solved, instead of sending it down to committee, it is being solved over the phone or over a drink. This has come about project by project and initiative by initiative and through greater necessity, better personal relationships and more effective decision making processes are being established.

The nature of the cross-border programmes have also changed in that some new initiatives focus more on synergy and developing the partnership process between members than on establishing parity. The Peace and Reconciliation Programme introduced in 1995 reflects this new approach in that it seeks to build better relationships and a more open decision making between cross-border partners. One interviewee from an RTA comments on the operation of the Peace and Reconciliation Programme:

Peace and Reconciliation monies are much more driven by the experience of cross-border partnerships and are just as interested in the number of cross-border meetings as the actual programme. They want to know about the meetings, about the relationship, about how often do you come north or south. We are drawing down a claim from Peace and Reconciliation and we must make sure we note that the tourism officer from Fermanagh District Council was at all the meetings. It was more important to do that than anything.

In the last few years the partnership process in cross-border co-operation has been undergoing transition. Decision making is less structured and ordered and is now conducted within a more informal process allowing the partners to open up and talk about problematic issues. Working on more projects over a period of time with limited staff, has helped to build working relationships and lay the necessary foundations to set up an open decision making process. Although building good relationships and an effective decision making process has been difficult and has taken a long time, one interviewee is of the opinion that this slow transitional process has been necessary for partnership development at the local project level, 'looking back, the period in the early 1990s can now be seen as a necessary kind of incubation period, where people got to know one another, let relationships build up, build dialogue and accept one another's processes'.

However, it must be pointed out that not all areas of partnership between the NITB and BF operate an open decision making process. In some cases decision making still remains only at executive level conducted through committees. Under this formal process there is little opportunity for open decision making among other members of the boards, who in effect do not undertake much cross-border co-operation or contact. One interviewee comments that partnership decision making at the executive committee level creates too much parallelism and restricts partnership development and synergy:

> The level of meeting and decision making between north and south in some cases still remains purely at the Chief Executive level or between personnel out in the markets. There are around 120 people in BF and 20 people in the product side, people responsible for outdoor pursuits, equestrian activities and cultural heritage but, with the exception of a small number of areas, most of them would not have any co-operation or

meetings with the NITB. The NITB produce their own product brochures and the southern people produce theirs and that is how it is.

Operational Matters in the Partnership Relationship between the Northern Ireland Tourist Board and Bord Fáilte

Strategic Issues

It must be remembered that co-operative partnerships are very loose in nature as authority is retained by each partner organisation, the interrelationships are informal and there is no commonly defined mission, structure or planning effort. Therefore, it is clear that co-operative partnerships by their design and nature do not have a common overall strategy.

Currently the partnership between the tourist boards is based on an informal, co-operative relationship meaning no overall strategy exists. In fact if a common strategy for the NITB and BF was formulated this would take the tourist boards into a more formal and integrative relationship. Developing a more integrative relationship, however, does not come under the remit of the tourist boards, and the emergence of a formal cross-border partnership body is a political decision. A common overall strategy for the partnership between NITB and BF is a decision which has to be made at government level and until such time the partnership will remain on a co-operative basis, as one interviewee from the NITB remarks:

> The formulation of one overall strategy for the tourist boards is a political decision as one board would be required to implement that strategy. At present there are two separate organisations with two different remits and the separate strategies are communicated to each other to allow for correlation and scope for a common approach. But the NITB does not want to pre-empt any political decision.

Although there may be no overall strategy the tourist boards do co-operate on matters of strategic direction and development. There is close liaison between the boards on strategic aims and objectives in relation to marketing approaches for targeted and segmented markets. In this way the tourist boards are provided the opportunity to identify common areas of strategy and develop strategic focus for the partnership. The development of a common strategic focus for the boards has been possible as the separate strategies of the NITB and BF are broadly similar, as one interviewee from the Department of Tourism, Sport and Recreation explains:

> Both strategies of the tourist boards are relatively similar. Each board wants to maximise the number of high spending tourists, deal with the problems of seasonality and to spread the benefits around the country leading to a greater regional balance. The tourism policies and strategies are very similar and there is a great deal of commonality on strategic matters. There is not a great difference in the philosophy of Bord Fáilte and the Northern Ireland Tourist Board and that makes it easier for co-operation.

In the marketing of the island of Ireland both boards have been co-operating to attract the maximum number of tourists to Ireland through the joint programmes known as OTMI and TBI. However, co-operation on strategic issues has largely been based on a loose *ad hoc* basis, making it difficult to formulate and apply a long term strategic vision for marketing. On this basis, concerns have been raised over the issue of sustainability. In co-operating and attracting more tourists to Ireland this may lead to the problems of mass tourism in ten or fifteen years time which could have a detrimental effect on the tourist product. One interviewee is firmly of the opinion that a common overall long term tourism strategy is needed for marketing Ireland:

> Ireland is promoted as a place for the discerning visitor based on the history, culture and green / environmental tourism. But it is turning into a mass market destination. This is not a great idea and the tourist boards need to address this. It is a huge benefit to go into a market place and sell Ireland as one entity without any hang ups about borders. But in my view the issue is to be selective about it. I don't want lager louts. The country needs to look very carefully about what it wants from tourism. The boards must look at a sustainable tourist policy for the island of Ireland that recognises it is not just a numbers game, that our product is unique and could be spoilt.

However, it must be recognised that co-operating in an uncertain political environment has made it difficult to formulate a long term strategic plan. Since the development of the peace process and following the 'Good Friday' Agreement there has been a cloud of uncertainty hanging over cross-border co-operation in tourism, as to whether the boards would be amalgamated into one implementation body or included as one of the 'matters for co-operation'. Even after the Trimble / Mallon statement (1998) which classified the role for tourism, uncertainly still remains on the stability of the 'Good Friday' Agreement and the peace process in general, particularly after the resignation of the Deputy First Minister, the issue of decommissioning and the publication of the Patten report on policing. Operating within this environment has made it impossible for the government departments and the boards to formulate a long term strategy for cross-border co-operation.

In the development of cross-border projects the tourist boards have also found it difficult to formulate a common strategic plan for the border region. One of the problems faced by the boards when seeking to apply a strategic approach is in dealing with the complex environment created by the number of different funding programmes. Within each of the programmes there are different priorities and objectives which have to be met before funding is awarded. With three or four funding programmes operating in the border region this has created confusion and raises difficulties in seeking to adopt a strategic approach. One member of the Department of Tourism, Sport and Recreation comments that due to the number of funding programmes and the difference in their priorities, strategic development is problematic and as a result cross-border tourism programmes are divorced from the main strategy:

> In the Operational Programme for Tourism, Bord Fáilte and the Department have a clear strategic overview of what tourist areas we wish to develop and where that will fit in with other projects for integrated development. However, cross-border programmes are seen as an add on from the Operational Programme and are distanced from the main strategy. One of the main problems is that the INTERREG, Peace and Reconciliation and IFI programmes each have their own particular set of rules and procedures and only certain types of specific projects can be awarded funding. Therefore, a lot of the projects that have been funded have met the requirements of the particular programme and not the needs of tourism development in the border region. Infrastructure has been developed which will not attract visitors and be a successful tourism commercial enterprise.

In the absence of a clear integrated strategy cross-border tourism development has tended to be focused on an *ad hoc*, project led basis.

Projects have been formulated largely in reference to the different funding programmes and not within an integrated strategic plan. Projects have not been developed on a tourism needs basis which leaves many initiatives vulnerable and unsustainable. The problems that have emerged in cross-border tourism development due to the absence of a clear strategy are well illustrated by the comments of one tourism consultant:

> I have been at meetings for cross-border tourism schemes in which Northern Ireland Tourist Board representatives would have said this is not the right project and it is not in the right place but it is driven by the need for the funding programmes (IFI) to spend money in that area. Funding dictates so much that is actually created in tourism. Where funding leads the whole proposition is faulty, the chemistry tends to be weak and the programme is structurally weak. A lot of cross-border co-operation falls into that category and you end up with some heritage project in the border region which attracts no visitors. The potential of funding has led to so much co-operation rather than organic cross-border co-operation which identifies an opportunity, presents a scenario with costings on it to the funders and the funders saying, 'we like the idea guys here is the money to do it.' There are conspicuous examples where it has worked but many examples where it has not. A lot of cross-border projects are driven by the need for the tourist boards just to be seen to be doing something, facilitated by EU and IFI funding, rather than saying this is a tourism product that will attract visitors.

It is clear from this interview that without an overall strategy, cross-border tourism has been developed on a funding led basis, establishing projects which may well collapse when the funding is exhausted. To exacerbate the problems of strategic development in tourism, it is also common that the success of projects is determined by the nature of the relationships between north and south rather than through specific commercial criteria. As political criteria have been used to judge the success of cross-border projects, this has lowered the priority of development based on tourism needs and smothered the importance of strategic development. The comments of one representative of a RTA reflect on the problem of using political criteria to determine the success of projects:

> I have seen so few cross-border projects that work and seen so many that fail. I am using the yardstick of selling more units, that you can say from a quantifiable point of view that they deliver x number of visitors, x number of bed nights and x number of spend per day. But the yardstick used in so

many cross-border projects that have failed is, has it politically worked?, are the councils happy?, is there the minimum number of letters of complaint in the local newspapers? It is a totally different set of standards, a totally different ball game. If you use hard criteria few of the projects are going to pass. But you ask the politicians and they will tell you, 'cross-border co-operation is going really well, we have a great relationship with Cavan or Fermanagh, we are doing great stuff here.' It is dabbling, it is politically safe, it is not being strategically driven by tourism marketers that are trying to bring more visitors to the northern part of Ireland, because that is what we are all about in the border counties.

From the Trimble / Mallon statement in December 1998 tourism has since been identified as a 'matter for co-operation.' New structures have been proposed which would see the creation of a new publicly owned limited company to market the island of Ireland, leaving BF and NITB to carry out certain tourist activities within their own jurisdictions (de Breádún 1988). Although the new structures have yet to be set up and a great deal of uncertainty still surrounds the arrangements, concerns have been raised that the new structures will not address the problem of strategic development. First of all, by maintaining the two tourist boards it is argued that each will be subject to their own separate political pressures which will distort and confuse strategic objectives and create parallel development. The following analysis has come from a tourism consultant:

> I have seen so many good strategies ruined by politics and this could be the situation for the new structures. For instance taking urban tourism, Dublin is a major European City destination and is now very popular, reputably second to Paris or London, that has a lot to offer and you would be foolish not to build on that. But what may happen politically, the strategy would say Belfast should be developed the same rather than saying the strengths of Northern Ireland are the northern coastline and very fine countryside that has not been spoiled like places in the south. There is a danger in trying to achieve too much parallel development. There is a need for an overall common strategy which clearly sets out what the product is and how the boards are going to develop and market that product.

Secondly, another issue that has been raised over the new structures is that strategic development will remain difficult as the two boards will still be focused on the own jurisdictions, looking after their own priorities and not the needs of their tourist industry throughout Ireland.

Inter Partnership Co-operation

The marketing strategy of the NITB is subdivided into three sections each representing different strategies and approaches to partnership. This strategy is centred on a customer base and the markets are segmented corresponding to the opportunities for attracting potential tourists to Northern Ireland. In the first market segment NITB has recognised that there are certain customers from the Republic of Ireland and Great Britain who visit Northern Ireland each year, so for this market the NITB exclusively promotes Northern Ireland as a holiday destination. Secondly, Northern Ireland can also be marketed as an all-Ireland destination and as part of an overall Irish product. In this approach the NITB can co-operate with BF to promote and attract visitors to Northern Ireland who principally travel to visit the traditional tourist centres in the south of Ireland. In the third market segment Northern Ireland, due to historical and cultural links, can also be regarded as a British tourist holiday destination. In this marketing policy NITB partner with the BTA to attract tourists from the long haul markets of, say, Australia, New Zealand and Canada. Therefore, in relation to the different approaches to marketing the NITB seeks to market Northern Ireland exclusively or to co-operate with the BTA or BF. Under this approach the NITB, through partnership, is able to increase the marketing and promotion of Northern Ireland and to attract a higher number of potential tourists.

However, in this marketing strategy tensions have been raised over the twin approach adopted by the NITB. In the south of Ireland there are concerns that the NITB is confusing and distorting the tourism image promoted in the partnership with BF. It is held that the NITB in co-operating with the BTA, is promoting two different tourism images and this is diluting and confusing the all-Ireland marketing strategy developed with BF. The comments of one interviewee from the Department of Tourism, Sport and Recreation capture these concerns, 'there is a feeling in the South within the Department and Bord Fáilte that the Northern Ireland Tourist Board are riding two horses and are making a tourist product that is essentially Irish, more British'.

Although certain tensions have been raised, the bilateral approach of the NITB can also benefit BF who can partner with the BTA to promote the British Isles as a tourist destination for long haul customers. With BF and the BTA working together, the south of Ireland can attract tourists who visit Britain and London first of all, but are also willing to see other parts of the islands. BF can then tap into the marketing potential of London and Britain and promote Ireland as an additional package.

Moreover, in a similar facilitative and directive approach to the relationship between the NITB and BF, both governments also see the partnership with the BTA as part of the wider political process. The 'Good Friday' Agreement has also included provision for a 'Council of the Isles' in which Regional Assemblies and Parliaments of Scotland, Wales and Northern Ireland are to work together in a Council with the government of the Republic of Ireland to address common problems and issues. Although the remit of the Council has yet to be finalised it is likely that tourism will be included as an area in which the Regional Assemblies and Irish Government can work together to promote the British Isles as a tourism destination. The comments of one interviewee from the Department of Tourism, Sport and Recreation provides some insight into a possible future role for the Council:

> Just like government involvement in North-South co-operation, movements have also been made to facilitate a tourism aspect to the Council of the Isles. In this approach Ireland, North and South, can jointly market the British Isles with the British Tourist Authority particularly in areas such as Australia and New Zealand. It will then be possible to develop and market tourism packages and tours of the British Isles to attract long haul tourists.

National Versus Local Tourism Development

In the co-operation between the tourist boards tension and conflict has developed between the national and local or regional level. Tensions have been raised in the north and south of Ireland over what role local interests should play in the development and promotion of tourism. Due to the wider availability of funding for tourism projects under programmes such as LEADER, INTERREG, Peace and Reconciliation and the IFI's tourism initiative, local and regional organisations have been eager to develop tourism as a means to regenerate their areas. Local and regional interests have developed tourism attractions and products, formulated brochures and marketed their localities. However, in this role the local and regional interests have come into conflict with the tourist boards which see that the development and promotion of tourism should be conducted at the national level. It is held that local tourism interests have little experience in tourism and are fragmenting and distorting the marketing strategy. One interviewee from the NITB comments on the difficulties and problems with local tourism interests becoming more assertive in tourism promotion and development:

> One of the difficulties when you are talking partnership is that many local groups in the border region see tourism as a panacea for regenerating their local parish or region. All the local tourism groups are scrambling to get brochures, employ consultants to do market research, go to trade shows and do promotions. We (Northern Ireland Tourist Board) have had a long battle over this issue over the last two years arguing that this is not the way to go. In terms of marketing you have to put your best foot forward, to promote the most attractive, sexy, glamorous elements of what will bring people to Ireland and you try and incorporate that within these groups. Local groups cannot go to all the trade shows to promote their own patch, you have to do it co-operatively. This approach gets a better return from that investment rather than duplicating repetitively.

Although the EU and IFI programmes have helped to facilitate greater co-operation between north and south and assisted in developing the border region, not all tourism interests should be promoted at the local level. Under the INTERREG programme in particular, both boards have faced difficulty in trying to convince local and regional interests that tourism is more efficiently and effectively promoted at a higher spatial scale. In co-operating on the INTERREG programme the boards have undergone a learning process and have developed a common approach to accessing the tourism potential of the border region. In this approach the NITB and BF have both been reluctant to fund cross-border projects which do not have clear tourism potential.

However, there is a possibility that the INTERREG 3 programme may be administered by the Cross-Border Local Authority Networks, the Irish Central Border Areas Network (ICBAN), North-West Regional Cross-Border Group (NWRCBG) and the East Border Region Committee (EBRC), as discussed in the pervious chapter. These Networks are partnerships of local authorities in the border region who are working together to seek to improve the economic and social problems in the border region. If these networks are charged with the responsibility of implementing the INTERREG 3 programme there are concerns that projects will be funded which are not specific tourism needs. There is an element of unease among the tourist boards that the Networks, not being experienced in tourism development, will fund local cross-border projects which will not be sustainable and will fragment tourism promotion. One interviewee from the NITB is concerned that the learning process undertaken by the two boards in accessing the tourism potential of the border region will be a wasted effort especially when considering that the Networks will have to undergo the same process:

> The Northern Ireland Tourist Board and Bord Fáilte would be well developed in their thinking as to what tourism entails. People think tourism is easy and that anyone can do it, you just stick a sign out the front door and the tourists will be queuing up. The institutions EBRC, ICBAN and the NWRCBG will never score on a tourism assessment. I have sat in on a number of meetings of the groups and they have a very basic understanding of tourism. They want to develop tourism in their area but they really have no concept of what it involves. I would find it frustrating if they end up with the money and started to undermine the years of work that the two boards have achieved. The Networks are four to five years behind and whether they want to go through the same learning process in tourism assessment of the border region and developing a common approach that the boards went though is another matter. The two boards have gone through a very steep learning curve and made progress and I would not like to see that wasted.

Positive Publicity

It has been mentioned earlier in this chapter that funding has been made available for the boards if co-operative arrangements were established. Therefore, it has been to the advantage of both boards to undertake positive publicity on the partnership relationship to attract more funding as one member of the NITB comments:

> Positive publicity for partnership between the boards can be very good for funding purposes as a lot of funding from the EU and IFI programmes is awarded on the basis that the boards are co-operating and working well together.

Although positive publicity may be seen as beneficial to improving relations, sharing experience and attracting funding, there is a sense that the NITB needs to be careful and not promote partnership with the south of Ireland too loudly. The NITB in partnership with BF, is still mindful that it is co-operating against a political backdrop and that a significant section of the Unionist Community do not wish to develop deeper links with the south of Ireland. In this case NITB is wary of actively promoting links with BF and conscious of not upsetting political sensitivities. The danger of the NITB promoting the partnership too publicly are recorded by one interviewee:

> If positive publicity in cross-border co-operation was conducted by Bord Fáilte this would not capture the imagination but the Northern Ireland Tourist Board on the other hand, have to watch their backs. There is a political backdrop to all of this and sections of the Unionist Community are still very wary about cross-border co-operation. If NITB were to promote greater co-operation with the south of Ireland and to use money for positive publicity this could cause ructions and they would probably have to spend even more money to conduct a public relations damage limitation exercise.

Conclusion

From analysing the relationship between the NITB and BF certain conclusions can be drawn over what are the underlying conditions impacting on the performance of Regional / National Transjurisdictional partnerships. First of all, this case study of the tourist boards shows that co-operating within a turbulent political environment and against a background of terrorist violence is an extremely difficult task. Political tensions create feelings of distrust and suspicion which cause agencies to minimise the extent of the relationship. Operating within a tense political environment has also created difficulties, particularly for the NITB, which is conscious of not upsetting political sensitivities and is apprehensive in its approach to co-operation. Peace and a stable political environment has been pivotal to the partnership between the tourist boards as the peace process has helped to weaken political tension and open up the relationship. However, random outbreaks of violence are placing strain on co-operation and essentially, partnership development depends on a stable peace.

In co-operating within a tense environment the EU and IFI have acted as convenors in bringing the boards closer together and facilitating greater partnership. It must be pointed out that the availability of external funding from the EU and IFI has acted to bring the boards together. By making the development of co-operative linkages a requirement for funding programmes, financial incentives have contributed to establishing and maintaining the partnership. In recent years the relationship has been given greater impetus by the two governments who have been actively seeking greater co-operation. The importance of government involvement in, and political will to support, Regional / National partnerships can be highlighted by contrasting the relationship between the NITB and BF which existed in four of five years ago when the tourist boards enjoyed a great deal of flexibility in cross-border arrangements and demoted the importance of co-operation.

Given that the tourist boards will benefit more by working together than individually, a more supportive environment has been created which has helped to drive the partnership forward. As the tourist boards will mutually benefit from co-operation this acts like an undercurrent in all aspects of the partnership. Despite facing certain difficulties, the partnership between the NITB and BF has been able to override problematic issues because co-operation is to the benefit of both organisations.

The imbalance between the tourist boards has also created difficulties for the partnership in the implementation of joint programmes and by raising sensitivities among members of the NITB who feel overshadowed by BF, the larger and more dominant partner. However, allowing northern tourism interests equal representation in decision making and more favourable promotional coverage has helped to quell tensions and sensitivities.

The experience of the NITB and BF has shown that the members of Regional / National partnerships can perceive each other as a threat. As the tourist boards and individuals within the organisations regard each other to be in competition, this has in certain cases, inhibited co-operation and increased tensions and feelings of suspicion and distrust. Differences in culture, priorities and stages of development between partner organisations can also create problems and frustrations in seeking to establish a common approach for partnership development.

In the decision making process between partners operating at the Regional / National Transjurisdictional level it is important that an open and fluid decision making process is enacted. Until the last number of years decision making between the NITB and BF has been conducted in a very structured and ordered fashion with both partners feeling reluctant to engage on a cross-border basis. However, due to greater government involvement and by working together over a period of time with a limited number of staff, better relationships have been established and this has provided a greater opportunity to develop an open and effective process.

Although co-operative partnerships by their design and nature do not contain a common strategy there is an argument to suggest that the relationship between the NITB and BF would benefit from the formulation of an overall strategy. Without a common strategy concerns have been raised over the sustainability of Irish tourism and the extent of co-operation between head offices in Ireland. In the absence of such a strategy cross-border projects have been developed on a funding led basis and not in relation to tourism needs. In this case projects have been established which may well have limited tourism potential and may not be economically viable.

In the development and implementation of cross-border tourism projects tensions have been raised between the national and local or regional level. Due to the availability of funding, cross-border projects have been established by a plethora of local groups which is fragmenting the development and promotion of tourism at the national level. The tourist boards have raised concerns that further devolution of tourism development will impinge on progress that has been made to date.

The experience of the partnership between the NITB and BF has supported the view that co-operating with other initiatives and partnerships will increase mutual benefit. Although there are tensions over the linkages established between the NITB and BTA, BF can also adopt a bilateral approach. To maximise the marketing potential of each area of the British Isles, the NITB, BF and BTA can establish a three way partnership to attract tourists from distant global markets.

Finally, developing positive publicity for the partnership has worked to attract funding for the boards and has the potential to develop a better partnership relationship. On the other hand however, it must be remembered that the political environment still remains tense and the NITB needs to be wary of upsetting political sensitivities by promoting greater links with the South of Ireland.

7 A Synthetic Model for Partnership Governance and the Wider Implications of Partnership for Public Policy

Introduction

To date very little is known and written about the conditions in which partnerships operate and how they affect performance. Researchers who have studied partnership performance have largely focused on identifying conditions for success or outlining steps of best practice. Research in this area however, has tended to be vague as partnerships are largely regarded as one entity. This has brought very little added value to the debate as partnerships are very diverse and complex structures. There are many different kinds of partnerships, they create different structures, involve different partners, set themselves different goals and operate under varying conditions. Each initiative requires a different approach and it has therefore become extremely difficult to outline steps of best practice as there is no-one partnership model. Therefore, in any discussion over the performance of partnerships it must be recognised that partnerships are diverse arrangements which operate under different and varying conditions.

Having evaluated the three case studies representing the different coalition building processes of co-operation, co-ordination and collaboration, and tested their experience against the framework set out in Chapter Two, it can be concluded that examining the conditions which affect the performance of partnerships is a difficult task. The analysis of the partnership case studies has presented a varied, lengthy and complex range of conditions. In certain instances, theory outlined in the literature such as the structure of stakeholder organisations (Rogers *et al*, 1982; Aldrich, 1977) did not apply to the case studies, whereas, in other instances, there was no corresponding literature for the conditions presented in the case studies. Autonomy and responsibility, inter partnership / organisational co-operation or the project and programme based approaches, are all conditions which were highlighted in the case studies but which had no reference in the literature. In addition, there are a limited number of conditions set out in the literature which apply to all three case studies.

Considering the complexity and variety of conditions which affect the performance of partnerships, it is the aim of this chapter to provide more in-depth analysis by developing a synthetic model for partnership governance. The model outlines the complex range of conditions which affect the performance of partnerships and these are subdivided into micro and macro conditions. Micro conditions are those which have been drawn from the analysis of the case studies and macro conditions refer to the wider conditions and policy implications of the research. Following the presentation and analysis of the model the chapter concludes with a discussion on the future of partnership governance.

A Synthetic Model for Partnership Governance

The model (Figure 7.1) shows the conditions which affect the performance of partnership governance at the micro and macro levels and the interrelationship between the conditions. At the micro level the conditions are clearly separated into four categories partnership operation, stakeholder / organisational, decision making and contextual conditions and within those categories are the conditions which affect partnership performance. However, what is also clear is that each category is multi-directional and is interrelated to the other and this highlights the complexity of conditions which affect partnership performance. In this way the model does not set out a recipe listing the sixteen important conditions for partnership success, but instead acknowledges the interrelationship of the conditions and how they act together to affect performance.

The model also outlines three macro conditions which refer to the wider tensions in the public policy arena which influence and impact on the development of partnerships. By outlining the conditions which affect the performance of partnerships, this model is important as it helps policy makers and stakeholders to understand the diversity of partnerships and the environment in which they operate. By understanding partnerships and their environment, public policies and the actions of stakeholder organisations can then be shaped to take these conditions into account. Ultimately, this can help to improve partnership performance. To begin to examine the model, this section starts by explaining each of the micro conditions, how they interrelate and affect the performance of partnership governance.

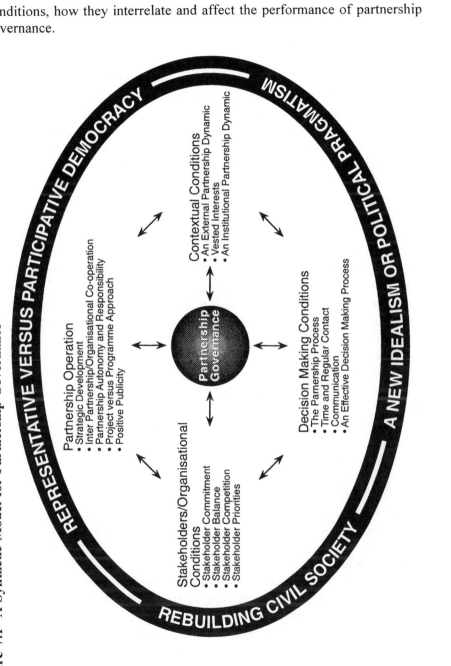

Figure 7.1 A Synthetic Model for Partnership Governance

(1) Partnership Operation

Strategic Development

The formulation of a strategy is outlined as an important condition which affects partnership performance as it brings the partners together and is a foundation from which operational functions of a partnership emanate. Partnership arrangements are difficult to manage as they involve a range of different stakeholders from different backgrounds. Indeed, the complexities of partnerships are clearly highlighted when reflecting on the development of the Local Authority Networks and the District Partnerships. In these case studies the partnerships have struggled to operate a programme of development as the diverse interests among the partners have caused confusion and created unwieldy organisations. The Local Authority Networks have suffered as each partner council has been pursuing local interests, while tensions and suspicions among different sectors has caused difficulties in the District Partnerships. However, the formulation of a common strategy has marked a watershed in the development of the partnerships. The strategies have forged a common purpose among the different partners, set out specific objectives and made the long term aims for development clear to all partners. Furthermore, when the different participants actually sat down to the task of formulating a strategy, this provided a focus, helping them to interact and contributing to the gelling process.

In the formulation of a strategy, evidence suggests that it is essential to undertake an extensive consultation process to involve the wider community. The importance of adopting an inclusive strategic planning process is well represented when comparing the experience of the District Partnerships and the NWRCBG. The strategy developed by the NWRCBG failed to be successfully implemented as it was not formulated in consultation with the local community. First of all, the basis of the NWRCBG's strategy, the North West Study, was formulated for the partnership by a group of private consultants which deprived the partners of ownership. As members of the NWRCBG did not develop the strategy they did not have a clear commitment to work towards its implementation. Secondly, the consultants had no first hand knowledge of the local area so they brought little added value to the planning process. The strategy sought to rebuild a regional policy for the North West but it was not integrated with the actions of other stakeholders namely, government departments and agencies, the business sector and community and voluntary groups. As a result, the strategy which was presented under the INTERREG programme was too ambitious, not integrated with the needs of the region and was refused EU funding by the two governments.

On the other hand, the District Partnerships adopted a wide consultation process to seek the views of their local constituency. In this proactive consultation approach the views of the most marginalised were collected and incorporated into the local strategies. This allowed the community to take ownership and ensured the strategies would 'make a difference' by reflecting local needs.

Following the failure of the North West Strategy to receive funding, the NWRCBG endorsed a similar consultation process to take into account the views of other stakeholders. The NWRCBG adopted a facilitative approach by encouraging greater involvement and participation and seeking to ensure the strategic plan will be integrated, relevant to the needs of the region and complementary with government policy.

The experience of the case studies, however, does not suggest that the deployment of consultants will lead to the failure of a strategic planning process. Evidence from the District Partnerships and the Local Authority Networks points out that there are instances in which the consultants can contribute to partnership success. In the District Partnerships consultants focused board members on strategic issues and offered advice and an independent viewpoint in discussions. In the Local Authority Networks consultants were able to provide assistance in specific areas in which they had greater expertise for example, statistical analysis. It can be seen that in each case the partnerships required a facilitative or specific role for the consultants, but insisted that decision making over strategy formulation was solely undertaken by board members. In short, consultants can improve the performance of partnerships provided the ownership of the strategy is centred and grounded with the board members.

Inter Partnership / Organisational Co-operation

As partnerships need to adopt an inclusive approach in the planning process, a similar approach must be applied in the implementation of the strategy. The Local Authority Networks have learned that focusing solely on their own particular sub-region each strategy is likely to have a detrimental effect on development of the border region. Formulating separate strategies induces competition between sub-regions, creates duplication of effort and leads to a zero-sum game. However, by establishing links between each of the Networks a common strategy for the border region can be formulated which will support and complement the specific needs of each sub-region.

In a similar vein, the District Partnerships have sought to establish links with other local initiatives developed through LEADER, the ABSAGS and the district councils. It is thought that by creating co-operative actions each initiative will be informed of the aims and objectives of the other, so an effective strategy and more focused approach to development can be undertaken.

By establishing links with other initiatives, evidence from the case studies suggests that partnerships can also double efforts in programme implementation. To improve programme output the partnership between the NITB and BF has established a tripartite relationship with the BTA. In this arrangement each tourism organisation can forward their own special attractions to compose a common package to encourage tourists from long haul destinations to visit Ireland and Britain.

Partnership Autonomy and Responsibility

In seeking to implement their strategy or programmes, tensions have been raised between the partnerships and central government. The Local Authority Networks and the District Partnerships have come into conflict with central government departments and the NIPB respectively, as they feel the operation of the partnership is being unnecessarily restricted to ensure that control rests with central government. In the District Partnerships there was concern in being overburdened by financial accountability measures and bureaucracy from the NIPB, which prevented them from adopting local innovative actions and exercising full autonomy. The Networks believed that the British and Irish Governments are unwilling to decentralise authority and so declined to participate in the formulation of strategies or provide financial assistance. In both instances the failure to achieve greater responsibility has created frustrations within the partnerships and tensions with central government.

On the other hand, the case studies have shown that, in seeking greater autonomy, partnerships have to be responsible and more mature in their actions. The NIPB has played a valuable role in the Peace and Reconciliation programme by assisting the fledgling District Partnerships in providing advice and practice in the formulation of strategies. Each of the partnerships had to learn that programmes must be implemented within certain guidelines and financial accountability measures. Likewise the Networks, in order to achieve more responsibility from government, have to demonstrate they can adopt a proactive approach and formulate an integrated strategic plan for the border region.

Ironically in the case of tourism, it is the partnership between the two tourist boards at the national level which is unwilling to grant autonomy to partnerships established at the local or sub-regional level. Due to the availability of EU and IFI funding for cross-border co-operation, a plethora of partnerships has emerged in the border region seeking to develop and promote tourism in their area. This has caused tension between the local and regional level and the tourist boards who see the emerging partnerships fragmenting the tourism message and distorting development in the border region. Interestingly, conflict has come to the fore between the tourist boards and the Local Authority Networks who are emerging as possible administrators of the INTERREG 3 programme. There are concerns that the Networks, in seeking a greater role in tourism, will inhibit progress in the border region and fragment the promotion of the island of Ireland by marketing their own sub-regions.

The Local Authority Networks and the District Partnerships have pointed to a clear trend in the development of partnerships at the local or regional level. As partnerships become more established and assertive they seek greater autonomy to fulfil their objectives. With greater autonomy however, partnerships must also demonstrate they are mature and can be receptive to the responsibilities of other public bodies.

The Project Versus the Programme Approach

From analysing the development of the case studies evidence is increasingly pointing to the value of the programme based approach for the implementation of partnership initiatives. One of the major difficulties with the project approach is that the partnerships have little responsibility for ensuring that strategic objectives will be fulfilled, which creates an implementation gap. In the District Partnerships the assessment of projects presented a demanding workload, leaving the partners little time to engage their constituents, improve the nature of the projects and to think strategically. Furthermore, under the project based approach the District Partnerships were depending on the local community to formulate applications; as a result, if those from the marginalised sections of the community did not forward an application, their needs could not be addressed. In the relationship between the NITB and BF the project approach has also restricted strategic development. Due to the range of programmes established under the EU and IFI, the tourist boards have formulated projects to comply with the aims of the different funding initiatives. This has ensured that development is taking place on a funding led basis, establishing *ad hoc* projects which may not be sustainable. To exacerbate the problem the success of projects is determined by political criteria, in how well the partners are working together on a cross-border basis, which has further diminished the importance of strategic development.

In recognising the weaknesses of the project based approach, the District Partnerships have now focused attention on formulating programmes. The programme approach allows the District Partnerships to identify themes for development which are closely related to those formulated in the strategy. The partnerships can then invite other stakeholders who have local knowledge and experience to develop and implement programmes. In this way the implementation gap is reduced as each programme is developed from the strategy, while the partnership is given time to think strategically and take direction. Therefore, the experience of the case studies would suggest that the programme approach is a condition which affects the performance of partnerships as it provides for greater strategic development.

Positive Publicity

Although not directly impacting on the implementation of a strategy, positive publicity is viewed as an important condition as it can facilitate wider involvement and a greater access to funds. Evidence from the District Partnerships for Peace and Reconciliation points to the value of positive publicity in increasing the profile of partnerships in their local community to encourage participation. Publicity was used to assist the consultation process and facilitate local accountability measures by organising community meetings to gauge local opinion and seek feedback on the work of the partnership. By introducing co-operation as a condition for the implementation of cross-border projects, the NITB and BF have also found it beneficial to undertake positive publicity in partnership. In promoting a positive co-operative relationship the NITB and BF have been able to attract more funding from the EU and IFI for tourism development.

Positive publicity however, has not received wholehearted support from all the partnership case studies. In the Local Authority Networks it was expressed that publicity should only be endorsed in cases where the attention and participation of the local community is warranted. As the Local Authority Networks have not received block funding, it was held there could be a danger of increasing the profile of the networks beyond their capacity and unnecessarily raising the hopes of the local community. Furthermore, the relationship between the NITB and BF has illustrated that care needs to be taken to assess the political environment. Although publicity was seen as an advantage for the tourist boards in the assessment of funds, both BF and the NITB in particular, have been unwilling to publicly promote their relationship. It is thought that due to the volatile political environment this could invoke sensitivities from the Unionist Community in Northern Ireland which would have negative repercussions for partnership.

(2) Contextual Conditions

An External Partnership Dynamic

In the case studies the external partnership dynamic in terms of geographic proximity and above all, the contentious political environment, has had a significant effect on the partnerships. A context of division between Nationalist and Unionist in Northern Ireland or between the North and South of Ireland has impacted on the performance of each case study, affecting the relationship between the partners and the operation of the partnerships. This is clearly highlighted in the experience of the Local Authority Networks. As a direct result of political sensitivities Armagh District Council, a Unionist controlled Council and an important strategic partner, declined membership of the EBRC and Limavady District Council temporarily resigned from the NWRCBG. In this instance the violence and political sensitivities over cross-border co-operation created distrust between the partners and restricted the development of a partnership relationship.

Operating within a contentious political environment has also influenced the type of coalition building processes which are ongoing in the partnerships. Commentators such as Elliot and Greenwood (1999) and Huxham (1993) maintain that a more effective partnership is created if the arrangement is established on a collaborative basis. Huxham contends that for partnerships to operate successfully a 'meta strategy' should be developed to set out the mission, objectives and strategy of the arrangement. In a similar way, Elliot and Greenwood comment that a degree of formal agreement is a necessary factor which allows a partnership to thrive. In all cases, each commentator advocates the formulation of a strategy, a formal arrangement and moves towards developing a collaborative process.

On first sight it would seem that the partnership case studies would support the views of Huxham and Elliot and Greenwood. In the absence of a formal strategy concerns have been raised over the direction and development of the partnership between the NITB and BF. At present, both tourist boards are co-operating together to maximise the number of visiting tourists but no clear strategy has been devised to set out the long term goals of co-operation. There is a danger that joint promotion will increase the number of tourists to Ireland beyond capacity and this could have a detrimental effect on the sustainability of the tourist product. Secondly, without clear direction provided by an overall strategy, cross-border tourism has lacked co-ordination and tended to be focused on an *ad hoc* funding led basis, creating projects which may be unsustainable and distort integrated development.

Although this highlights the importance of formulating a common strategy, the experience of the case studies would point out that in not all instances should a partnership strive to establish a formal collaborative process. Evidence from the tourist boards suggests that a loose co-operative arrangement has been the suitable approach. At the national level political sensitivities are heightened as establishing formal cross-border arrangements immediately raises questions over national sovereignty and constitutional issues. To avoid being dragged into a political debate, the relationship between the NITB and BF has been deliberately organised on a co-operative informal basis. For this reason the boards have not been able to develop a common strategy as they do not want to be seen pre-empting any political decision which has to be taken by government. Therefore, although commentators have argued that a formal collaborative partnership is more effective, the context in which partnerships operate needs to be taken into account. The relationship between the NITB and BF illustrates that, in difficult and tense circumstances, it is more appropriate to adopt a loose arrangement to provide an inclusive process and allow opportunities to build relations and maintain dialogue.

To further express the importance of a relaxed and supportive external environment, it is interesting to reflect on the development of the partnerships after the paramilitary cease-fires of 1994 and 1997. The peace process has managed to build a more positive environment on the island of Ireland which has, in turn, influenced relationships within the partnerships by quelling the feelings of suspicion and providing an opportunity to break down barriers. The transition in the nature of the relationships between the partners, from deep suspicion and distrust to one of greater understanding, clearly demonstrates the influence of the external partnership environment. However, the advent of the peace process has not meant that the feelings of distrust and suspicion between the partners have been completely eliminated. Trust and confidence have been established but the underlying political environment can still occasionally upset progress and hinder relations. For instance, some Unionist politicians in the Local Authority Networks are reluctant to promote greater links with the south as this may affect chances of re-election.

In the EBRC geographical conditions also created underlying difficulties in developing a common approach and implementing projects and programmes. As Newry and Mourne District Council and Louth County Council areas have a similar economic and social make up and geographical proximity, they have developed a number of core projects. This has created a central axis within the network leaving Monaghan County Council and Down District Council to feel peripheral in the partnership, which causes tensions between the partners.

Vested Interests

The external partnership dynamic is an important condition affecting partnership performance as it impacts on other areas such as the relationships between the partners, decision making and the operation of partnerships. However, the case studies have shown that other factors can be weighted against negative external conditions which can help bring partnerships together and maintain relations. One issue which had a bearing on the partnerships was that each partner had a vested interest in working together. In the case studies, vested interests of the partners have been represented through two issues, stakeholder synergy and access to additional funding. In the Local Authority Networks and the District Partnerships, there was a recognition among the partners that the needs of the sub-region or local area would be more readily addressed in partnership than acting individually. By concentrating on improving the economic and social needs of their local district or region this has helped to forge a common purpose between the partners and divert attention away from divisive political issues. Similarly, both tourist boards acknowledged that co-operating together will reduce the costs of duplication and increase the promotion of the island of Ireland. Aiming to achieve synergy has brought the different partners together from different backgrounds and helped to reinforce partnership relationships in the goal of achieving a greater collective purpose. Secondly, in each of the case studies additional funding from the EU and the IFI, or the potential to access funding, has played an important role in developing partnership arrangements. As the EU and IFI have placed partnership as a condition to access funding, this has acted as a financial incentive for working together.

An Institutional Partnership Dynamic

In developing partnership linkages within a contentious political environment, the case study stakeholders have been also assisted by other institutions. The EU, IFI and central government have brought a new dynamic to the partnerships in bringing the partners together and strengthening partnership relationships.

As the European Commission is perceived to be an independent body it has earned the trust of each of the partners in the case studies. This has been an important factor as Unionist politicians had initially been reluctant to sit alongside Sinn Féin in the District Partnerships, and were suspicious of the motives behind cross-border co-operation between the tourist boards and the Local Authority Networks. As an independent body, the Commission has been able to work with both communities in Northern Ireland, Nationalist and Unionist, and this has quelled political tensions and sensitivities. This role could not have been played by government as suspicions would have been raised about underlying motives, making it difficult to earn the trust of participants.

By contrast, the IFI has adopted a different approach to developing partnership arrangements. As the IFI was established shortly after the Anglo-Irish Agreement, the Unionists have tended to view the fund as providing support to the initiative. Consequently, the IFI has not been perceived as an independent body and has found it difficult to earn the trust of both communities in Northern Ireland. However, this has not prevented the IFI from being influential in facilitating partnership arrangements. The

IFI has adopted a backstage role in working with the tourist boards to further partnership arrangements. In this approach the IFI has been very proactive, probably more so than the EU who were restricted to funding joint initiatives within set guidelines. Adopting a flexible and backstage role has allowed the IFI to facilitate productive partnership arrangements between the tourist boards.

As the EU and IFI have facilitated and maintained partnership in the case studies, particularly during the difficult initial stages, within the last number of years central government has added a new impetus to partnership. From the announcement of the paramilitary cease-fires in 1994 and 1997 and the development of the peace process, the relationship between the NITB and BF has now become intertwined with the wider political issue of improving North-South relations and establishing a peace settlement on the island of Ireland. Both governments now play a greater role in directing the partnership between the NITB and BF and ensuring that the boards prioritise co-operative actions. The relationship has been carefully managed and directed by government to ensure it can contribute towards the new institutional arrangements established under the 'Good Friday' Agreement.

(3) Decision Making Conditions

The Partnership Process

Before a partnership undertakes operations, such as formulating a strategy or adopting a programme approach, the case studies have shown that a partnership process must first be established. It is within the process that the partners get to know one another on an individual basis, build relationships, develop trust and confidence and establish the necessary procedures to operate and develop a partnership.

For example, in the District Partnerships and the relationship between the NITB and BF, it was also found that an established process had first to be set in place before programmes could be implemented. It must be remembered that when adopting the project based approach the District Partnerships were in the initial stages of development, a time when each of the partners was building relationships. During the early phase of the District Partnerships the partners needed an opportunity to get to know one another, develop understanding and achieve quick identifiable outcomes. Given that the partnerships are seeking to establish themselves and set up structures and procedures, it is difficult to consider the immediate formulation of programmes for action. In the Peace and Reconciliation programme it was not until the partnerships had passed the embryonic stage in which the members had matured, grown in confidence and reviewed their expenditures, that a programme approach could be adopted. Furthermore, in the development of tourism initiatives, partners also needed the opportunity to develop a process considering the sensitivities surrounding cross-border co-operation and the role that individual personalities have played, prioritising organisational goals and creating tensions at world travel markets.

Whilst developing a partnership process, including establishing relationships and building trust and confidence, is a condition which affects performance, it is a process which requires continued effort. Developing a partnership process is conducted between participants and there are two main conditions which have facilitated individual contact in the case studies, time and regular contact and good communication channels.

First of all, time is needed to achieve a properly balanced and stable partnership and for the participants to build relationships and establish trust. In the District Partnerships eighteen months after relationships had been developed, a re-nomination process for the voluntary / community sector participants and the re-election of local councillors changed the composition of the boards. This upset the partnership process as relationships and trust had to be rebuilt with the new participants. In the development of cross-border tourism projects and the Local Authority Networks, time to build relationships and establish linkages has provided the opportunity for each of the participants to establish relations and confidence, remove the formality and ordered nature of the relationships and ultimately, improve the decision making process.

On a similar note, regular contact between the members is also important to building a partnership process. In ICBAN the main partnership board, the Network, meets only twice a year and this makes it difficult for the members to get to know one another and to build good knowledge of current developments. As a result, this has impinged on the decision making process as members found it difficult to continuously establish relationships and participate in informed discussions.

Secondly, evidence from the case studies suggests that effective communication channels have to be set in place. Communication among participants is a central feature as it informs all partners of current developments and assists partnerships in formulating a common approach. Due to the demanding workload and the need to adopt an inclusive process, a number of District Partnerships divided the assessment of project applications among a number of sub-committees. However, problems then arose as certain areas within the partnership locality were receiving an over allocation of funding. The basic problem was that communication between sub-committees broke down which meant funding decisions were taken without the knowledge of the other members.

Moreover, considering that each of the partnerships are operating within a contentious political environment, communication and language skills have been important in helping to establish good personal relations and build an effective decision making process. At the local project level in the tourism partnership, contact between members of District Councils, RTAs and the elected representatives is undertaken at a personal level, almost on a day to day basis. At that level language skills are important in quelling political sensitivities, making individuals feel comfortable and building reconciliation. Language skills were also cited as helping to dampen political sensitivities in the District Partnerships for Peace and Reconciliation. With a range of different sectors in one board, the debating and negotiating skills worked to ease tension, articulate ideas and facilitate decision making, particularly when discussing contentious issues.

An Effective Decision Making Process

An effective decision making process can be regarded as a condition which improves partnership performance as it builds interpersonal relations as part of the partnership process, invokes debate and facilitates the development and operation of the partnership. To enable an effective decision making process a number of factors are important. First of all, considering the variety and diversity among each of the partners, the case studies have shown that an inclusive decision making process is a central factor. To develop a common approach, the District Partnerships established an inclusive decision making process by formulating sub-committees in which all members could actively participate. With an inclusive process this has ensured fair and equal representation which has helped to build an environment of trust and understanding among the different sectors. Establishing trust through inclusive decision making structures has also been the aim of the Local Authority Networks. The

NWRCBG recognised the need for a common approach to regional development and established a consensus or unanimous decision making procedure. Allowing each participant to air individual views establishes an inclusive unifying approach in which the partners can move forward together.

An inclusive approach has also facilitated a more effective decision making process between tourism interests in the implementation of cross-border programmes. The political sensitivities over cross-border co-operation and the imbalances between the tourism industry North and South have created a hostile partnership environment, making it difficult for the partners to engage in a decision making process. Allowing for equal representation or parity between the cross-border partners has ensured an inclusive approach guaranteeing equality and equity and helping to allay fears over being dominated by a larger partner.

However, as the partnerships have progressed the value and the need for an inclusive process has diminished. As the partners have developed relationships and started to break down barriers the partnerships have found the inclusive decision making process too rigid and lengthy. For example, in the relationship between the tourist boards, the insistence that an equal number of participants meet on a cross-border basis has established a structured procedure. Under this system there is little opportunity to engage in an informal and open basis which has hindered decision making and limited progress. Similarly, the NWRCBG are formulating programmes which means difficult decisions over the allocation of funds and development of the region have to be made. Under the consensual approach the Network has not been able to make quick decisions as unanimous decision making is a slow procedure.

The inclusive approach can place a burden on the partnership, it requires a lot of time and is best suited in the initial stages of partnership development when the partners are beginning to get to know one another. In recognition of this problem, each of the Networks have established executive organisations of a number of individuals who can lead the direction of the partnerships, focus on strategic issues and make quick decisions. Executive organisations can create a more effective decision making process as they provide an engine for partnership development, leaving the main boards to debate and discuss more specific operational matters.

A second important factor was that the partnership case studies established an informal decision making process which allowed the participants to discuss contentious issues. In the Peace and Reconciliation programme a clear distinction can be made between the District Partnerships, which established an informal decision making process, and those which discussed the basic programme issues. Within an informal decision making process, participants could readily discuss difficult issues such as sectarianism which allowed the partnerships to tackle one of the main problem areas. To assist the process a number of partnerships invited the Community Relations Council to set out methods of good practice of how to discuss concepts such as the 'glass curtain', single identity work and problems of avoidance. In this way the partnerships have established procedures to deal with the problem areas and work towards the goals of the programme. By contrast, in the partnerships which established a restrictive decision making process, the contentious issues were not discussed in an open and up front manner and the problem areas in relation to community relations and peace and reconciliation were effectively ignored. Furthermore, in the relationship between the NITB and BF similar problems have emerged. In the initial stages of partnership the boards rigidly adhered to their agenda, which prevented informal discussion between participants and denied the opportunity to address problematic issues and share experience.

Thirdly, the Chairmen have also undertaken an important role in the partnerships by facilitating an ordered decision making process among the participants. In the District Partnerships the Chairman was often able to offer facilitative leadership of the board by raising contentious issues, organising meetings and giving direction. Other Chairmen adopted a more consensual style and offered a joint / rotating chair to appease the different sectors. This worked to develop a common approach and ensure equal balance and representation within the board. The Local Authority Networks benefited from a Chairman who co-ordinated the partnership board (Main Committee EBRC) informing participants of current events and promoting the regional perspective. The rotational chair, operated by the Networks, has also helped to develop a common organisational approach by allowing each of the partner councils to hold the position.

Finally, the case studies have demonstrated the importance for the representation of members to correspond to the partnerships spatial level of operation. In the Local Authority Networks, difficulties have emerged over local councillors not being able to adopt a sub-regional view in the formulation of projects and programmes. Councillors in the networks are elected to represent their local area and in being tied to the interests of their locality, find it difficult to take a holistic or sub-regional approach. With councillors representing a parochial view this creates tensions as each council member seeks to voice their own local interests in the decision making process.

Problems over the representation of members and the spatial operation of the partnership have also been reflected in the District Partnerships. Representatives of the voluntary / community sectors have been nominated to the District Partnerships by a provincial organisation NICVA, who have allocated members to different localities. This has created difficulties for the partnerships as the members did not know the local needs and issues and could not make effective decisions. Secondly, the representatives were not familiar with the other local participants which made it difficult for the members to get to know each other, have contact on a daily basis and build trust and confidence.

(4) Stakeholder / Organisational Conditions

Stakeholder Commitment

To work in a partnership arrangement with other stakeholders over a long period of time, organisations need to bring a high level of commitment to the process. In the District Partnerships members were placed under an intense amount of pressure analysing application forms within a limited time frame. This caused stress among the board members who found it difficult to fulfil the demanding routine. In working towards and completing these tasks, each of the board members showed full commitment to the partnership which ensured that the members would work together in a consistent approach and implement the partnership programme.

Commitment of each of the councils in seeking to work together and improve the region, has managed to maintain the partnership relationship in the Local Authority Networks. During the 1970s and 1980s the EBRC and NWRCBG struggled for existence when support from government was not forthcoming and when cross-border co-operation was not fashionable nor profitable. During this time it was the commitment of the partners which held the Networks together and maintained relations. However, now as funding for a secretariat has been awarded and the Networks seek to develop a common strategy, further commitment is required from the councils. At this stage questions have been raised over certain partners and whether they are prepared to provide more commitment if funding is not forthcoming. In the EBRC the partner councils did not provide funding for the secretariat in the interim between INTERREG 1 and 2. In this instance the absence of further commitment has caused frustration and tension within the partnership and hindered progress.

Stakeholder Balance

In the relationship between the NITB and BF, imbalance in power has caused problems in the implementation of joint initiatives and created tension between the boards. As there is a larger and more mature tourism industry in the south of Ireland, BF can be regarded as a more significant tourist board than the NITB. This imbalance has been reflected in the partnership relationship and has raised northern sensitivities over co-operation, in being overshadowed by a larger more dominant organisation. Sensitivities over co-operation have largely come to the fore at world travel markets when the differences in numbers and staff between the NITB and BF are magnified. Tensions arise as the smaller number of NITB staff feel overshadowed by the larger number of personnel from BF.

Given the difficulties and tensions surrounding the imbalance in strength between the boards, allowances have been made in the formulation of joint programmes. For instance, in the TBI and OTMI, the northern tourism industry has received a disproportional amount of publicity and coverage when compared to the size of the industry in the north and the financial contributions made by the NITB. Although this may have caused certain tensions and disagreements over funding, it can be argued that granting the NITB favourable representation on co-operative all-Ireland marketing programmes has helped to alleviate fears and sensitivities over being dominated by a larger partner.

Within the District Partnerships differences in strength and confidence also existed between the elected representatives and the voluntary / community members. In some instances members from the voluntary / community sector felt overawed by the District Partnerships as meetings were held in the District Council Chambers and conducted in a very formal atmosphere. Voluntary / community representatives tended to shy away from participating in discussions as they felt intimidated by councillors who were more familiar with the surroundings, the business of partnership and debating techniques. In recognising the difficulties and disadvantages of the voluntary sector, the District Partnership sought to rectify the imbalance by conducting meetings at a neutral venue and in an informal process. This helped to facilitate a decision making process in which all members could feel they can equally contribute.

Stakeholder Competition

Co-operation between the NITB and BF has also highlighted the difficulties of working together if both partners see each other as competitors. Tensions have been created between the boards who, being different economic entities, regard each other as competitors for in coming tourists. Problems arise in the home markets as the NITB and BF compete for tour operators to programme holidays to either the north or south of Ireland. In these circumstances it becomes difficult to promote partnership, as trust and understanding often breaks down with both boards suspiciously monitoring the actions of the other to prevent encroachment into one another's market. This case study highlights the problems in a relationship if the partner organisations perceive each other as a threat. If the partners distrust one another this makes it difficult to establish good relations and develop the partnership.

Stakeholder Priorities

In the development of partnership, the experience of the case studies would support the view that a major problem with partnerships occur when each of the partners have different priorities. The problems in reconciling different partner priorities were clearly evident in the District Partnerships which had to complement the different priorities and cultures of the public, private, and voluntary / community sectors, trade unions and locally elected representatives. This proved to be a very difficult task with tensions becoming apparent between the voluntary / community sector and the local councillors. Tensions were raised with councillors claiming they had greater democratic authority and therefore warranted a more prominent position on the partnerships than the voluntary and community members.

Difficulties in partnership development were also created with the participation of the business sector who did not conform easily to the values and culture of the programme. Other partners such as the councillors and the voluntary / community sector could easily identify with terms such as social inclusion, community capacity building and peace and reconciliation, whereas the business representatives, trained to focus on quantifiable inputs, throughput and outputs, regarded those themes as nebulous. Consequently members of the business community found it difficult to apply their skill and understanding to the partnerships and their attendance at meetings declined.

Problems with different cultures and partner priorities have created obstacles to partnership development between the NITB and BF. In co-operation both tourist boards have different priorities in the types of tourist products and attractions they wish to see developed and promoted. As tourism in the south of Ireland has experienced periods of favourable growth, the industry has reached a stage of maturity in the tourism life cycle and does not require further development. As a result the role and activities of BF have had to change, having virtually all emphasis on marketing rather than the development of projects. In contrast, the industry in Northern Ireland has not developed to the same extent and still requires significant infrastructural development to improve the tourist product. Differences in the needs and priorities of the tourist boards have created problems for the relationship as limited commonality exists when developing common linkages which restricts partnership development.

Conditions Affecting Partnership Governance at the Macro Level

With the development of partnerships there are a number of policy issues and tensions at the macro level which have implications for partnership governance and can impact on the development of the partnership approach as a whole. From the experience of the case studies three themes have emerged.

Representative Versus Participative Democracy

Central to the emergence of the partnership approach in public policy has been the changing roles of the voluntary / community sector and local government, and the rising tensions between the strains of participative and representative democracy. In the development of partnerships one of the major considerations has surrounded the extent to which the voluntary / community sector should be involved in governance. In Britain, urban initiatives adopted by government within the last ten years have actively sought the participation of the voluntary / community sector. Through the partnership approach, programmes such as the Single Regeneration Budget (SRB) and City Challenge have sought to facilitate the participation of the voluntary / community sector in the development and delivery of local regeneration strategies (Nevin and Shiner, 1995; Bailey, 1993). Following the attention on public / private partnerships in the 1980s, in the 1990s it is now acceptable 'to bring the community back in' (Robinson and Shaw, 1991, p.2).

With the inclusion of an increasingly influential voluntary / community sector, this has challenged the traditional role of local authorities and raised concerns over the democratic credentials of partnerships. Many commentators such as Hutchinson (1994), Hutchinson and Foley (1994), Bailey (1997) and Lezierski (1990), see the rise of community involvement altering the democratic balance of an area and weakening accountability. The main focus of the argument is that councillors can claim to be representatives of the whole community, while community / voluntary members tend to represent more specific or sectoral interests. Therefore, as the voluntary / community sector begins to play a more important role in partnerships, decisions over public money are increasingly being made by organisations which are not representative or have not been directly elected by the public.

On the other hand, Lowndes *et al* (1997) argue that the inclusion of the voluntary / community sectors improves governance by encouraging participative democracy. It is held that unrepresentative voluntary / community groups can fill the 'democratic deficit' in local politics caused by the political apathy and subsequent low turnout at elections at that level. Secondly, Lowndes *et al* contend that the voluntary / community sector can complement the formal democratic process by providing a direct voice for marginalised or excluded groups who are disassociated from the system of government. Indeed, from a study of local development in the Republic of Ireland, Walsh (1997/98) maintains that partnership between the local authority and community representatives was perceived by the local authority to be in better tune with the needs of the area. In addition, the partnership provided a conduit to the local authority for sharing information and providing understanding which has assisted the local authority to improve relations with the local population.

Tensions over participative and representative democracy have been prominent in the Local Authority Networks and the District Partnership experience. In both case studies difficulties emerged with councillors being suspicious of the voluntary / community sector usurping their role as elected representatives. By the same token the voluntary / community members distrusted the councillors, believing the latter resented the involvement of community representatives and were reluctant to share power in a partnership arrangement. Within the District Partnerships the role of the voluntary / community sector has caused concerns over accountability. Voluntary / community members were nominated by a province wide organisation, the NICVA, who in certain cases, appointed members to different local districts. This weakened the accountability within the organisations as partnership members were not representative of their local areas. Furthermore, little opportunity existed for other voluntary / community groups, which were not aligned to NICVA, to become involved in the programme.

Despite this, it can be argued that the voluntary / community sector has improved local accountability. As discussed in Chapter 3, from the imposition of direct rule, Northern Ireland has been devoid of a system of accountable government. The Secretary of State, who has no constituency base, is the main locus of power, while essential public services such as health, education and housing, operate under appointed boards (Knox, 1996). By involving the voluntary / community sector to deliver the Peace and Reconciliation programme, this has improved local accountability by allowing them to make contributions in the District Partnerships. After the difficult and initial stages, the voluntary / community members and elected representatives have worked well together, drawing on the experience of both sectors, complementing the strains of participative and representative democracy creating greater ownership of decisions at the local level.

Tensions between representative and participative democracy have caused divisions among participants and cast a continuous cloud over partnership arrangements. It is clear that these tensions need to be reconciled if partnerships are to improve their performance and become a permanent feature in public policy. However, evidence from the District Partnerships in the case study material has demonstrated that voluntary / community members and elected local representatives can work together. In this instance the inclusion of voluntary / community members in local governance has complemented the role of elected representatives, provided a voice for the socially and politically excluded and improved accountability. However, it is also clear that the nomination process must ensure that members from the voluntary / community sector are fully representative of their organisations.

Rebuilding Civil Society

By involving voluntary / community representatives and encouraging the development of participatory democracy it is also argued that this can enrich civil society. This view is held by Clark (1995) and Hadenius and Uggla (1996) who maintain that participation by voluntary / community groups in governance encourages local communities to express their concerns, find out about the activities of government and hold officials to account. With voluntary and community groups acting together this provides a voice for the disadvantaged and excluded sections of society and gives them an opportunity to protect their own interests. As a result, Hadenius and Uggla state that this strengthens civil society as collective action embeds the social virtues of trust among citizens and facilitates the development of a pluralist political democracy.

This view can be applied to the experience of the District Partnerships in Northern Ireland. From its inception, the Peace and Reconciliation programme has been seen as a grass roots initiative designed to encourage and facilitate a bottom up approach to social and economic development. The language of the programme, focusing on terms such as social inclusion, capacity building and peace and reconciliation, has been 'user friendly' for the voluntary / community sector, helping them to adapt quickly to the partnerships. Evidence of the full participation of the community / voluntary sector is well represented in the District Partnerships as members experienced a true learning process. After making decisions on funding projects, members from the sector started to understand the reasons behind bureaucratic checks and balances and the difficulties in funding applications with limited resources. This has given the voluntary / community sector in Northern Ireland a true experience of working in governance arrangements, challenging decisions and conducting the business of government. What is even more striking in the partnerships is that the voluntary / community sector includes representatives from across the political spectrum who have worked well together and have developed trust and co-operation with the other sectors. On this basis, the inclusive District Partnership arrangements have helped to rebuild civil society in Northern Ireland which in the last thirty years has been characterised by social exclusion, disenfranchisement, alienation, distrust and sectarianism.

This argument is also subscribed to by Williamson *et al* (1999) who, in their study of the District Partnerships, comment that the voluntary

/ community sector has made an important contribution to the partnerships by taking a strong lead, ensuring the policies were sensitive to local needs and tackling issues of accountability and financial probity. They conclude that the partnerships have helped establish a basis of trust between neighbours deeply divided by history and ethnicity and that the role of the voluntary / community sector has been germane to the task of rebuilding civil society.

An established strong and vibrant civil society provides a solid foundation on which partnership governance can be built. With greater participation and active citizenship, partnerships can foster these new energies and skills to build an informative and more inclusive decision making process.

A New Idealism or Political Pragmatism?

Another consideration for the development of the partnership approach in public policy concerns the wider role and purpose of partnerships. Much debate has focused on whether partnerships have been adopted for pragmatic political reasons or are part of a new idealism to achieve wider government or macro goals For instance, currently attention has been focused on the partnership approach under the Labour Government in Britain and whether it is a pragmatic response to public expenditure restrictions or an attempt to facilitate a stakeholder society. Falconer (1999) documents this debate by first referring to Falconer and Ross (1998) who argue that the Labour Government has embraced the partnership approach in order to court private finance and effect more efficient public service provisions in the light of committed expenditure ceilings. On the other hand, Falconer cites Hutton (1997) who contends that the partnership approach, by involving public, private and voluntary / community organisations in governance, will build a stakeholder society. It is argued by Hutton that the stakeholder society is one in which all have a common interest and is based on the 'acceptance of responsibilities as well as assertion of rights and changing culture' (Falconer 1999, p.178).

Other debates over the motives or underlying reasons behind partnerships have been centred on urban policy under Conservative Governments. Lawless (1991), Deakin and Edwards (1993) maintain that adopting public-private partnerships in urban regeneration programmes, was not just simply an attempt to lever private finance, but was concerned with promoting the enterprise culture in the public sector. Mackintosh

(1992) refers to governments implicit agenda as 'transformation', a process whereby, in working together, the private sector seeks to reform the culture and values of the public sector. Boyle (1989) comments that through public-private partnerships, government is abdicating responsibility for regeneration and 'privatising local economies via the back door.' Similarly, Hastings (1996) refers to the study by Sheffield City Polytechnic (1991) and its analysis of the bids under the first round of City Challenge. This study concluded that those bids which were successful tended to acknowledge an implicit agenda of changing the culture of local government.

Sabel (1996) takes this debate further and argues that partnerships need to invoke institutional reform and become part of a wider government project to deal with an increasingly complex and interdependent world. In a study of local development partnerships in the Republic of Ireland for the OECD, Sabel sees partnerships having two purposes and operating at two levels. At one level partnerships are centred on a project led basis and are solely introduced to address local economic and social problems and as a means to appease constituents living in disadvantaged areas. Sabel regards these types of partnerships as amorphous organisations representing a collection of varied and evolving projects. At another level, partnerships can be part of a wider government ideal of bringing different sectors and influences together to deal with the negative consequences of an increasingly complex and interdependent world. It is held that partnerships can be used as a mechanism to extend and reinforce socially inclusive concertation in Ireland. Sabel argues that partnerships are more effective if they influence and inform the activities of government and initiate a participative approach to development at the local and national levels.

When reflecting on the experience of the case studies there is an argument to suggest that central government, in facilitating partnership, is seeking to achieve a wider goal. For example, in the relationships between the tourist boards both the British and Irish Governments have had an influential effect in managing and directing greater partnership linkages. From the development of the peace process, the two governments have been eager to show that tourism can be highlighted as an area for cross-border co-operation which can contribute to the implementation of the 'Good Friday' Agreement. This case study clearly highlights the role that government has played in facilitating partnerships within the last number of years and would point out there is an implicit agenda. Other than creating greater synergy and drawing down additional funding, government has a wider goal of using partnership as a mechanism to reconcile interests North and South and establish a lasting settlement on the island of Ireland.

Certainly after analysis of the Peace and Reconciliation programme the role of partnerships in implementing a series of projects would suggest that the programme also was a pragmatic response to combating social exclusion and disadvantage following the cease-fires of 1994. However, from examining the design of the District Partnerships there is an argument to suggest that the programme has a wider agenda. As previously discussed, by involving business, trade unions and the voluntary / community sector in partnership arrangements along with the public sector and local councillors, this will cumulatively help to shape civil society in Northern Ireland. In this approach partnership can be seen as a mechanism to facilitate participation and inclusion of different sectors in governance to build civil society.

In addition, as mentioned earlier in this chapter, the EU and IFI have played a significant role in facilitating and maintaining partnership arrangements. It can also be argued that the EU and IFI are developing partnerships as a means of achieving wider goals of promoting reconciliation and improving cross-border economic opportunities. In aiming towards these goals, the EU and IFI have established partnerships which are reshaping the working and political relations in Northern Ireland and the island of Ireland. Furthermore, by facilitating and supporting partnerships the EU and IFI have also influenced British and Irish Government policy towards cross-border co-operation between the NITB and BF.

This view is supported by Williamson (1999) who argues that the European Commission, through various initiatives such as the Poverty Programme, has influenced British and Irish social policy. Williamson states that there is now a convergence of local social and economic development policy in the two parts of Ireland, being shaped by European funding opportunities, based on a continental approach to public administration which calls for an inclusive approach to the participation of a third sector. It is held that partnership initiatives in Northern Ireland such as the Making Belfast Work programme (Appendix) and urban and rural based partnerships in the Republic of Ireland are examples of the influence of the European Commission. The Commission, therefore, has a prominent role developing partnerships in other policy areas and spatial fields, and not only on a cross-border basis. Through partnership, what is emerging is more co-ordination between the North and South of Ireland and a greater convergence of policy on the island of Ireland as a whole.

The experience of the case studies demonstrates that partnerships can be used as a mechanism to achieve a wider goal. Although each initiative has the central aim of implementing a series of projects and improving service delivery, the partnerships are working towards greater goals of building civil society, promoting reconciliation and contributing to the 'Good Friday' Agreement. By being included as part of a wider government ideal, this will enable partnership governance to go beyond the basic project approach and elevate partnerships as a central feature in public policy.

Developing the Synthetic Model

This book is focused on identifying and discussing conditions which affect partnership performance within the framework set out in the literature comprising contextual, organisational, decision making and operational issues. One problem however, with this framework is that it views partnership as a rigid organisation divided into separate and distinct functions. On the other hand, commentators such as Lowndes and Skelcher (1998) see partnerships as fluid, evolutionary arrangements adopting different structures at different stages of development. It is held that strategies to develop effective partnerships must take into account the changing life cycle of partnership development as different stages require different approaches. This view of partnership is supported by the experience of the case studies which can be seen as more fluid organisations constantly changing and developing. The application of any rigid framework to the study of partnerships, fails to take into account the transitional nature of partnerships. A flexible approach which analyses stages of development is also required.

It can therefore be suggested that the duration of partnership arrangements could have been used as a variable in the mapping exercise in Chapter 3. The duration of partnership development embraces the variety of partnerships and would possibly provide greater insight into the variety and diversity of different partnership arrangements. For further analysis on the conditions which affect partnership performance it would, therefore, be of benefit to apply a longitudinal research approach for future study. This would examine the conditions associated with partnership governance over a period of time and provide the opportunity to develop a three dimensional model.

Conclusion: Whither Partnership Governance?

When reflecting on the case studies and discussing the wider implications of the findings for partnership governance, it is also necessary to examine the weaknesses of partnership and the limits of the approach. One problem in advocating the implementation of partnerships is that they will increase environmental and organisational complexity. This point is explored by Cebulla (1996) and Tilson *et al* (1997) who comment that mass production of partnerships makes it difficult to adopt a common approach, creates organisational proliferation and duplication of effort.

The multifarious existence of partnership arrangements in Northern Ireland, as outlined in Chapter 3, provides a clear example of the complexity of partnership governance. In Northern Ireland different kinds of partnerships have been applied to a range of policy areas and operate across a variety of spatial levels. Partnerships have been developed on a rapid and *ad hoc* basis and this has caused difficulties co-ordinating efforts due to competition, duplication and fragmentation.

Problems with the explosion of partnership initiatives is demonstrated in the relationship between the NITB and BF. Both tourist boards have faced difficulties in trying to forge a common approach to the development of the border region and the promotion of the island of Ireland. The proliferation of partnership arrangements at the local and sub-regional level has fragmented the tourism message, distorted strategic development and caused duplication in tourism projects. This case study clearly shows the limitations of the partnership approach. The implementation of too many partnership initiatives creates fragmentation, increases confusion among participants and limits strategic development.

Another difficulty surrounding the partnership approach is the dependence of stakeholders on additional funding. Martin and Oztel (1996) and Peck and Tickell (1995) contend that major problems occur when funding is exhausted and the partners have not devised a clear exit or forward strategy, causing the partnership to collapse. In the initial stages of partnership between NITB and BF, co-operation was weak as the boards prioritised their own interests and maintained almost an artificial relationship for the purpose of receiving financial resources. In addition, questions over the sustainability of the Local Authority Networks also remain. To date the Networks have received minimal amounts of funding from the EU INTERREG programme, in essence just enough to fund a secretariat. If substantial funds are not awarded to the Networks under INTERREG 3, individuals and partner councils have stressed that their membership may be reviewed. These case studies point out the limitations inherent in partnerships. Partners depend on additional funding to resource the initiative while too much emphasis on financial rewards leads to fragile and artificial relationships which are not sustainable.

Problems of partnership arrangements are also contained in trying to forge a common approach among the different partners. Woodburn (1985) argues that this is a very difficult task as different partners have different and often conflicting objectives, different views on organisational roles and a range of perspectives on how to approach problems. Woodburn concludes by commenting that what is needed is effective management of the different partners. In a similar vein, as mentioned earlier in this chapter, problems emerged with different partners having different priorities.

It can be concluded that there are inherent difficulties contained within the partnership approach. Partnerships are not a panacea which can be readily applied to all areas of public policy to improve policy formulation and implementation. The case studies support the views of Darwin (1999, p.137) that 'partnerships are volatile and fragile things and need to be handled with care.' If these problems inherent in partnerships are not addressed then partnerships will fail to be seen as an effective mechanism to deal with an increasingly complex and interdependent world. The case studies suggest that an overall framework in the form of an institutional or government structure is required to oversee partnerships, particularly to ensure common policy development, allocate funding and provide advice and guidelines in management. Launching wider institutional structures for different partnership initiatives would be timely considering the volume of partnership arrangements in Northern Ireland and on the island of Ireland. The institutional structure proposed for partnerships could be in the shape of the NIPB which provided guidance, support and focus in the development of the District Partnerships.

Indeed, the concept of a regional partnership in Northern Ireland has recently been advocated by the NIPB in the current debate surrounding the implementation of the second Peace programme from 2000-2004 (NIPB, 1999). The proposed regional partnership is to be comprised of representatives of central government, local government, statutory bodies, voluntary / community sectors, the social partners, the private sector and intermediary funding mechanisms. As a means to achieve greater coherence and complementarity, the regional partnership would have the responsibility of drawing up guidelines for collaborative action for twenty six local partnerships. It is envisaged that the regional partnership would have more authority than the original NIPB as it would determine the appropriate funding to each local partnership, approve the composition of the boards, assess the complementarily of other programmes, provide area collaboration between local partnerships and be responsible / accountable for its own funds.

Although there are limitations in the partnership approach, it must be stated that potential exists for partnerships to be a central feature in governance arrangements. In reflecting on the findings of the case studies, lessons can be drawn from the partnerships which have implications for future governance.

In the first instance, the case studies highlight that the partnership approach can be adopted by local authorities to create a more focused and coherent approach. This thesis has continuously cited the problems of fragmentation, segmentation and confusion in the public sector environment and how partnerships have contributed to this complexity. Indeed, environmental complexity is well represented in the map of partnership arrangements (see Figure 3.1) which clearly shows the plethora of partnerships operating in Northern Ireland, particularly at the local level. It can be argued however, that these problems can be addressed by allowing local authorities a central position in partnership development.

Evidence of a possible co-ordinating, strategic role for local government is emerging from the case studies as local authorities have been important to the development of all three partnerships. Being located in a prominent position at the local level, local authorities have the potential to establish linkages and formulate a strategic framework for development. Through partnership, local authorities can establish a common vision from which stakeholders can become involved in governance activity and develop a more effective approach to local development.

The experience of the District Partnerships has also highlighted the value of partnerships in encouraging participation, inclusiveness and a bottom up approach. In the District Partnerships a broad consultative and participative planning process created strategies to target disadvantage and establish ownership at the local level. In this instance, greater participation facilitated synergy and helped develop innovative projects and programmes to deal with complex problems such as social exclusion. However, in Northern Ireland, these developments are only occurring at the local level while government at the macro level under direct rule continues to be characterised by complacency and administrative inertia (Knox, 1999). To effectively address complex problems such as social exclusion and urban and rural disadvantage a participative partnership framework could be applied both at the macro and local level in Northern Ireland. Establishing a participative partnership framework including voluntary / community representatives, trade unions and the business sector, would facilitate the formulation of a common approach and ensure sustainable benefits of economic and social development would be extended to a wider range of communities. Moreover, a participative partnership framework would move the partnership approach away from the politically pragmatic project based approach, to become a mainstream element of governance. On this basis, partnerships assume two functions: a 'supply side' approach, concentrating on project delivery and a 'demand side' approach, helping communities articulate their concerns and participate in development processes (Clark, 1995).

An overall framework would also provide a institutional mechanism to facilitate networking and understanding between partnerships. Currently, too much emphasis is being placed on developing new and innovative processes and procedures while existing partnerships have a wealth of experience which tends to be overlooked. For example, by facilitating good relationships and building trust and confidence through inclusive partnership processes, the case studies have highlighted elements of good practice. In an effort to achieve a greater balance between good practice and innovation, such models of good practice need to transferred across partnerships to reduce duplication, improve understanding and create opportunities for developing financial leverage.

The arguments in favour of a participative partnership approach at the macro level can be supported when reviewing the experience in the Republic of Ireland. From the early 1990s, the Irish Government has been actively pursuing an inclusive partnership approach to strategic policy through the National Economic and Social Forum (NESF) and latterly, the Partnership 2000 agreement. The NESF was established in 1993 and is comprised of traditional social partners, trade unions, employers and farm associations and representatives of voluntary / community sectors. The aim of the NESF is to develop economic and social policy initiatives in partnership with government and private business. This partnership at the macro political level has created consensual agreement and has played an important strategic role in the development of an active labour policy (O'Donnell and Thomas, 1998). Consequently, throughout the 1990s, partnership at the macro political level has continued to adopt an inclusive approach and involves a wider range of social and economic interests, including voluntary / community representatives. The current partnership agreement, Partnership 2000, has established broad strategic guidelines on budgetary policy and social agreements which the partners have negotiated and agreed. According to O'Donnell and Thomas (1998) this has contributed to economic growth and reconfigured the relationships between representative and participative democracy which is fostering new forms of deliberative democracy.

What is also interesting from the experience in the Republic of Ireland, is that the partners in the agreement have acknowledged the limits of partnership at the macro level. It was understood that partnership at the national level, however, successful as it was in addressing macro economic difficulties, could not guarantee prosperity to the long term unemployed and socially excluded (O'Donnell and Thomas, 1998). As a result, the national agreement was extended to include local development and a range of participative partnerships were established at the local level. Local partnerships in the Republic of Ireland have also been set up by the EU and with this, the possibility of extending the participation in economic and social reconstruction has been realised (Sabel, 1996). Although problems such as institutional and democratic legitimacy are evident in the partnership arrangements, Sabel argues that by establishing a partnership framework in which evaluation and policy learning are ongoing, this can maximise effort, co-ordinate activity between the local and national level and improve accountability.

In learning from the experience of the Republic of Ireland a participative partnership approach would also be of value for the North-South Ministerial Council (NSMC) and the cross-border bodies proposed under the 'Good Friday' Agreement. Previous cross-border initiatives launched at the national level have been top down in nature and have failed to make a significant impact on strategic development (O'Dowd, 1994). Partnership would create greater participation and improve policy formulation and implementation as the local communities in Northern Ireland and the Republic of Ireland will be widely consulted. In addition, a participative partnership approach in the NSMC and the Council of the

Isles will broaden ownership of the peace process / settlement and ensure that the wider community will have a stake in peace. Partnership and participation in the new institutions is also important and timely, given recent trends in the fall of membership of political parties and rising economic polarisation in both the North and South of Ireland (Heath, 1999). These trends are creating greater social exclusion and marginalisation on the island of Ireland which can be combated through partnership and a genuine bottom up approach in the new institutions.

In addition, transferring a participative partnership approach to the NSMC would further strategic development in the border region as planning would be conducted on a trans-national level rather than on a cross-border basis. Formulating exclusively cross-border programmes limits the potential for development in the border region as planning is essentially premised on the existence of the border. In applying a partnership approach within the NSMC and cross-border bodies, a more effective strategy would be developed as spatial planning is organised on an all-Ireland basis. This facilitates a strategic co-ordinated approach as the border is not seen as an international frontier or a peripheral region in both jurisdictions, but rather is incorporated into the policies and strategies of both governments.

By establishing a participative partnership framework in Northern Ireland and on a cross-border basis, this will complement the partnership agreement in the Republic of Ireland and provide an effective response to dealing with a complex and fragmented policy environment. Furthermore, in the light of an increasingly interdependent shared power world, the framework could also be extended to certain polices under the Council of the Isles also proposed under the 'Good Friday' Agreement.

However, if partnerships are to progress as a central feature of governance, central government must devolve more autonomy. In the case studies clear tensions emerged between partnerships and central government over the balance between autonomy and delegated responsibility. The partnerships argued that central government are unwilling to decentralise, whereas central government maintain that partnerships are unable to facilitate strategic direction and be financially accountable. In this tension between autonomy and delegated responsibility, evidence from the case studies suggests that it is the unwillingness of central government to decentralise which needs to be addressed as partnerships have matured in terms of moves towards formulating integrated strategies and implementing programmes within financial guidelines. Civil servants have been slow to recognise the progress achieved by partnerships and thus there is a need for reform in government departments to facilitate delegation and improve co-operation with partnership initiatives.

Developing a participative partnership framework at the local and macro level in Northern Ireland and on a cross-border basis also has potential to rebuild civil society. According to Hadenius and Uggla (1996) the state has the ability to strengthen civil society by establishing institutions and polices which enhance co-operation with the voluntary / community sector. It is argued that recognising voluntary / community groups as legitimate organisations and taking them into consideration when making policies, is important to the growth of civil society as individuals are more likely to join organisations which they perceive to possess a degree of power. On this basis, establishing a participative partnership framework will develop a vibrant civil society. Moreover, the proposed creation of a Civic Forum under the 'Good Friday' Agreement provides an ideal opportunity to strengthen civil society in Northern Ireland and develop a more participative approach at central government level. Together, participative partnerships and the Civic Forum, will nurture the required trust and co-operation among communities required to reconcile, and deal with, the increasingly fragmented and polarised social order acknowledged by Healey (1996) and facilitate pluralist policy making and greater accountability in Northern Ireland.

Developing civil society is important as it helps to build a culture of democracy in Northern Ireland which to date has been characterised by political exclusion, distrust and sectarianism. Participation in governance arrangements allows voluntary and community groups to become involved in democratic activities and gives them the opportunity to learn democratic skills. Furthermore, Hadenius and Uggla (1996) argue that by taking part in democratic processes citizens come to understand other views which creates a growing mutual concern and public spirit. Taking this point further, participative partnerships can also be seen to have a wider purpose in promoting understanding and reconciliation within the context of division. Although partnerships are primarily regarded as a service delivery mechanism, it is the process within partnerships which can make them a unique instrument. Evidence from the case studies suggests that partnerships, through their notions of co-operation, sharing and building relationships, can bring Unionist and Nationalist constituencies together to work towards common goals. The partnership process developed trust and confidence which helped to break down barriers and provide a foundation for partnership operation.

It is a challenge for the NSMC and cross-border bodies to build reconciliation throughout the island of Ireland. Commentators such as Murray (1999) have expressed concern that under current reconciliation initiatives, relationships are not being developed at the national level and that cross-border co-operation is creating a 'new partitionism' between Northern Ireland and the border counties of the Republic and the rest of Ireland. Indeed, in each of the case studies relationships have been developed at the local level, between local actors within Northern Ireland (in the District Partnerships) and between councillors and local tourism interests from Northern Ireland and the border counties of the Republic (in the Local Authority Networks and co-operation between the NITB and BF). By adopting an inclusive partnership approach the North-South Ministerial Council will encourage participation and build relationships and trust throughout the island of Ireland. The case studies have demonstrated that although the partnerships operate within a context of division in which there is no previous culture of partnership, relationships can be established based on trust and understanding which can break down barriers between participants. This is a clear indication that the new institutional arrangements, proposed under the 'Good Friday' Agreement, can contribute to building reconciliation within Northern Ireland and on the island of Ireland. Not least, the case studies can provide a solid foundation on which these new institutions can be built.

The development of a partnership is fuelled by the need to adopt a shared response to an increasingly complex, fragmented and interdependent world. Provided this environment remains, partnership activity is likely to increase and partnerships will become a central feature in public policy and indeed, in mainstream governance. A participative partnership framework in Northern Ireland and on a cross-border basis, has the potential to deal with the current economic, social and political challenges. Partnerships, within Northern Ireland, on the island of Ireland and between Ireland and Britain, can provide the opportunity to strengthen civil society, facilitate pluralist policy making and greater accountability, address social exclusion and above all, develop relations and work towards reconciliation. In conclusion, by fulfilling their potential, partnerships can ultimately help to realise this vision of a 'New Ireland.'

Appendix:
Mapping Partnerships in
Northern Ireland

To complement the map of Northern Ireland partnerships and the description of partnership governance in Chapter 3, this appendix outlines each of the partnership arrangements included in Figure 3.1. As discussed in Chapter 3, in order to classify partnerships in terms of their coalition building processes and level of spatial operation, detailed information was needed on each partnership. On this basis partnerships in Northern Ireland were examined against an analytical framework, illustrated in Chapter 3, which refers to the number of partners, aims and objectives, structures and functions of partnerships. It is the aim of this appendix to present this information on each partnership included in the study. Based on the categorisation in Table 3.1, this appendix will be broken into three parts A, B and C representing the different spatial levels in which partnerships operate in Northern Ireland, the *Local*, *Sub-regional* and the *Regional* levels. The first section, A, includes partnerships which operate at the local level in Northern Ireland and these are sub-divided into two areas, Local partnerships and Local - Transjurisdictional partnerships. In section B partnerships operating at the sub-regional level are mapped out and these were divided into Sub-regional partnerships and Sub-regional - Transjurisdictional partnerships. The final section, C the Regional level, is again sub-divided into two categories of partnerships, Regional partnerships and Regional / National Transjurisdictional partnerships.

Part A: Local Level Partnerships

Local

In Northern Ireland there are a range of partnerships operating at the local level. There are a number of different types of partnerships, involving different partners with different goals, implementing different strategies. The partnerships have been established across a number of policy areas for instance, rural development, urban regeneration, local economic development, education, health and employment.

One of the most prominent policy areas of partnership activity operating at the local level in Northern Ireland is urban regeneration. In urban regeneration a number of different partnerships have been established to regenerate the cities of Belfast and Derry. Urban regeneration falls under the remit of the Department of the Environment (DoE) which has widely embraced the partnership approach. It is stated in the corporate framework that the DoE has adopted a partnership approach to a range of urban regeneration measures in an attempt to, 'promote a comprehensive approach to tackling social, economic, physical regeneration and redressing disadvantage of cities, towns and villages in Northern Ireland' (DoE (1) 1996, p.17).

Making Belfast Work

Within the DoE's urban regeneration programme there are five partnership arrangements all implemented at the local level. One of the most long-standing partnership arrangements developed under the DoE's urban regeneration programme is the Making Belfast Work Initiative (MBW). The MBW initiative was launched in 1988 and has since shifted from a top down to a bottom up community partnership approach. The overall aim of the partnership is to,

> Strengthen and better target the efforts being made by the community, the private sector, and the government to tackle in partnership the economic, social and environmental problems which affect people in the most disadvantaged areas of Belfast, through increasing opportunities for residents of the MBW area to secure employment and improving the quality of life (MBW, 1996, p.4).

The MBW programme seeks to develop a coherent strategy for Belfast by facilitating partnership between all the relevant parties. MBW regards partnership as a seminal concept and has sought to encourage relationships with, 'other Government departments, public bodies, the private sector and the local communities. The development and facilitation of area partnerships is a crucial part of future strategy' (MBW, 1996, p.5).

The MBW initiative has established six teams throughout the city which provide targeted resources to the local communities in line with the objectives of the programme. It is envisaged that these teams should act as key players in taking the lead to encourage and facilitate area partnerships. At present work is continuing to strengthen partnerships in the North, South, East and West of the city. However, one of the more longer standing partnerships developed under the MBW programme is the Greater Shankill partnership. The Greater Shankill partnership brings together actors involved in the regeneration process: the business sector, community organisations, statutory bodies all of whom are elected onto the partnership board. Two major initiatives on the Shankill, which have been supported by the partnership, are the Urban Early Years Programme funded by the European Commission and MBW, and a Millennium bid which has reached the final stages of selection. Area forums on training, women, young people, education, sport and employment have also been facilitated by the partnership. Education has been a primary focus for investment by MBW in the Greater Shankill area in 1996/97 and the team has worked with the Belfast Education and Library Board (BELB), the Department of Education (DENI) and the local forum of schools to improve both the provision and uptake of opportunities.

To implement the strategies for education and training formal structures for the Greater Shankill Partnership were established in 1993. These included an Interim Partnership Board, a Support Team and an Elected Representatives Group each with complementary responsibilities. The Partnership Board is comprised of fifteen members including MBW, statutory bodies, local communities and Church groups and the private sector businesses in the area. The role of the Partnership Board is to develop the strategy and endorse the programmes. The Support Team has seven members representing local interests and has the role of preparing strategic programmes for key areas. The elected representatives group includes the local representatives from the Shankill in Belfast City Council, who advise the support team. In the Shankill partnership it is the process of collaboration that is binding the relationship. The collaboration process in the partnership can be highlighted in a number of ways. First of all, the partnership has developed a new formal organisational structure with clearly defined roles for each participant, in the Partnership Board, the Support Group or the Elected Representatives Group. Secondly, the partnership has adopted a comprehensive planning strategy which has included developing joint strategies and measuring success in terms of impact on the needs of those served. The strategy of the partnership to improve education along with the BELB, DENI and the local forum of schools is a case in point.

The Londonderry Initiative

In a similar programme to the MBW initiative, the DoE has also developed a partnership approach to urban regeneration in the City of Derry. The programme is known as the Londonderry Initiative of which the overall strategy is to,

> release the full potential of the most disadvantaged areas of Derry to become vital parts of a dynamic, prosperous and successful City by creating new opportunities for positive change through imaginative local action in partnership with others (DoE (3), 1997, p.3).

As a means to implement the locally based partnerships the department has established six community partnerships which include representatives of all interests in the disadvantaged areas of the city. The department recognises that the six partnerships cannot take an over arching view of regeneration and so an Urban Regeneration Group has been set up to oversee the partnerships and implement a more strategic regeneration approach. According to the strategy, membership of the Urban Regeneration Group will include a partnership of up to three representatives from, Derry City Council (5), the voluntary and community sectors (5), the statutory sector (3), the private sector (3) and chaired by the Londonderry Development Officer from the DoE. It is the Urban Regeneration Group which will have the responsibility for policy formation, implementation, monitoring and evaluation of the initiative. Local community strategies and programmes will be devolved down to the six local area partnerships by the Urban Regeneration Group. Funding for the initiative from its launch in December 1988 to the end of 1994/95 financial year has totalled £17.01 million, representing around an annual allocation of £2.84 million (DoE (3) 1997).

From viewing the remit and function of the Urban Regeneration Group it is clear that the partnership relationship is a collaborative one. The partnership has overarching control of the initiative and the development of a strategy which has involved comprehensive planning and the adoption of a number of projects. It is clear that authority is determined by the partnership with individual goals being fully committed to the implementation of a long term strategy to regenerate the city.

Laganside Development

Another partnership arrangement involving the DoE has developed under the remit of the Laganside Corporation in Belfast. In 1989 the Laganside Corporation was established by government to redevelop land along the river Lagan and to improve the quality of the river. The Corporation was charged with redeveloping about 140 hectares of land in the city. The Corporation is a public corporation with a Chairman and board members appointed by government, the Corporation has secured public sector investment amounting to £49 million, including £32 million from a DoE grant and a £3 million from the European Union. The Corporation's success is largely dependent upon a large range of partnerships. The partnership approach is adopted in two ways,

1. The Corporation seeks to widely consult and work closely with landowners along the river bank, local communities and other interested bodies to determine the most appropriate development strategy.
2. The redevelopment of land is dependant upon partnership with the landowners, mostly from Belfast City Council, and the commitment of the private sector (Laganside, 1996, p.6).

Probably the most interesting multidimensional partnership arrangement in the Laganside Corporation is that which is operating to develop the Gasworks. Belfast City Council as landowners is progressing the development of the site in partnership with the Laganside Corporation, private and voluntary bodies, the Queens University of Belfast and in consultation with the local community. Interaction between the partner organisations in the Laganside development is based on a co-ordinative process. Some joint planning has been developed to regenerate the Gasworks site but each individual organisation firmly retains its own authority and accountability.

Belfast and Derry City Centre Partnership Boards

In another effort to regenerate Belfast and Derry, City Centre Partnership Boards have been established. The Belfast Partnership Board was established in early 1996 to develop in consultation with the people of Belfast, the long term vision of the city to the year 2025 and to oversee the realisation of that vision. The Board has been established as a Company Limited by guarantee and consists of between twenty-five to thirty representatives from the statutory, business, trade union and community / voluntary sectors as well as Councillors from Belfast City Hall. The board has its own secretariat and is jointly chaired by the Minister for the Environment and a nominee from the council. The aim of the partnership is to set out a broad framework, 'which has been widely debated and agreed by the citizens of the city and within which public agencies, the business sector and local communities can work together in achieving more prosperous, more equitable, more vibrant and exciting city' (NIIS, 1995, p.2).

A similar partnership structure was established in Derry in 1995 involving the public, private, statutory and community spheres. The Partnership Board in Derry is chaired jointly by the Mayor of Derry City Council and the DoE's Permanent Secretary. The main role of the Partnership Board is to take an overarching view of the long term physical regeneration of the city and to formulate a strategy after consultation with the local community. The Partnership Board has been established as a new organisational structure in the form of a public company limited by guarantee with all representatives sharing equal risk and developing joint strategies. This leads firmly to the position that the partnership is working under a collaborative relationship.

Urban Partnerships

Not only have the DoE been involved in establishing partnerships for urban regeneration at the local level but the European Commission has also introduced an urban partnership initiative. The Urban Programme seeks to award funding to local partnerships in deprived urban areas and is designed to, 'help find solutions to the serious socio-economic problems experienced by supporting schemes for economic and social revitalisation and environmental protection' (European Commission, 1995, p.8).

Support from the programme is focused on four main areas, supporting new economic networks, training, work experience and related schemes for young people, improving facilities in the health and safety fields and providing support for infrastructure and environmental improvement measures. To receive funding and support the area must have developed innovative strategies to deal with one of the main areas and above all, the local area must be able to demonstrate that their strategies build a partnership between the community and the agencies of government, the private sector and voluntary organisations. In Northern Ireland a number of areas have developed partnerships and drawn funding from the Urban initiative, namely, the Shankill, as previously discussed in this appendix, and Upper Springfield areas of Belfast and the Creggan, Fountain and Bogside / Brandywell areas of Derry.

In the Upper Springfield area of Belfast a partnership known as the Upper Springfield Development Trust was established to implement and administer a programme seeking to address the needs of the teenage and young adult population (11-21 year olds) in the area. The programme is largely operated through the Trust's Management Committee which is comprised of, 'four representatives from the statutory agencies, three representatives from the private sector and nine representatives elected from the Upper Springfield Community' (Upper Springfield Development Trust, 1995, p.13). To address the needs of the Youth in the area the Trust developed a strategy in which the main objectives were to,

> improve the employment profile of the area's young people in terms of quality and sustainability; increase the take up of education / training opportunities in the area by young people; maintain and increase participation in mainstream youth activities and encourage greater partnership and co-operation between the statutory and voluntary players who have an input in the area (cited by Hughes and Carmichael, 1995, p.15).

Under the programme other partnerships have been established with various statutory agencies. The Upper Springfield Development Trust has developed co-operative partnership links with statutory agencies such as the Belfast Education and Library Board, the Training and Employment Agency and the Department of Education, in an attempt to co-ordinate and complement services created through the project, to ensure maximum effectiveness of mainstream resources and to create an integrated programme package. The partnership relationship within the Upper Springfield Development Trust is a collaborative process. The partnership is organised through formal linkages in the Management Committee with new goals and missions being developed. Secondly, a new strategy was formulated which involved comprehensive joint planning between the partners. Finally, the Trust's Management Committee has the responsibility for monitoring the effectiveness of the programme.

DoE and Local Community Regeneration Programmes

Aside from the major regeneration initiatives in Belfast and Derry, the DoE has also been active on the partnership front in the regeneration of towns and villages in the rest of Northern Ireland. The DoE, with the assistance of the International Fund for Ireland (IFI), has developed a number of programmes aiming to involve local communities in the development and rejuvenation of their areas. In each programme a partnership relationship is established between the IFI, DoE and the local communities. The IFI and the DoE give support and funding to local communities and groups who develop their own strategy. No joint planning occurs as the authority, ownership and accountability of the strategies rests solely with the local communities and groups. Each programme is therefore based on a co-operative partnership process.

Community Regeneration Improvement Scheme (CRISP)

In much of a similar initiative to the DANI's Community Based Regeneration project, the DoE and the IFI have developed the Community Regeneration Improvement Scheme (CRISP). The CRISP scheme is designed to assist smaller towns and villages with a population of less than 10,000 in disadvantaged areas of Northern Ireland. It is administered by the DoE and co-funded by the IFI under whose auspices it was founded in 1990. Between 1990-1996 45 CRISP schemes have been approved (IFI, 1996). The role of the IFI and the DoE in the scheme is largely to provide support for the community based economic core projects, including assistance for environmental improvements and to support private sector projects aiming to regenerate vacant and derelict properties.

Community Economic Regeneration (CERS)

This programme is targeted at areas of disadvantage in towns with a population of over 10,000 and offers grants and loans to community groups who have proposals for economic orientated projects. The programme is administered by the DoE and its aim is to, 'stimulate economic activity, improve confidence and community development, provide retail and industrial facilitates, reduce unemployment and improve the environment' (IFI, 1996, p.23). The programme has assisted 14 projects with a total investment of over 26 million.

Urban Development Programme

Through the rehabilitation of properties for commercial purposes and the improvement of public spaces, this programme continues to make a major contribution to the economic and social regeneration of town and village centres. An important feature of the programme is the Community Property Development Scheme (CPDS). First introduced in 1994, this scheme targets a selected list of priority towns in Northern Ireland and offers assistance to local cross-community groups to regenerate derelict key buildings in the commercial centres for economic use.

Another major area of partnership activity at the local level in Northern Ireland is in the field of local economic development. The role of district councils received a major boost under the Local Economic Development Measure in the Single Programming Document for Northern Ireland Structural Funds 1994-1999. This measure was designed to build complementarity with the work of IDB and LEDU, to provide support for groups pursuing local economic development objectives, and to enhance new business formation and local entrepreneurship. In order to draw down funding, the Department of Economic Development (DED) requested that local authorities commit themselves to the formation of district development strategies and subsequent action plans. Some £8 million of structural funds was allocated for implementation up until 1997. The DED has appointed the Local Economic Development Unit (LEDU) to act as co-ordinating agent to establish greater, 'involvement in development and implementation of 26 council strategies for local economic development' (LEDU, 1996, p.22).

Greater Craigavon Partnership

One council which has involved LEDU in formulating its strategy for local economic development is Craigavon Borough Council. As a means to implement the strategy, the council has established the Greater Craigavon Partnership (GCP) which is an amalgam of local private, voluntary, community and statutory interests. The partnership also contains a number of local organisations and partnerships committed to improving economic regeneration of the area, for example, Lurgan Forward, Brownlow Ltd, Portadown 2000, Craigavon Rural Development and the Business Centre. The mission statement of the partnership is to, promote and secure a successful self-sustaining and competitive enterprise culture for the Borough. Our goal is to strive to make Craigavon an alternative place in which to invest, work and live through industrial, commercial and community development (GCP, 1995, p.1).

The partnership aims to establish 80 new businesses, encourage the development of 50 hectares of service land, 36,000 square metres of additional factory and commercial space and to strengthen the living standards of the borough residents.

The Greater Craigavon Partnership is a partnership based on a co-operative process. The partnership is a loose affiliation of organisations and interests which are bonded together with the sole commitment of fostering economic prosperity in the Borough. The partnership functions on a good will basis without any legal status and does not seek to control or direct the resources of member organisations. Accountability firmly rests with each individual partner.

Portadown 2000

Considering that the Greater Craigavon Partnership is also an amalgam of other local partnerships it is interesting to identify and highlight one of the partnerships. Portadown 2000 was established in 1994 with the aim of securing the physical regeneration of the town and promoting the image of Portadown. Portadown 2000 is a partnership comprising representatives from the Portadown Chamber of Commerce, Craigavon Borough Council, the Craigavon Standing Conference of Women's Organisations, Portadown Architects group, Business in the Community and a permanent full time Chief Executive. Portadown 2000 has a wide remit in regeneration in Portadown and the partnership works in co-operation with Craigavon Borough Council and the statutory and voluntary agencies. For example, in developing the roads, work was conducted by Portadown 2000 along with the DoE and Ulsterbus. In improving the public park, sports facilities and the development of a Marina, the partnership sought the aid of the Northern Ireland Tourist Board and in establishing the new public library, the partnership worked alongside the Southern Education and Library Board.

Portadown 2000 is a collaborative partnership relationship. The partnership has been established as a company limited by guarantee with authority and accountability resting with the Board of Directors. The partnership has developed a number of joint strategies and equal risk is shared by all participants in the partnership.

Derry Investment Initiative

The Derry Investment Initiative also aims to improve the local economy of the Derry region but instead of developing a local economic strategy such as the Greater Craigavon Partnership, the Initiative focuses largely on attracting overseas investment. The Derry Investment Initiative was established in April 1997 and is comprised of a multidimensional range of participants including Derry City Council, Londonderry Chamber of Commerce, University of Ulster at Magee, DoE, LEDU, Business in the Community and John Hume MP, MEP. The partnership aims to regenerate the region of Derry by attracting overseas investors and promoting the region as an ideal European location for mobile US investment. Before the partnership was established, links had been forged with the US Department of Commerce and major US industries, companies and universities, through exchange visits and conferences. In April 1997 members of the partnership travelled to a number of locations in the US, for example, Silicon Valley, with the aim of attracting industry to the Derry region. The Derry Investment Initiative is a co-operative partnership with each of the participants drawn together to promote investment. The partnership operates on an informal basis with each participant acting independently of each other and only co-operating on mutual, infrequent projects such as the visit to the US in April 1997.

Rural Community Based Regeneration

Rural development is another area which has been associated with development of local partnerships in Northern Ireland. The main thrust of the partnership approach adopted by the DANI is located within the Rural Development Programme implemented in 1992. In the DANI there is a recognition of the value of rural development being fostered and maintained at the local level and therefore one of the main aims of the Rural Development Programme is to adopt,

> A careful and progressive approach to development, recognising the need for building capacity of local communities to help themselves in the first instance and then providing appropriate financial support for the projects

which arise from the process of community economic development (DANI, 1996, p.13).

A community based regeneration project has been launched within the Rural Development Programme in an attempt to bring the DANI's Rural Development Division closer to the local communities by working in partnership. The project, which is funded by the Rural Development Division and in part by the European Union structural funds, aims to provide rural communities with the expertise to implement their own proposals. At present, the project is engaging with 450 local community groups and provides assistance in many ways. The project assists local communities to formulate local development plans and implement projects promoting the diversification of the rural economy and encouraging the growth of local community enterprise. Groups such as the Seeconnel Initiative have received funding to develop tourism accommodation and the Ardboe Development Association have received assistance in establishing a business park to attract and develop local community enterprise.

Furthermore the Rural Development Council (RDC), an independent body funded by DANI, is also active in the area of rural community development. At the core of the RDC's new strategy is the, 'provision of specialist services to assist communities with this process and particularly to develop good projects which can contribute to job creation in disadvantaged areas' (RDC, 1996, p.11).

The DANI's Community Based Regeneration project and the RDC's programme are similar in many ways, with both programmes giving assistance to local community groups and organisations. The partnership relationship which has been established is a co-operative relationship. In the co-operative process the mission and goals of the local organisations are only taken into account whenever the DANI and the RDC decide whether to allocate funding to the groups. No joint planning is undertaken as the DANI and the RDC give assistance to the groups who are developing their own plans.

The Rural Development Programme also aims to integrate the communities into local partnerships comprising a number of key actors. Indeed, the establishment of local multidimensional partnerships is a consistent theme throughout the programme. The strategic aim of the programme seeks to, 'stimulate the economic and social revitalisation of the most disadvantaged rural areas of Northern Ireland through partnership between the public, private and community sectors' (DANI, 1996, p.14).

Area Based Strategies

One of the programmes seeking to establish local multidimensional partnerships is the Area Based Strategies initiative. The Area Based Strategies adopt a different approach to the Community Based Regeneration Project as they aim to develop local partnerships or area based strategy action groups made up of representatives of the community within the area to which the strategy applies, the local authorities, central government, statutory bodies and the private sector. In the partnerships a strategy manager is put in place and a sum of £1 million is provided to lever in other funding to trigger regeneration activity to meet the costs of the strategy. The essence of the Area Based Strategy approach is found in,

> local ownership of the process of consultation, of decision making, and of the implementation of the resulting strategy, and of its management. A high degree of adaptation to the strategy to the specific needs of the area and a high degree of leverage of other funds by resources dedicated to the strategy (DANI, 1996, p.27).

It is clear that the partnership relationship developed under the Area Based Strategies is more intertwined or developed than co-operation would suggest. For instance, the partnership has developed an overall strategy and has control or ownership of a consultation process, decision making and implementation of that strategy. The essential relationship in the Area Based Strategies is co-ordination. This is because the partnerships develop a single project specific strategy, whereas in a collaborative relationship one or more projects are undertaken. Secondly, the actors involved have particular roles on the partnership but each function relatively independent of each other; interrelated roles and formal division of labour are not established. Finally, although there is some sharing of leadership and risk most of the authority and accountability in the area partnership falls to the individual organisations. In a collaborative process however, leadership is dispersed, control is shared and mutual between all the organisations in the partnership.

The European Commission has also been involved in developing partnership programmes in Northern Ireland for rural development. LEADER 2 is the EU Community Initiative on rural development which is designed to address problems which are common in many rural areas throughout the member states: rising unemployment, increasing economic insecurity, the migration of best educated young people and the disappearance of local services. The programme aims to, 'promote the development of the rural economy by stimulating local action groups and other rural bodies to adapt innovative measures which contribute to rural development at the local level' (European Commission, 1995, p.6).

LEADER 2 is administered by the DANI but implemented through local action groups, collective bodies and local partnerships. At present 24 LEADER groups have been established including 15 local action groups and 9 other collective bodies. The EU and the DANI have allocated over £15 million of funding to the local action groups who largely operate in clearly defined geographical areas corresponding broadly to a number of the district council areas of Northern Ireland. The spirit of LEADER 2 is to promote decision making responsibilities and control at the local rural community level and in this light LEADER provides support for innovative measures in the,' acquisition of skills, including technical support for the creation of local partnerships, analysis of local areas and the formulation of local development strategies' (European Commission, 1996, p.6).

With advice and support from the LEADER programme, local communities have established partnerships which have the ability to undertake decision making responsibilities and develop some project specific planning. Under the programme co-ordinative partnerships have been set up at the local community level. However, the relationship between the local partnerships and the programme developers in the DANI is purely a co-operative relationship based on an advisory supportive role.

The Fermanagh University Partnership Board

The Department of Education has also been at the forefront in establishing multidimensional partnerships at the local level. Within the last number of years, the DENI have been actively encouraging Universities to make their services more accessible. In the Department of Education's Strategic Plan, it states that one way to achieve this is for Universities to, 'improve links with further education colleges and work with district councils to improve access in remote areas' (DENI, 1996, p.24).

Two areas in which the Queen's University of Belfast and the University of Ulster have sought to improve their accessibility in remote areas are Armagh and Fermanagh. In both instances, the university partnerships have been developed with the local district council to set up a university outreach centre. In Armagh, a partnership between the Queen's University of Belfast and Armagh District Council has established an outreach centre of the Queen's University in Armagh City, and a University in rural Fermanagh has been established due to the work of a partnership between Fermanagh District Council and the University of Ulster. The initiative in rural Fermanagh is most interesting and can be highlighted as an example of a local multidimensional partnership for education. In 1995 a formal partnership arrangement was established known as the Fermanagh University Partnership Board. The Board was first of all comprised of the University of Ulster and Fermanagh District Council as lead partners but also included, Fermanagh Training Ltd, Fermanagh College of Further Education, Enniskillen College of Agriculture and representatives from the voluntary and private sectors. The aim of the partnership is to establish an outreach centre of the University of Ulster in Fermanagh and to implement a number programmes to improve education in rural Fermanagh. One programme is the Fermanagh Higher Bridges Project of which the main focus is to improve Information Technology provision in rural communities. Information Technology facilities will be improved for use in the further education college and secondary schools and to establish community learning through distance education for the unemployed. Small companies in the area will also benefit in terms of education and research in marketing and finance. Within the partnership the business representatives will look for gaps in the provision of University education and bring their local expertise and knowledge of what skills employers need. It is hoped that the partnership will regenerate community life through employment, education and economic growth.

The partnership of the Fermanagh University Partnership Board is a formal relationship which has the responsibility for formulating and implementing project specific planning. Within the partnership there is some sharing of leadership and control. Authority, however, is not determined by the partnership as each participant retains individual authority and accountability. The coalition building process within the Fermanagh University Partnership Board is co-ordination.

Partnership in the Health and Social Services: Health Trusts and the Voluntary / Community Sector

In recent years the concept of partnership has had a strong influence in the development of the strategy for the Department of Health and Social Services (DHSS). Indeed, the term partnership is included as one of the main mechanisms to achieve the aims of the department. It is stated that what is needed is,

> strong alliances and partnerships between a very wide range of organisations, and not just those in health and personal social services. The wider statutory, voluntary, community and private sectors, as well as individuals and their families, have just as an important role to play in promoting health and social well being (DHSS, 1997, p.2).

The idea of partnership has permeated throughout the department involving all health boards and social service trusts across the province. It is the role of the health and social service trusts to deliver services at the local level. In this role the trusts now seek to work in partnership with local voluntary and community groups to deliver services which are appropriate and relevant for the local area. The partnership approach adopted by the DHSS differs from urban regeneration or local economic development as the Trust seeks to 'work in partnership' or establish 'partnership links' with local community and voluntary groups. In areas of partnership activity for example, urban regeneration, a specific partnership programme is adopted.

With the trusts working with local community and voluntary agencies, this is seen by the DHSS as developing a community development approach. The DHSS has established community development as an underlying principle which is defined in the annual report as,

> A way of working, informed by certain individuals which seek to encourage communities to tackle for themselves the problems which they face, and which aim to empower them to change things by developing their own skills, knowledge and expertise and also by working in partnership with other groups and statutory agencies (DHSS, 1997, p.13).

Trusts and the Local Community

An example of one trust which has embraced the community development approach is the South and East Belfast Health and Social Services Trust. The South and East Belfast Trust is keen to develop a community development approach by engendering, "trust and understanding by developing stronger partnership between the community and the trust" (South and East Belfast Trust, 1997, p.10).

The South and East Belfast Trust has been engaged in a community capacity building programme designed to raise awareness of the inherent value of the community and the trust working in partnership. The trust also seeks to develop closer linkages with the area partnerships established under the Making Belfast Work Initiative. In this role the trust representatives give advice and expertise to the partnerships operating programmes of health care. The partnership approach adopted between the trust and the community is a co-operative relationship. At present, partnership interaction is developed on an informal basis and functions largely to seek the views of the community, to raise awareness and build capacity for the delivery of future services.

Trusts and the Voluntary Sector

Trusts have also developed partnership links with the voluntary sector which are more formal co-ordinative arrangements. In the South and East Belfast Trust, voluntary groups have been contracted out to operate services on their behalf, particularly in the areas of elderly care and mental illness. Each year the Eastern Health Board spends over £2 million on contracting out for the four trusts in the region. The South and East Belfast Trust also aims to contract out services to local community groups. However, this development is at the pilot stage. Working in partnership through a contract basis is a more formalised method of interaction. The trusts co-ordinate action together with the voluntary groups to deliver a particular service but each organisation still functions separately maintaining its own authority and accountability.

District Partnerships for Peace and Reconciliation

In 1995 the European Commission adopted the European Union Special Support Programme for Peace and Reconciliation (EUSSPP&R) for Northern Ireland and the border counties of Ireland, with the aim of maintaining peace and reconciliation following the paramilitary cease-fires of the previous year. The overall aim of the programme is to,

> reinforce progress towards a peaceful and stable society and to promote reconciliation by increasing economic development and employment, promoting urban and rural regeneration, developing cross-border co-operation and extending social inclusion (Commission of European Communities, 1995).

As well as focusing on the above mentioned five priority themes administered by central government and Intermediary Funding Bodies, the programme also includes the establishment of district partnerships. The District Partnerships number twenty-six corresponding to each of the district council areas and have the responsibility of harnessing the energies and talents of local groups in the pursuit of the common goals of the programme. In the first phase of funding, the District Partnerships have been allocated a total of almost £46.7 million to be distributed across four programme priorities, Employment 19%, Urban and Rural Regeneration 19%, Social Inclusion 44%, Productive Investment and Industrial Development 18%. The District Partnerships in reflecting the interests of the local area, must comprise one third each, local councillors, voluntary / community, business / trade union interests as well as statutory organisations. The primary aim of each of the District Partnerships has been to formulate and implement a local action plan detailing social and economic projects to best meet the needs and goals of the programme. After a lengthy consultation the District Partnerships have also formulated a strategy document which has been used as a framework for processing applications. To administer and oversee the district partnerships a further new partnership has been established, the Northern Ireland Partnership Board (NIPB). The NIPB is made up of elected representatives (8), voluntary / community (7), private sector representatives (3), Trade Unions (3) and one Rural Development Council nominee. The NIPB is a company limited by guarantee and is chaired by the Permanent Secretary of the DoE.

The District Partnerships established under the EUSSPP&R are a form of collaborative partnership. The partnerships have developed new organisational structures and, in certain instances, established themselves as a company limited by guarantee. The District Partnerships have formulated their own joint strategies after extensive planning and consultation. A large number of the projects have been undertaken by the district partnerships and in some cases District Partnerships have decided to develop a programme approach. Within each of the partnerships control and mutual and risk is shared by all the participants.

Local Transjurisdictional

Local partnerships have not only been established within Northern Ireland, partnerships also operate at the local level in Northern Ireland and at the

local level in another national jurisdiction. The main area in which local -
transjurisdictional partnership have been established is the field of
economic development.

The Partnership of Belfast City Council and Novia Scotia

Local authorities in Northern Ireland have been active in establishing links
with other partners outside the European Union. One example of this type
of partnership is that which has been developed between Belfast City
Council and the Provincial Government in Novia Scotia. The main aim of
the partnership is to further economic development and trade between the
two areas by matching companies which could trade together. Funding for
the partnership has been awarded by the economic development arm of
Belfast City Council. The partnership is still in developmental stages but a
number of visits have taken place with alliances being fostered between
companies. Belfast City Council and the Provincial Government of Novia
Scotia have signed a memorandum of agreement aiming to improve trading
and economic links. The agreement also refers to improving cultural links
as Novia Scotia contains a large proportion of people from Ulster Scots
descent. Although the partnership is still in its embryonic stages, it can be
said that the relationship has been established on an as needed basis with
each form of government strictly maintaining its own form of authority,
accountability, independence and leadership. The partnership has,
therefore, established a co-operative relationship.

*Co-operation Ireland (formally Co-operation North) Local Authority
Linkages Project*

An example of local - transjurisdictional partnerships are those established
under the Co-operation Ireland Local Authority Linkages Project. Co-
operation Ireland is a charity based organisation which was established in
1979 in response to the challenge of conflict and violence in Northern
Ireland. It is a non political, non-religious organisation which aims to,
"overcome destructive prejudices and promote joint activities on a cross
border, cross community basis" (Co-operation North, 1996, p.2).

In an attempt to meet these aims, Co-operation Ireland has
developed a number of programmes: the Youth, Education and Community
Programme, an Economic Co-operation Programme and a Media
Programme. In the Economic Co-operation Programme, for example, the

aim of Co-operation Ireland is to, 'encourage cross-border business contacts (which all) foster new economic opportunities as well as strengthening established enterprises' (Co-operation North, 1996, p.2).

Under the theme of economic co-operation, a number of partnerships have been established through the Local Authority Linkages Project. This programme is part funded by the Bank of Ireland and in 1996 links were established between Larne Borough Council and Dun Laoghaire / Rathdown Borough Council, Ballymena Borough Council and Castlebar and Carrickfergus Borough Council and Wexford County Council. The partnership between Carrickfergus Borough Council and Wexford County Council was established in 1996 and includes a number of programme areas. First of all, under the theme of tourism, accommodation providers in both council areas conducted exchange visits and a seminar is due to be held in Carrickfergus by tourism providers from Wexford on partnerships in marketing. Secondly, in the business links programme, personnel from large companies were transferred to companies in the other council area in an effort to exchange good business practice. Small business seminars were held covering joint areas of interest, for example, town regeneration and the promotion of small businesses. Finally, a community programme has operated cultural and sporting exchange visits between community groups, sports and historical groups and photographic groups. The partnerships established under the Local Authority Linkages Project are as the facilitating body suggests, co-operation. The relationship between Carrickfergus Borough Council and Wexford County Council is an informal one, with each council acting and functioning as a separate organisation and with interaction ongoing on an as needed basis.

ECOS-OUVERTURE

The European Union (EU) have also been actively involved in establishing partnerships at the local - transjurisdictional level. The European Commission has adopted the Ecos-Ouverture programme which seeks to increase exchanges between the local authorities in the EU with those in Central and Eastern Europe. The aim is to establish partnerships to aid the local authorities in Central and Eastern Europe to bolster the development of democracy and the market economy (Murray and Smyth, 1996). Through partnership, local authorities can enhance local government expertise on a mutual basis through practice exchange visits, cultural enrichment and the creation of new investment and marketing opportunities. In Northern Ireland eight district councils have been involved in partnerships with Central and Eastern European countries under the programme.

Down District Council has been involved in partnership with local authorities in Bulgaria and Greece. The partnership operated under the guidelines of the programme set by the European Commission and the aim was to develop best practice for craft enterprises which would, in itself, improve the local economy and aid tourism. The partnership existed between March 1996 and October 1996 in which a number of training workshops were organised along with conferences and meetings.

The partnership relationship operating under this programme was the co-operative process. The aim of the partnership arrangement was to organise a number of training workshops and meetings in which to share information and establish best practice. In this relationship no specific project planning was conducted with interaction being largely centred on a loose arrangement of information sharing and networking.

The European Union Employment Programme

In addition, the EU has developed a programme to establish partnerships across the EU operating at the local level with the aim of improving employment practices. The Employment and Development of Human Resources is a European Union (EU) programme which has helped to facilitate partnerships between various companies and businesses throughout the EU. The main aim of the programme is to,

> support innovative and transnational measures to improve the working of the labour market and stimulate the growth of employment opportunities for women, improving the job prospects for the disabled and facilitating the integration of young people in the labour market (European Commission, 1995, p.5).

The programme is divided into three areas, Employment Now, Horizon and Youthstart. The Employment Now programme aims to reduce the numbers of unemployed women and to improve the position of those already in work mainly by innovative and transnational measures. The programme has been widely adopted in Northern Ireland with many companies and organisations working to improve the position of women in the workplace. For example, the Brownlow Community Trust, a limited company and charity based organisation in Craigavon has adopted a project under the programme to offer, 'employability skills for women and return to work education and training programmes both of a general nature and within the office environment' (Proteus, 1996, p.8).

To assist the programme, the Trust has established links with European partners in the South of Ireland, England and Spain. Each of the partners share information, network, and identify good projects and practice concerning women's employment. The partnership is also working to develop a methodology to identify barriers for women at work and a joint conference was also held in Waterford for representatives from all the partner organisations. The partnership is a co-operative process in that it is a loose affiliation of members which interact on an infrequent basis, (the partnership has met only on four occasions within the last two and a half years), largely to share information, network and support each other.

Part B: Sub-Regional

The Tyrone Economic Development Initiative

The Tyrone Economic Development Initiative (TEDI) is a sub-regional partnership which aims to promote economic development within the County of Tyrone. The partnership is a company limited by guarantee and is comprised of representatives from four district councils, Cookstown, Strabane, Omagh and Dungannon and representatives from the private sector. The TEDI operates on a non-profit making basis and has the responsibility for promoting and developing business opportunities for Tyrone companies at home and abroad. The partnership works along with business and statutory organisations in operating a number of key functions. First of all, it provides information and support services to over 300 companies in the Tyrone area and assists them in identifying export opportunities. Secondly, TEDI works alongside the local councils and the Industrial Development Board (IDB), implementing a number of programmes to assist companies in winning increased sales and also acting as a regional voice for Tyrone, lobbying government on economic development issues.

The TEDI operates under a collaborative partnership arrangement. The initiative has established a new organisational structure, in terms of a company limited by guarantee, and has adopted a range of long term projects and joint strategies. The company operates on a formal basis with authority being determined by the collaboration.

Partnerships in Health and Social Services: Health and Social Services Boards and the Voluntary / Community Sector

To complement the partnership links established by the Trusts, the Health and Social Service Boards also aim to work in partnership with the voluntary and community sectors. Within the DHSS it is the role of the four Health Boards to access need and purchase health and social care. The health boards seek to work in partnership with voluntary and community groups, health and social service trusts and other providers of services to assess local need and devise a strategy which is appropriate for the particular sub-region.

The Eastern Health Board in devising its strategy has sought to adopt and develop a community development partnership approach. The Eastern Health Board aimed to ensure that all key individuals were in a position to influence the decision making process. This meant that consultation was undertaken with community groups, local councillors, Trust Senior Managers, Trade Union representatives and key individuals as to the principles, goals and approach that such a strategy should adopt. All themes and areas of the strategy were considered and specialist views of organisations were sought. For example, Mencap was consulted over mentally handicapped / disabled service provision and the board worked closely with the Royal National Institute for the Deaf to identify the needs of the deaf in the community.

It can be seen that the partnership process adopted with the community and voluntary sectors within the DHSS is co-operation. In formulating the strategy and implementing programmes the DHSS has sought the views and ideas of local voluntary and community groups. This is a form of community development partnership with the relationship being established on an informal as needed basis.

Sub-regional - Transjurisdictional

The East Border Region Committee

One partnership which has been established between the North and South of Ireland is the East Border Region Committee, a Local Authority Cross-Border Network. The East Border Region Committee was established in the late 1970s and is a partnership between Down District Council, Newry and Mourne District Council and Monaghan and Louth County Councils. The main aim of the partnership is to improve economic development through rural development, tourism, local town regeneration, agriculture, roads and infrastructure development. Another two such partnerships exist: The Irish Central Border Area Network which is a partnership between Fermanagh and Dungannon District Councils and Cavan and Leitrim County Councils and the North West Regional Cross Border Group, which includes Derry City Council, Limavady Borough Council, Strabane District Council and Donegal County Council. The East Border Region Committee is not a funding organisation but lobbies and works with governmental organisations. For example, in economic development the partnership would work with LEDU or the NITB and with the DoE when seeking to improve the roads. The partnership is a co-ordinative process in that a formal relationship exists in terms of a Main Committee and an Executive. The Main Committee is comprised of 6 elected representatives and 2 council officials from each of the four councils, making 32 council members. A foreign affairs representative from Dublin and a representative of the Central Secretariat in Belfast sit on the board and MPs and TDs are also invited.

Recently, Banbridge and Armagh District Councils have been invited to join the Committee and Banbridge are currently attending meetings in an observer capacity. The Main Committee meets every month to discuss and debate matters and authorise proposals. The Executive on the other hand, comprises a Council Chairman and a Regional Development Officer. It is in the Executive that most of the operational work of the partnership is carried out, formulating proposals and working with other organisations and government departments and agencies. Through the Committee and Executive each participant has established roles of co-ordinating the operation of the partnership. Until recently the partnership has functioned largely with funding from each of the Councils. However, the East Border Region Committee, the Irish Central Border

Area, the North West Cross Border Group and the Irish Central Border Area Network now have a secretariat funded through the INTERREG 2 programme.

At present the East Region Border Committee is still a co-ordinating, lobbying body working alongside government departments and agencies. However, under the INTERREG programme new developments may take place. The Irish Central Border Area, The North West Regional Cross Border Group and the East Region Border Committee have joined the Association of European Border Regions. It is the aim of the INTERREG programme to develop these regional partnerships and encourage them to develop area strategies for their partnership locality. This would further institutionalise the partnerships and possibly bring them into a more collaborative process.

Part C: Regional

The final level of partnership operation in Northern Ireland is the National / Regional level. As mentioned at the beginning of this chapter this level includes partnerships which operate throughout Northern Ireland at the Regional level or throughout Northern Ireland and another national jurisdiction, the National / Regional- Transjurisdictional level.

The Private Finance Initiative

The Private Finance Initiative (PFI) is a programme designed to deliver higher quality and more cost effective public services in government departments and agencies by establishing better links with the private sector. In Northern Ireland there are a number of public - private sector partnerships which have been implemented across the region under the Finance Initiative (PFI). The PFI was introduced to bring,

> the public sector more directly into the provision of public services, with the public sector as an enabler and, where appropriate, guardian of the interests of the users of customers of public services (HM Treasury, 1995, p.1).

At present the PFI in Northern Ireland is in early stages of development. However, steps have been taken to implement the initiative in the DoE, the

DENI and the DHSS. For example, the DENI established a Central PFI Unit in June 1996 to co-ordinate PFI activity. A strategy was devised to test the scope of PFI solutions in the schools and Further Education College sectors. The strategy involved a wide ranging market sounding exercise which sought the views of private sector companies throughout the UK on how best high priority school capital projects could be progressed through PFI. In addition, a number of pathfinder projects were established to procure accommodation and services for two Further Education Colleges and four Secondary Schools. These projects are at various stages of the procurement process. One of the projects, the rationalisation of the teaching accommodation in the North West Institute of Further and Higher Education is planned to reach contract award stage by the end of 1997. Similarly, the DoE is also in various stages of the procurement process and in one instance, advertisements have been published in the Official Journal of the EC for the provision of sewage and treatment works at Bangor and Kinnegar through the Water Executive.

Relationships between the public and private sectors established under the PFI are a form of co-ordinative partnership. Under PFI, relationships between the public and private sector is centred on a formalised basis with interaction focused on one specific project of definable length, for example, a formal contract to provide a sewage treatment works. In PFI projects the public and private organisations co-ordinate action together to facilitate a project but, clearly, authority and accountability remain with the individual organisations.

The Department of Education for Northern Ireland and the Training and Employment Agency

In Northern Ireland a partnership arrangement has been established between the Department of Education for Northern Ireland (DENI) and the Training and Employment Agency (T&EA), with the aim of improving education and training skills. In Northern Ireland, overall responsibility for meeting the needs of industry lies with the T&EA but there is a close relationship with the education sector, particularly in the provision of vocational courses in further education colleges. It is thought that training providers in schools could work together in shared development of the national framework of vocational qualifications for 14-19 year olds. It is stated in the Department of Education's strategic plan that,

The Northern Ireland Education Service, in partnership with the training sector, will work towards the National Targets for Education and Training (NTETs) which reflect the government's commitment to training levels and improving the qualifications of the workforce in the UK as a whole (DENI, 1996, p.6).

In view of the aim to work in partnership, structures have been set up to ensure co-ordination between the DENI and the T&EA which include: an overall strategy, a policy and co-ordination group, a vocational qualifications group and an Interdepartmental Executive. In relation to the strategy, both the DENI and the T&EA recognise the value of working together to raise the training and education levels for young people. In the school curriculum, a broad vocational emphasis has been adopted for pupils in the two years before compulsory school leaving age. The education sector has recognised that the knowledge must be closely related to the demands of adult working life and the introduction of General National Vocational Qualifications (GNVQ) has enhanced this position. Secondly, in 1995, the DENI and T&EA published a report describing existing education and training strategies for the 14-19 year old group and how these might be developed further in achieving parity of esteem between vocational and academic progression routes. This raised important issues which were also picked up by the Dearing Report on the review of Qualifications for 16-19 year olds published in March 1996. Also in 1995, the DENI and the T&EA jointly published a review of careers guidance and in May 1996 published a consultation paper on life time learning.

In the Jobskills programme the function of the Interdepartmental Executive is to advance education provision. The programme, therefore, combines the specific skills based orientated approach of the T&EA with a knowledge based provision from the DENI.

The partnership between the DENI and the T&EA has also adopted a single Education and Training Inspectorate (ETI). The ETI assesses quality in both education and training and ensures that there is continuity and coherence in the experiences offered to young people in schools, colleges, training establishments and in the work place. Indeed, in recognition of the interface between education and training, one Minister has been given responsibility for both the DENI and the T&EA.

It can be seen that the partnership between the DENI and the T&EA has developed a clear strategy and a basis for equal interaction given the existence of an overall strategy and a policy and co-ordination group. Joint mechanisms have formalised the relationships and communication roles have been established. Definitive channels for partnership working have also been created through the Education and Training Inspectorate and the Interdepartmental Executive. The DENI and the T&EA work together in partnership in what is a complementary area but they still function independently of each other. The DENI maintains sole responsibility for the curriculum and responsibility still rests with the T&EA for programmes such as Jobskills. With most of the authority and accountability remaining with the individual organisations, it can be clearly seen that the partnership relationship developed between the DENI and the T&EA is a form of co-ordination.

Industrial Development Board - The Northern Ireland Partnership

A second public - private partnership established in Northern Ireland is that between the IDB and the Northern Ireland Partnership. The NIP is an international voluntary network of senior business and professional people who come from Northern Ireland or who have worked, lived or studied there and wish to contribute to its economic development. The partnership between the IDB and the NIP has three objectives, to support IDB's inward investment drive, to help identify business and trade opportunities for Northern Ireland and to help promote Northern Ireland as a viable business location (IDB, 1997, p.1).

This partnership is still in the early stages of development but it can be stated that the partnership arrangement is a co-operative relationship. The relationship is informal and ad hoc with each organisation working together on an as needed basis with no joint strategy making or planning and each organisation functioning as separate independent bodies.

Industrial Development Board - Business Community

As well as establishing links with the NIP to improve business and trade opportunities in Northern Ireland, IDB is also active in developing partnership links with the wider business community. Indeed, building relationships with the business sector has been the cornerstone of the IDB's strategy. In December 1990 the IDB published its strategy for the 1990s in which one of the guiding principles was that, 'government and the private sector should in partnership tackle the issues of growth and competitiveness on a sectoral basis' (IDB, 1996, p.6).

Consequently the IDB has met regularly with the employer and employee representative organisations, management consultancy, accountancy and economic research bodies to discuss industrial development issues. Since 1993 the Board has participated in outside visits to meet client companies and business representatives. The partnership process in this relationship is also a co-operative relationship in that the IDB interact with the private sector on an informal basis largely to provide support, share information, identify good practice and to network.

Industrial Research and Training Unit - Academia

Partnership arrangements have also been established between the Industrial Research and Training Unit (IRTU) and the Queens University of Belfast and the University of Ulster in the area of industrial research. It is envisaged that the strategy developed by QUB and the University of Ulster should, 'further promote the increasing synergies between the regional industry and academia and the contributions of Universities to commercially orientated research projects' (IRTU, 1995, p.11).

On a similar basis as the IDB, the partnership relationship established between the IRTU and the University is co-operation. Each of the organisations function completely separately, with no joint planning being developed. The relationship is largely an informal one with information being conveyed as needed.

National / Regional Transjurisdictional Level

Government departments and agencies have also developed partnership links in other national countries. Cross border partnerships with the Republic of Ireland are now the more prominent partnerships operating at this level.

Northern Ireland Tourist Board - Bord Fáilte

A partnership relationship was established in 1995 between the Northern Ireland Tourist Board (NITB) and Bord Fáilte to market the island of Ireland as a tourist destination for overseas visitors. It is stated that the

NITB will be working on two fronts in the campaign, firstly, 'in co-operation with Bord Fáilte, to attract visitors to the island and, second, to encourage as many of them as possible to spend part of their holiday in Northern Ireland when they arrive' (NITB, 1995, p.13).

The marketing campaign of the NITB and Bord Fáilte has been funded £6.8 million by the European Union, the International Fund for Ireland and public and private sector contributions. Marketing and the development of cross-border tourism programmes are largely the main functions of the relationship with interaction being developed on an as needed basis. Both of the organisations function separately with authority and accountability resting with the independent organisations. The partnership is, therefore, centred on a co-operative relationship.

Industrial Development Board - Irish Trade Board

The Industrial Development Board (IDB) and the Irish Trade Board (ITB) have also developed a partnership which is very similar to the relationship between Bord Fáilte and the NITB. A partnership was established in 1992 between the IDB and the Irish Trade Board with the aim of co-operating further to, 'develop cross border trade and promote the scale of local products and services outside the island of Ireland' (IDB, 1996, p.3).

Within the last number of years the organisations have worked together to aid cross border trade. Joint literature has been produced outlining a directory of companies producing goods and services in Ireland. It is hoped that companies will be able to use the directory to identify new market opportunities North and South of the border. In promoting the sale of products outside Ireland, representatives from the two organisations travelled to Russia to promote Irish companies and products and to identify new trade opportunities. As with the tourism partnership this relationship is also on a co-operative basis. Interaction is on an indefinite and informal as needed basis, with little joint strategy making. Furthermore, each organisation maintains its own independence and lines of accountability and authority.

Industrial Research and Training Unit - US Department of Commerce – Academia

In recent years a transjurisdictional partnership has been established between the IRTU, the United States Department of Commerce and academia in Northern Ireland and the US. The IRTU's Corporate Plan sets out the main aim of the partnership, 'to develop the economic opportunity offered by the peace process by including and implementing a research and development collaborative agreement between Northern Ireland and the US' (IRTU, 1995, p.7).

The partnership is still in the development stages. However, the relationship established is a co-operative process in that contact between the organisations is continued on an informal way with interaction on an as needed basis. No joint planning is conducted and authority rests solely with the individual organisations.

Industrial Research and Training Unit – Enterprise Ireland (formally Forbairt)

Cross border partnership links have also been established in the field of industrial and technological research. The Industrial Research and Training Unit has developed a partnership with Enterprise Ireland (Forbairt), a government agency in the South of Ireland, to improve scientific services. The partnership is funded by the International Fund for Ireland (IFI) under a joint North / South technology programme and aims to, 'increase the competitiveness of Irish Industry and strengthen the economies of both parts of the island through promotion and technological change' (IRTU, 1995, p.24).

This partnership is centred on a co-operative basis in which both organisations interact on an informal as needed basis, mainly to share resources, information and expertise.

Bibliography

Aldrich, H. (1977), 'Visionaries and Villains', *Organisations and Administration*, vol. 8, no. 3, pp.23-40.

Anderson, J. (1994), 'Problems of Inter State Economic Integration, Northern Ireland and the Irish Republic in the European Community', *Political Geography*, vol.13, no.1, pp.53-72.

Anglo Irish Joint Studies (1981), *Joint Report and Studies,* November 1981.

Aughey, A. (1996), 'Local Government', Chapter 11 in Aughey, A and Morrow, D. (eds), *Northern Ireland Politics*, London and New York, Longman. pp. 94-103.

Bailey, N. (1993), 'Picking Partners for the 1990s', *Town and Country Planning,* vol.62, no.6, pp.136.

Bailey, N. (1994), 'Towards a Research Agenda for Public-Private Partnerships in the 1990s', *Local Economy*, vol.6, no.4, pp.292-305.

Bailey, N. (1997), 'Competitiveness, Partnership – and Democracy? Putting the 'local' back into London Government', *Local Economy*, vol.12, no.3, pp.205-219.

BDO-Stoy Hayward (1998), *'East Border Region Committee - The East Border Development Strategy'*, March 1998.

Bennet, R.J and Krebs, G. (1994), 'Economic Development Partnerships: An Analysis of Policy Networks in the EC-LEDA Local Employment Development Strategies', *Regional Studies*, vol.28, no.2, pp.119-140.

Berham, E.M. (1996), 'Local Government and Community-Based Strategies: Evidence from a National Survey of a Social Problem', *The American Review of Public Administration*, vol.26, no.1, pp.71-93.

Birrel, D. and Wilson, C. (1993), 'Making Belfast Work: An Evaluation of an Urban Strategy', *Public Administration*, vol. 41, no.1, pp.40-56.

Bord Fáilte (1970), *Bord Fáilte Eireann - Irish Tourist Board: Report and Accounts for year ended March 31st 1970.*

Bord Fáilte (1972), *Bord Fáilte Eireann - Irish Tourist Board: Report and Accounts for year ended March 31st 1972.*

Bord Fáilte (1989), *Report and Accounts 1989.*

Bord Fáilte (1997), *Tourism Facts.*

Boyle, R. (1989a), 'Partnership in Practice', *Local Government Studies*, vol.15, no.2, pp.17-27.

Boyle, R. (1989b), 'Partnership in Practice: An assessment of public-private collaboration in urban regeneration – A case study of Glasgow Action', *Local Government Studies*, vol.15, no. 2, pp.17-28.

Brady, Shipman and Martin, (1979), *'The Erne Catchment Area Study'* volume 2 Report prepared for the Governments of the UK and Ireland and the Commission of the European Communities.

Brindely, T. and Stoker, G. (1988), 'Partnership in Inner City Urban Renewal - a critical analysis', *Local Government Policy Making*, vol. 15, no.2, pp.3-11.

Browne, G. (1997), Presentation on the mid-term evaluation of the INTERREG Tourism Measure.

Bryson, J.M. and Crosby, B. (1992), *Leadership for the Common Good*, San Francisco: Jossey-Bass.

Buckely, P.J. and Klemn, M. (1993), 'The decline of tourism in Northern Ireland: the causes', *Tourism Management*, vol. 14, no.3, pp.184-195.

Busteed, M. (1994), 'The Irish Border - From Partition and Confrontation to Co-operation?', *Boundary Bulletin*, vol. 4, pp.13-17.

Cebulla, A. (1996), 'Making Partnerships Work", Whose City? - Visions of Belfast', *Fortnight Supplement*, No.348.

Clarke, J. (1995), 'The State, Popular Participation, and the Voluntary Sector', *World Development*, vol. 23, no.4, pp. 593-603.

Clarke, M. (1996), 'Urban Policy and Governance', *Local Government Policy Making*, vol. 23, no.1, pp.13-19.

Clarke, W. and O'Cinneide, B. (1981), *'Understanding and Co-operation in Ireland: Tourism in the Republic of Ireland and Northern Ireland'*, Paper 5, Co-operation North, Belfast and Dublin.

Colman, T. (1997), 'Perspectives from Local Government', paper presented to *New Partnerships in Local Government Conference*, 28th January, 1997. London.

Combat Poverty Agency (1995), *Making Partnerships Work: A Handbook on Involvement in Local Development Partnerships*, Combat Poverty Agency, September 1995.

Commission of the European Communities Office in Northern Ireland (1995), 'Special Support Programme for Peace and Reconciliation in Northern Ireland and the Border Counties of Ireland 1995-1999', *Eurolink Supplement 9*, Belfast EC.Office.

Co-operation North (1983), *North-South Co-operation In Ireland: 5 Years of Progress 1979-1983.*

Co-operation North (1996), *Co-operation North Annual Report.*

Coopers and Lybrand (1990), *The North West Study - Final Study Report*, April 1990.

Coopers and Lybrand and INDECON (1994), report for Joint IBEC/CBI Northern Ireland Council *'A Corridor of Opportunity'*, May 1994.

Coopers and Lybrand (1997), *'Special Support Programme for Peace and Reconciliation and the Border Counties of Ireland 1995-1999, Mid Term Evaluation Final Report'*, July 1997.

Coventry City Council (1996), *Partnership Constitution – Influence, Responsibility and Accountability*, Coventry City Council, November 1996.

Craigavon Borough Council (1994), *Craigavon Economic Development strategy- Achievement in the Making 1994-2000.*

Darwin, J. (1999), 'Partnership and Power', in Montanheiro, L. Haigh, B. Morris, D. and Linehan, M. (eds), *Public and Private Sector Partnerships: Furthering Development*, Sheffield Hallam University, pp.125-139.

Deakin, N. and Edwards, J. (1993), *The Enterprise Culture and the Inner City*. London: Routledge.

de Bréadún, D. (1998) 'A late late show of achievement by consensus', *Irish Times*, 19th December, p.6.

Deegan, J. and Dineen, D.A. (1997), *Tourism Policy and Performance – the Irish experience*, London, International Thompson Business Press.

de Groot, L. (1992), 'City Challenge: Competing in the Urban Regeneration Game', *Local Economy*, vol. 7, no. 3, pp.196-210.

De Neufville, J. and Barton, S.E. (1987), 'Myths and the Definition of Policy Problems: An Exploration of Home Ownership and Public-Private Partnerships', *Policy Sciences*, vol. 20, no. 1, pp.181-206.

De Witt, J. Kettl, D.F. Dyer, B. and Lovan, W.R. (1994), 'What Will New Governance Mean for the Federal Government?', *Public Administration Review*, vol. 54, no. 2, pp.170-175.

Department of Agriculture for Northern Ireland (1996), *The Northern Ireland Rural Development Programme - A Review of Progress 1990-1996.*

Department of Economic Development (1989), 'Tourism in Northern Ireland – A View to the Future', DED.

Department of Economic Development (1995), *Growing Competitively. A Review of Economic Development Policy in Northern Ireland.*

Department of Education for Northern Ireland (1996), *Strategic Plan for Education 1996-2000.*

Department of the Environment for Northern Ireland (1995), European Union Special Support Programme for Northern Ireland and the border counties of Ireland 1995-1999, European Structural Funds Guidelines on District Partnerships, Sub-programme 6.

Department of the Environment for Northern Ireland (1) (1996), *Corporate Framework for the Department of the Environment for Northern Ireland.*

Department of the Environment for Northern Ireland (2) (1996), *Your Guide to the Department of the Environment and its Agencies.*

Department of the Environment (3) (1996), *The Londonderry Initiative Regeneration Strategy 1996-1999.*

Department of the Environment (4) (1996), *Outline Strategy Proposals 1996-1999.*

Department of Health and Social Services (1997), *Health Well-being: Into The Next Millennium.*

DG for Research (1996), *Cross-Border Inter-Regional Co-operation in the European Union*.

Economic and Social Committee of the European Communities (1983), *Irish Border Areas Informational Report*, Brussels.

Elliot, M. and Greenwood, M. (1999), 'Making a Difference: Building the Process into Collaborative Partnerships', in Montanheiro, L. Haigh, B. Morris, D. and Linehan, M. (eds), *Public and Private Sector Partnerships: Furthering Development*. Sheffield Hallam University, pp.159-175.

European Commission (1994), *European Structural Funds INTERREG Programme Ireland and Northern Ireland 1994-1999*.

European Commission (1995), *Community Initiatives in Northern Ireland 1991-1999. Now, Euroform, Horizon 1991-1994, Employment Adapt 1995-1999*.

European Commission (1996), *Finance From Europe- A guide to grants and loans from the EU*.

Falconer, P.K. (1999), 'Better Quality Services: Enhancing Public Service Quality Through Partnership in the UK', in Montanheiro, L. Haigh, B. Morris, D. and Linehan, M. (eds), *Public and Private Sector Partnerships: Furthering Development*, Sheffield Hallam University, pp. 175-189.

Fitzpatrick, J. and McEniff, J. (1992), "Tourism", Chapter 5 in *Ireland in Europe: A Shared Challenge - Economic Co-operation on the island of Ireland in an Integrated Europe'*, Dublin Stationery Office, pp. 125-143.

Foyle Fisheries Commission (1995), *Annual Report 1995*.

Gent, E. (1992), 'The Future of Local Government- the Case of Nottingham', *Public Money and Management*, vol.12, pp.15-21.

Goodman, J. (1996), *Nationalism and Transnationalism*, Avebury.

Goodwin, M. (1992), 'The Changing Local State', in Cloke, P. (ed.), *Policy and Change in Thatcher's Britain*, Oxford: Pergamon, pp.77-97.

Grattias, A. and Boyd, M. (1995), 'Beyond Government: Can the Public Sector Meet the Challenges of Public-Private Partnering?', *Optimum*, vol. 26, no.1, pp. 3-14.

Gray, B. (1989), *Collaborating. Finding Common Ground for Multiparty Problems*, San Francisco, Jossey-Bass.

Greater Craigavon Partnership (1996), *Greater Craigavon Partnership Newsletter*.

Hadenius, A. and Uggla, F. (1996), 'Making Civil Society Work, Promoting Democratic Development: What Can States and Donors Do?', *World Development*, vol. 24, no.10, pp.1621-1641.

Hall, R. Clark, J. P. Giordano, P. C. Johnson, P.V. and Van Roekel, M. (1977), 'Patterns of Interorganisational Relationships', *Administrative Science Quarterly*, vol. 22, pp. 457-474.

Hannigan, K. (1994), 'A Regional Analysis of Tourism Growth in Ireland', *Regional Studies*, vol. 28, no. 2, pp.208-215.

Hannigan, K. (1995), 'Tourism Policy and Regional Development in Ireland: An Evaluation', paper presented to *Regional Studies Association Conference*, Maynooth, Co. Kildare, 14th September 1995.

Hastings, A. (1996), 'Unravelling the Process of 'Partnership' in Urban Regeneration Policy', *Urban Studies*, vol. 33, no. 2, pp.253-269.

Hayes, M. (1997), 'The Operation of the Public Sector in Northern Ireland, as seen by someone with Central Government, Local Government, Statutory Bodies and Regulatory Experience', Review of Northern Ireland Administrative Arrangements, May 1997, Essay No 6.

Hayton, K. and Gray, J. (1996), 'Developing Partnerships - Public Involvement, Private Control?', *Town and Country Planning*, vol.65, no. 3, pp. 85-87.

Healey, P. (1996), 'Consensus-Building Across Difficult Divisions: New Approaches to Collaborative Strategy Making', *Planning Practice and Research*, vol.11, no.2, pp. 207-216.

Heath, A. (1999), 'Ireland North and South: Continuity and Change', paper presented to Quest (Queens University Belfast) Conference, *Agreeing to Disagree? The Voters of Northern Ireland*, Queens University Belfast, 22nd June 1999.

Hennessey, T. (1997), *A History of Northern Ireland 1920-1996*, Gill and Macmillian.

HM. Treasury (1995), *Private Opportunity, Public Benefit. Progressing the Private Finance Initiative.*

House, H. (1990), 'The Border That Wouldn't Go Away: Irish Integration in the EC', *New York Law School Journal of International and Comparative Law*, vol, 11, nos, 1&2, pp.229-247.

Hughes, J. and Carmichael, P. (1996), 'UK Territorial Management and Urban Policy: Evidence from N. Ireland,' *Ulster Papers in Public Policy and Management*, No 67, University of Ulster.

Hughes, J. Knox, C. Murray, M. and Greer, J. (1998), *Partnership Governance in Northern Ireland: The Path to Peace*, Oak Tree Press, Dublin.

Hurely, A. Archers, B. and Fletcher, J. (1994),'The Economic Impact of European Community Grants for Tourism in the Republic of Ireland', *Tourism Management*, vol. 15, no. 3, pp.203-214.

Hutchinson, J. (1994), 'The Practice of Partnership in Local Economic Development', *Local Government Studies*, vol. 20, no. 3, pp.335-334.

Hutchinson, J. and Foley, P. (1994), 'Partnerships in Local Economic Development: The Management Issues', *Management Research News*, vol. 17, nos, 7-9, pp. 50-54.

Hutton, W. (1997), *The State to Come*, London, Vintage.

Huxham, C. (1991), 'Facilitating Collaboration: Issues in Multi-Organisational Group Decision Support in Voluntary, Informal Collaborative Settings', *Journal of Operational Research Society*, vol. 42, no. 12, pp.1037-1045.

Huxham, C. (1993), 'Collaborative Capability: An Intra Organisational Perspective on Collaborative Advantage', *Public Money and Management*, vol. 13, no. 3, pp. 21-29.

Huxham, C. and Vangen, S. (1996), 'Working Together: Key Themes in the Management of Relationships between Public and Non-Profit Organisations', *The International Journal of Public Sector Management*, vol. 9, no. 7, pp. 5-18.

Industrial Development Board for Northern Ireland (1996), *Annual Report and Accounts 1995-1996*.

Industrial Development Board for Northern Ireland (1997), *Northern Ireland Partnership, Working for Work*.

International Fund for Ireland (1996), *Annual Report 1996*, International Fund for Ireland.

INTERREG Programme Document 1995.

Ireland – National Development Plan 2000-2006 (1999), The Stationery Office, Dublin.

Irish Tourist Industry Confederation (1998), *Strategy for Growth Beyond 2000 - A Strategic Framework*.

Jacobs, B. (1994), 'Networks, Partnerships and the EU Regional Economic Development Initiatives in the West Midlands', *Policy and Politics*, vol. 25, no. 10, pp.39-50.

Jay, R. (1995), 'Democratic Dilemmas', *Fortnight*, no. 345, pp.16-17.

Jezierski, L. (1990), 'Neighborhoods and Public-Private Partnerships in Pittsburgh', *Urban Affairs Quarterly*, vol. 26, no. 2, pp.217-249.

Kickert, M. Elijn, E.H. and Koppenjan, J. (1997), 'Introduction: A Management Perspective on Policy Networks' in Kickert, M. Elijn, E.H. and Koppenjan, J. (eds), *Managing Complex Networks: Strategies for the Public Sector*, London: Sage, pp. 1-11.

Knox, C. (1996), 'The Democratic Deficit: A Partnership Approach in Northern Ireland.' *Ulster Papers in Public Policy and Management* No 58. University of Ulster.

Knox, C. (1997), 'Local Government, its operation since the Macrory Report and its potential for the future', *Review of Northern Ireland Administrative Arrangements*, Essay No 2.

Knox, C. (1999), 'Northern Ireland: At the Crossroads of Poltical and Administrative Reform', *Governance*, vol. 12, no. 3, pp.311-329.

Kooiman, J. (1993), 'Governance and Governability: Using Complexity, Dynamics and Diversity', Chapter 4 in Kooiman, J. (ed), *Modern Governance: New Government – Society Interactions*, Sage Publications, pp.35-51.

Laganside Corporation (1996), *Annual Report 1995-1996*.

Langton, S. (1983), 'Public Private Partnerships: Hope or Hoax?', *National Civic Review*, vol. 72, no. 5, pp.255-261.

Lawless, P. (1991), *Public-Private Sector Partnerships in the United Kingdom*. Sheffield: Centre for Regional Economic and Social Research, Newbury Park, Sage.

Lawless, P. (1994), 'Partnership in Urban Regeneration in the UK: The Sheffield Central Area Study', *Urban Studies*, vol. 31, no. 8, pp.1303-1324.

Lee, J.J. (1989), *Ireland 1912-1985*, Cambridge University Press.

Lennon, R. (1995), 'The Challenge of Northern Ireland Tourism', *Cornell Hotel and Restaurant Administration Quarterly*, vol. 36, no. 5, pp.82-86.

Local Economic Development Unit (1996), *Annual Report 1995-1996*.

Lowndes, V. Nanton, P. McCabe, A. and Skelcher, C. (1997), 'Networks, Partnerships and Urban Regeneration', *Local Economy*, vol. 11, no.4, pp. 333-343.

Lowndes, V. and Skelcher, C. (1998), 'The Dynamics of Multiorganisational Partnerships: An Analysis of Changing Modes of Governance', *Public Administration*, vol. 76, no.3, pp. 313-333.

Lyne, T. (1990), 'Ireland, Northern Ireland and 1992: The Barriers to Technocratic Anti-Partitionism', *Public Administration*, vol. 69, pp.417-433.

Mackintosh, M. (1992), 'Partnership: Issues of Policy and Negotiation', *Local Economy*, vol. 7, no.3, pp. 210-225.

Making Belfast Work (1996), *1996 Report*.

Marino, A. (1999), 'Public and Private Sector Partnerships in the Tourism Sector: Some of the Italian and Spanish Experiences' in Montanheiro, L. Haigh, B. Morris, D. and Linehan, M. (eds), *Public and Private Sector Partnerships: Furthering Development*, Sheffield Hallam University, pp. 345-355.

Martin, S. and Oztel, H. (1996), "The Business of Partnership. Collaborative-Competitive Partnerships in the Development of Business Links", *Local Economy*, vol. 11, no. 2, pp.131-143.

Mattessich, P. and Monsey, B. (1992), *'Collaboration: What Makes it Work'*. Amherest, H. Wilder H. Foundation, Minnesota, St. Paul.

Mayo, M. (1997), 'Partnerships for Regeneration and Community Development', *Critical Social Policy*, vol. 17, no. 3, pp.3-26.

McArthur, A. (1993), 'Community Partnership - A Formula for Neighbourhood Regeneration in the 1990s?', *Community Development Journal*, vol. 28, no. 4, pp.304-315.

McArthur, A. (1995), 'The Active Involvement of Local Residents in Strategic Community Partnerships', *Policy and Politics*, vol. 23, no. 1, pp.61-71.

McNulty, M. (1995), 'Impact on Tourism on the Irish Economy', *Accountancy Ireland*, vol. 27, no.6, pp. 43-44.

Meadowcroft, J. (1997), 'Planning for Sustainable Development: Insights from the Literatures of Political Science', *European Journal of Political Research*, vol. 31, pp. 427-454.

Meehan, E. (1997), 'The work of the smaller non-departmental public bodies, and their aptness and capacity for the responsibilities entrusted to them', *Review of Northern Ireland Administrative Arrangements*, Essay No 4.

Miles, M.B. (1979), 'Qualitative Data as an Attractive Nuisance', *Administrative Science Quarterly*, vol. 24, pp.590-601.

Morrison, J. and Livingstone, S. (1995), Reshaping Public Power: Northern Ireland and the British Constitutional Crisis, Modern Legal Studies, London, Sweet and Maxwell.

Morrow, D. (1996), 'Filling the Gap: Policy and Pressure Under Direct Rule' Section Five in Aughey, A. and Morrow, D. (ed.), *Northern Ireland Politics*, London and New York, Longman, pp.147-157.

Moxon-Browne, E. (1992), "The Impact of the EC" Chapter 4 in Hadfield, B. (ed.), *Northern Ireland: Politics and the Constitution*, Open University Press, pp. 89-103.

Murray, D. (1999), 'Tracking progress', in *No Frontiers North-South Integration in Ireland*, Democratic Dialogue No 11, Belfast, Regency Press.

Murray, M. and Dunn, L. (1996), *Revitalising Rural America: A Perspective on Collaboration and Community*, John Wiley and Sons.

Murray, M. and Smyth, M. (1996), 'Local Authority Partnerships in Central and Eastern Europe: A Northern Ireland Perspective', *Economic Outlook and Business Review*, vol. 11, no.4, pp.32-39.

Nevin, B. and Shiner, P. (1995), 'The Left, Urban Policy and Community Empowerment: The First Steps towards a New Framework for Urban Regeneration', *Local Economy*, vol. 10, no. 3, pp.218-229.

Northern Ireland Council for Voluntary Action (1997), *Building Peace, Piece by Piece*, August 1997, Belfast.

Northern Ireland Economic Council (1997), '*Rising to the Challenge: The Future of Tourism in Northern Ireland*', Report 121.

Northern Ireland Information Service (1995), *Creation of a Belfast City Centre Partnership Board, 20th December, 1995.*

Northern Ireland Partnership Board (1999), Northern Ireland Partnership Board Working Paper "EU Peace Programme 2000-2004: Proposed Implementation Model for the Locally Based Regeneration and Development Strategies Priority", Autumn 1999.

NITB (1969), *22nd Annual Report 1969*, Northern Ireland Tourist Board.

NITB (1970), *23rd Annual Report 1970*, Northern Ireland Tourist Board.

NITB (1971), *24th Annual Report 1971*, Northern Ireland Tourist Board.

NITB (1972), *25th Annual Report 1972*, Northern Ireland Tourist Board.

NITB (1973), *26th Annual Report 1973*, Northern Ireland Tourist Board.

NITB (1985), *37th Annual Report 1985*, Northern Ireland Tourist Board.

NITB (1992), *Annual Report 1992*, Northern Ireland Tourist Board.

NITB (1995), *Corporate Plan 1995-1998.*

NITB (1995/96), *Annual Report 1995/96*, Northern Ireland Tourist Board.

NITB (1996/97), *Annual Report 1996/97*, Northern Ireland Tourist Board.

NITB (1998a), *Corporate Plan 1998-2001*, Northern Ireland Tourist Board.

NITB (1998b), 'Special Edition Tourism Strategy', *Tourist* 4(1), Northern Ireland Tourist Board.

North West Region Cross-Border Group (NWRCBG) (1995), *'A Cross-Border Proposal for Development for the North West Region'*, Operation Programme for Globalised Assistance, October 1995.

O'Donnell, R. and Teague, P. (1993), 'The Potential and Limits to North-South Economic Co-operation', Chapter 9 in *The Economy of Northern Ireland – Perspectives for Structural Change,* London, Laurence and Wishart, pp. 240-271.

O'Donnell, R. and Thomas, D. (1998), 'Partnership and Policy Making' Chapter 7 in Healey, S. and Reynolds, B. (ed.), *Social Policy in Ireland, Principles, Practice and Problems*, Dublin: Oak Tree Press, pp. 225-241.

O'Dowd, L. (1994), *Whither the Irish Border? Sovereignty, Democracy and Economic Integration in Ireland*, Centre for Research and Documentation, Belfast.

O'Dowd, L. and Corrigan, J. and Moore, T. (1994), *'The Irish Border Region: A Socio-Economic Profile'*, Department of Sociology and Social Policy, The Queens University of Belfast.

OECD (1990), *Partnerships in Rural Development.* Paris, OECD.

Official Journal of the European Communities 1994 NoC 180/61.

Official Journal of the European Communities 1994 NoC 180/65.

O'Looney, J. (1992), 'Public-Private Partnerships in Economic Development: Negotiating the Trade-off Between Flexibility and Accountability', *Economic Development Review* , vol, 14, no. 22, pp.14-22.

O'Neill, M. and Fitz, M. (1996), 'Northern Ireland Tourism: What Chance Now?', *Tourism Management*, vol. 17, no. 3, pp.161-163.

Osbourne, D. and Gaebler, T. (1992), *Reinventing Government*, Reading, Addison, M.A.

Overseas Tourism Marketing Initiative (1997), *'OTMI Review of the Year 1997'*.

Paisana, A. and Oliveira, P. (1999), 'The Role of the Public and the Private Sectors in Regional Development: The Case of the AveValley in the North of Portugal' in Montanheiro, L. Haigh, B. Morris, D. and Linehan, M. (eds), *Public and Private Sector Partnerships: Furthering Development,* Sheffield Hallam University, pp. 453-465.

Pearce, D.G. (1990), 'Tourism in Ireland - questions of scale and organisations', *Tourism Management*, vol. 11, no. 2, pp.133-153.

Peat, Marwick, Mitchell and Co and Stokes, Kennedy, Crowley and Co. (1977), *'Cross-Border Communication Study for the Londonderry and Donegal Area'*, Volume 1, Summary Report prepared for Governments of the UK and Ireland and the Commission of the European Communities.

Peck, J. and Tickell, A. (1995), 'Too Many Partners: The Future for Regeneration Partnerships', *Local Economy*, vol. 8, no. 3, pp. 251-265.

Peters, B.G. and Pierre, J. (1998), 'Governance Without Government? Rethinking Public Administration', *Journal of Public Administration Research and Theory*, vol. 8, no. 2, pp. 223-243.

Prior, D. (1996), 'Working the Network: Local Authority Strategies in the Reticulated Local State', *Local Government Studies*, vol. 22, no. 2, pp.92-103.

Pycroft, C. (1996), 'Local Partnerships and Strategic Alliances for Economic Development: the need for Economic Development Audits', *International Review of Administrative Sciences*, vol. 62, no. 1, pp.109-123.

Rhodes, R.A.W. (1994), 'The Hollowing Out of the State: The Changing Nature of the Public Service in Britain', *Political Quarterly*, vol. 65, no. 2, pp.138-152.

Rhodes, R.A.W. (1996), 'The New Governance: Governing Without Government', *Political Studies*, vol. 44, no.4, pp. 652-668.

Rhodes, R.A.W. (1997), 'Foreword', in Kickert, W. Elijn, E.H. and Koppenjan, J. (eds), *Managing Complex Networks: Strategies for the Public Sector*, Sage: London.

Rittel, H.W. and Webber, M.M. (1973), 'Dilemmas in a General Theory of Planning', *Policy Sciences*, vol. 4, pp.155-169.

Robb, H.M. (1995), 'The Border Region: A Case Study' Chapter 12 in D'Arcy, M and Dickson, T. (eds), *Border Crossings Developing Ireland's Island Economy,* Dublin, Gill and Macmillian, pp. 133-143.

Roberts, N. C. and Bradely, R. T. (1991), 'Stakeholder Collaboration and Innovation: A Study of Public Policy Initiation at the State Level', *The Journal of Applied Behavioural Science*, vol. 27, no. 2, pp.209-228.

Robinson, F. and Shaw, K. (1991), 'Urban Regeneration and Community Involvement', *Local Economy*, vol, 6, no1. 1, pp. 61-73.

Robson, B. Bradford, M. and Deas, I. (1994), *Relative Deprivation in Northern Ireland.* Policy Planning and Research Unit, Occasional Paper no 28. Centre for Urban Policy Studies, Manchester University.

Rogers, D.L. Whetten, D.A. Halport, B.P. Mulford, C.L. (1982), *Interorganisational Co-ordination*, Iowa State University Press, Ames, Iowa.

Rural Development Council (1995), *Strategic Plan 1995-1999.*

Rural Development Council (1996), *Annual Review 1996.*

Sabel, C. (1996), *Ireland: Local Partnerships and Social Innovation.* Paris: OECD.

South and East Belfast Social Services Trust (1997), *Community Development Strategy: Executive Summary.*

Stake, R.E. (1995), *The Art of Case Study Research.* Sage Publications.

Stake, R.E. (1998), 'Case Studies', in Denzin, N. K. and Lincoln, Y. S. (eds), *Strategies of Qualitative Inquiry*, Sage Publications, pp. 86-110.

Skelcher, C. McCabe, A. and Lowndes, V. with Nanton, P. (1996), *Community Networks in Urban Regeneration. 'It all depends who you know....!'*, Policy Press.

Stationery Office (1994), '*Tourism 2000-Guide to the Operational Programme for Tourism 1994-1999*', Government Publications Sales Office, Dublin.

Stenberg, E. (1993), 'Preparing for the Hybrid Economy: The New World of Public-Private Partnerships', *Business Horizons*, vol. 36, no. 6, pp.11-16.

Stephens, N. and Symons, L.J. (1956), 'The Lough Erne Drainage Scheme', *Geography* XL1, pp.123-26.

Stewart, M. (1994), 'Between Whitehall and Town Hall: The Realignment of Urban Regeneration Policy in England', *Policy and Politics*, vol. 22, no. 2, pp.133-145.

Stewart, J. (1996), *Local Government Today*. London, Local Government Management Board.

Sweeney, P. and Gaffikin, F. (1995), *Listening to the People*, Making Belfast Work, March 1995.

The Agreement (1998), Agreement Reached by the Multi-Party Talks, Belfast.

Tilson, B. Morrison, J. Beazely, M. Burfilt A. Collinge, C. Hall, S. Loftman, P. Nevin, B and Srbljanin, A. (1997), 'Partnerships for Regeneration. The SRB Challenge Fund Round One', *Local Government Studies*, vol. 23, no.1, pp.1-15.

Titterington, A.J. and Lennon, R. (1995), 'Northern Ireland: Prospects for Hotel Investment and Tourism Recovery', *Cornell Hotel and Restaurant Administration Quarterly*, vol. 36, no. 5, pp. 87-93.

Trimble / Mallon Statement (1998), 'Trimble - Mallon Statement on what was agreed', *Irish Times*, 19th December, p.6.

Upper Springfield Development Trust (1995), *Report of Upper Springfield Development Trust 1995.*

Walsh, J. A. (1997/98), 'Best Pracrice in Local Development - The Ballyhoura Model' *Pleanáil*, vol. 14, pp.129-153.

Walsh, J. (1998), 'Local Development and Local Government in the Republic of Ireland: From Fragmentation to Integration?', *Local Economy*, vol. 12, no. 4, pp.320-341.

Webb, A. (1991), 'Co-ordination: A Problem in Public Sector Management', *Policy and Politic*, vol. 19, no. 4, pp.229-241.

Wheeler, R. (1996), 'Special Issue on Empowerment', *Local Government Policy Making*, vol. 22, no. 4, pp. 3-8.

Wilks-Hegg, S. (1996), 'Urban Experiments Limited Revisited: Urban Policy Comes Full Circle?', *Urban Studies*, vol. 33, no. 8, pp.1263-1279.

Williamson, A. (1999), 'Development Partnerships in Ireland, North and South: The European Union's role in shaping policy in Ireland's two jurisdictions', *Association for Voluntary Action Research in Ireland Research Series*, University of Ulster.

Williamson, A. Scott, D. and Halfpenny, P. (1999), 'Rebuilding Civil Society in Northern Ireland: The Community and Voluntary Sector's Contribution to the EU Peace and Reconciliation District Partnership Programme' in Montanheiro, L. Haigh, B. Morris, D. and Linehan, M. (eds), *Public and Private Sector Partnerships: Furthering Development*, Sheffield Hallam University, pp. 665-687.

Wilson, A. and Charlton, K. (1997), '*Making Partnerships Work. A Practical Guide for the Public, Private, Voluntary and Community Sectors*', The Joseph Rowntree Foundation, York Publishing Services Limited.

Wilson, D. (1993), 'Tourism, Public Policy and the Image of the Northern Ireland Since the Troubles', in O'Connor, B. and Cronin, M. (eds), *Tourism in Ireland: A Critical Analysis*, Ireland, Cork University Press, pp.138-162.

Wood, D.J. and Gray, B. (1991), 'Toward a Comprehensive Theory of Collaboration', *The Journal of Applied Behavioural Science*, vol. 27, no. 2, pp.139-163.

Woodburn, I. (1985), 'Management of Urban Economic Partnerships', *Local Government Policy Making*, vol. 2, no. 2, pp. 9-15.

Index